WordPress 5 Complete
Seventh Edition

Build beautiful and feature-rich websites from scratch

Karol Król

BIRMINGHAM - MUMBAI

WordPress 5 Complete
Seventh Edition

Commissioning Editor: Amarabha Banerjee
Acquisition Editor: Devanshi Doshi
Content Development Editor: Keagan Carneiro
Technical Editor: Jinesh Topiwala
Copy Editor: Safis Editing
Project Coordinator: Pragati Shukla
Proofreader: Safis Editing
Indexer: Tejal Daruwale Soni
Graphics: Alishon Mendonsa
Production Coordinator: Nilesh Mohite

First published: November 2006
Second edition: June 2009
Third edition: January 2011
Fourth edition: November 2013
Fifth edition: April 2015
Sixth edition: August 2017
Seventh edition: February 2019

Production reference: 1270219

Published by Packt Publishing Ltd.
Livery Place
35 Livery Street
Birmingham
B3 2PB, UK.

ISBN 978-1-78953-201-2

www.packtpub.com

To my mother, who taught me the value of finding purpose through hard work.

– Karol Król

`mapt.io`

Mapt is an online digital library that gives you full access to over 5,000 books and videos, as well as industry leading tools to help you plan your personal development and advance your career. For more information, please visit our website.

Why subscribe?

- Spend less time learning and more time coding with practical eBooks and Videos from over 4,000 industry professionals

- Improve your learning with Skill Plans built especially for you

- Get a free eBook or video every month

- Mapt is fully searchable

- Copy and paste, print, and bookmark content

Packt.com

Did you know that Packt offers eBook versions of every book published, with PDF and ePub files available? You can upgrade to the eBook version at www.packt.com and as a print book customer, you are entitled to a discount on the eBook copy. Get in touch with us at customercare@packtpub.com for more details.

At www.packt.com, you can also read a collection of free technical articles, sign up for a range of free newsletters, and receive exclusive discounts and offers on Packt books and eBooks.

Contributors

About the author

Karol Król is a WordPress developer, professional blogger, and writer. He has been building expertise in WordPress ever since his early years at the Silesian University of Technology (Poland), where he graduated with an MSc in computer science. Early in his career, he worked as a freelance website developer for several years. Later on, he decided to shift his interest toward popularizing WordPress as the perfect solution for all web-based projects, and devoted his time to growing his writing career. To this day, his articles have been featured on websites including About.com, MarketingProfs.com, SmashingMagazine.com, Adobe.com, CodeinWP.com, NIO.tips, and many more.

I'd like to thank everyone at Packt for working with me and making this book a reality. Also, many thanks to everyone who supported me along the way. Finally, I'd like to thank the WordPress community for building and constantly improving this incredible tool. If it wasn't for you guys, I'd be out of work.

About the reviewers

Olivier Pons is a highly skilled developer who's been building websites for many years. He's a teacher in France at the University of Sciences of Aix-en-Provence, CESI, and three other institutions, where he teaches Python, Django, advanced JavaScript, nginx, Apache, and Linux. In 2011, he left a full-time job as a PHP expert to concentrate on his own company, HQF Development. He currently runs a number of websites, and you will easily find his web development blog if you search for *Olivier Pons*. He's currently making a Unity MCQ mobile application, which works together with a Django website. He also helps big companies and CTOs in making the best choice for their web projects.

> *I would like to thank my family and friends for their never-ending support. I am also thankful to Packt Publishing and its amazing collection of videos, without whom none of this would be possible. I'd also like to thank the author of the book, for putting together a very helpful guide for WordPress users as well as Pragati Shukla for giving me the opportunity to review this amazing book.*

Rakhitha Nimesh Ratnayake is a freelance web developer, writer, and open source enthusiast. He has over nine years' experience in developing WordPress applications and plugins. He develops premium WordPress plugins for individual clients and the CodeCanyon marketplace. User Profiles Made Easy and WP Private Content Pro are the most popular plugins developed by him. Rakhitha is the creator of WPExpertDeveloper, where he shares his latest WordPress plugins. *Building Impressive Presentations with Impress.js* was his first book, which was published by Packt Publishing. He is also the author of the first three editions of *WordPress Web Application Development, published by Packt*. In his spare time, he likes to read books and spend time with his family.

Packt is searching for authors like you

If you're interested in becoming an author for Packt, please visit authors.packtpub.com and apply today. We have worked with thousands of developers and tech professionals, just like you, to help them share their insight with the global tech community. You can make a general application, apply for a specific hot topic that we are recruiting an author for, or submit your own idea.

Table of Contents

Section 3: Non-Blog Websites

Preface

WordPress 5 Complete, Seventh Edition, will take you through the complete process of building a fully-functional WordPress site from scratch. The journey goes all the way from teaching you how to install WordPress to the most advanced topics, such as creating your own themes, writing plugins, and even building non-blog websites. The best part is that you can do all of this without losing your shirt along the way. Moreover, once you get some practice, you will be able to launch new WordPress sites within minutes (that's not a metaphor, by the way; this is as true as it gets).

This book guides you along the way in a step-by-step manner, explaining everything there is to know about WordPress. We'll start by downloading and installing the core of WordPress, where you will learn how to choose the correct settings in order to guarantee a smooth experience for yourself and your visitors. After that, this book will teach you all about content management functionalities for your site, from posts and pages to categories and tags, all the way to media, menus, images, galleries, security, administration, user profiles, and more. Next, you will find out what plugins and themes are and how to use them effectively. Finally, you'll learn how to create your own themes and plugins to enhance the overall functionality of your website. Once you're done with *WordPress 5.0 Complete, Seventh Edition*, you'll have all the knowledge required to build a professional WordPress site from scratch.

Who this book is for

This book is a guide to WordPress for both beginners and those who have slightly more advanced knowledge of WordPress. If you are new to blogging and want to create your own blog or website in a simple and straightforward manner, then this book is for you. It is also for people who want to learn how to customize and expand the capabilities of a WordPress website. You do not require any detailed knowledge of programming or web development, and any IT-confident user will be able to use this book to produce an impressive website.

What this book covers

Chapter 1, *Introducing WordPress*, explains what makes WordPress such excellent software for running your website (whether it's a blog or not). WordPress is packed with world-class features and is so flexible that it really can do anything you want. It has a wealth of online resources. Additionally, it's super easy to use, and you need no special skills or prior experience to use it. Last but not least, it's free!

Chapter 2, *Getting Started with WordPress*, describes how to install WordPress on a remote server and change the basic default settings of your blog.

Chapter 3, *Creating Blog Content*, teaches everything you need to know in order to add content to your blog and then manage that content. We go through how to write your first posts, and how to work with categories, tags, and comments.

Chapter 4, *Pages, Media, and Importing/Exporting Content*, explores all the other types of content that WordPress is capable of handling. You'll be able to create static pages that aren't part of your ongoing blog, add various types of media to your posts, and create appealing image galleries to display photos and other images.

Chapter 5, *Plugins – What They Are and Why You Need Them*, explains what plugins are, why to use them, how to use them, where to get them, and how to keep up to date with any new and useful plugins that get released to the community.

Chapter 6, *Securing Your WordPress Website*, introduces the topic of website security and how it relates to WordPress. Even though WordPress is pretty secure from the get-go, learning the principles goes a long way and can save you a lot of trouble further down the road.

Chapter 7, *Choosing and Installing Themes*, describes how to manage the basic look of your WordPress website. You also get to learn where to find themes, why they are useful, and how to implement new themes in your WordPress website.

Chapter 8, *Customizing your Website Appearance/Design*, explores how to manage widgets and navigation menus, along with how to work with the basic layout customization features to further enhance the capabilities of your entire website. Also covers the WordPress Customizer, an easy-to-use interface that allows you to tweak how your current theme looks and performs.

Chapter 9, *Developing your Own Theme*, explains how to create your own theme. With just the most basic HTML and CSS abilities, you can create a design and turn it into a fully-functional WordPress theme.

Chapter 10, *Social Media Integration, Podcasting, and HTTPS*, explores social media integration, podcasting, and HTTPS, which is all about making your website more secure by adding an additional level of encryption to browser-website communication.

Chapter 11, *Developing Plugins, Widgets, and an Introduction to the REST API*, teaches you everything you need to know about creating basic plugins and widgets: how to structure your PHP files, where to put your functions, and how to use hooks. This chapter also teaches you how to add management pages and build widgets that are run by a plugin.

Chapter 12, *Creating a Non-Blog Website, Part One – The Basics*, explores the endless possibilities of WordPress when it comes to using it to launch various types of websites. This chapter presents the first batch of our non-blog websites and explains in detail how to build them on top of a standard WordPress installation.

Chapter 13, *Creating a Non-Blog Website, Part Two – E-Commerce Websites and Custom Content Elements*, goes through some additional types of non-blog websites and also presents some of the technical aspects of building them.

To get the most out of this book

In order to follow along with the examples in this book, you'll need the following:

- A computer
- A web browser
- A plain text editor
- FTP software

You might consider a text editor that highlights code (such as Coda, TextMate, HTMLKit, and so on), but a simple plain text editor is all that's required. You may like to run a local copy of WordPress on your computer, in which case you may need a server such as Apache and MySQL installed (though WAMP, XAMPP, or MAMP can take care of all that for you). But even this is not necessary, as you could do the entire thing remotely.

Download the example code files

You can download the example code files for this book from your account at www.packt.com. If you purchased this book elsewhere, you can visit www.packt.com/support and register to have the files emailed directly to you.

You can download the code files by following these steps:

1. Log in or register at www.packt.com.
2. Select the **SUPPORT** tab.
3. Click on **Code Downloads & Errata**.
4. Enter the name of the book in the **Search** box and follow the onscreen instructions.

Once the file is downloaded, please make sure that you unzip or extract the folder using the latest version of:

- WinRAR/7-Zip for Windows
- Zipeg/iZip/UnRarX for Mac
- 7-Zip/PeaZip for Linux

The code bundle for the book is also hosted on GitHub at https://github.com/ PacktPublishing/WordPress-5-Complete-7th-Edition. In case there's an update to the code, it will be updated on the existing GitHub repository.

We also have other code bundles from our rich catalog of books and videos available at https://github.com/PacktPublishing/. Check them out!

Download the color images

We also provide a PDF file that has color images of the screenshots/diagrams used in this book. You can download it here: http://www.packtpub.com/sites/default/files/downloads/9781789532012_ColorImages .pdf.

Conventions used

There are a number of text conventions used throughout this book.

CodeInText: Indicates code words in text, database table names, folder names, filenames, file extensions, pathnames, dummy URLs, user input, and Twitter handles. Here is an example: "If you're installing WordPress on your local server, just be sure to place the WordPress files in the correct webroot directory on your computer.

A block of code is set as follows:

```
.site-footer {
  float: right;
  padding: 20px;
}
```

Bold: Indicates a new term, an important word, or words that you see onscreen. For example, words in menus or dialog boxes appear in the text like this. Here is an example: "Now, click on **Install WordPress**."

Warnings or important notes appear like this.

Tips and tricks appear like this.

Get in touch

Feedback from our readers is always welcome.

General feedback: If you have questions about any aspect of this book, mention the book title in the subject of your message and email us at customercare@packtpub.com.

Errata: Although we have taken every care to ensure the accuracy of our content, mistakes do happen. If you have found a mistake in this book, we would be grateful if you would report this to us. Please visit www.packt.com/submit-errata, selecting your book, clicking on the Errata Submission Form link, and entering the details.

Piracy: If you come across any illegal copies of our works in any form on the Internet, we would be grateful if you would provide us with the location address or website name. Please contact us at copyright@packt.com with a link to the material.

If you are interested in becoming an author: If there is a topic that you have expertise in and you are interested in either writing or contributing to a book, please visit authors.packtpub.com.

Reviews

Please leave a review. Once you have read and used this book, why not leave a review on the site that you purchased it from? Potential readers can then see and use your unbiased opinion to make purchase decisions, we at Packt can understand what you think about our products, and our authors can see your feedback on their book. Thank you!

For more information about Packt, please visit `packt.com`.

Section 1: WordPress

This section covers everything that you must know about WordPress as a newcomer to the platform. This is your WordPress 101.

This section will cover the follow chapters:

- Chapter 1, *Introducing WordPress*
- Chapter 2, *Getting Started with WordPress*
- Chapter 3, *Creating Blog Content*
- Chapter 4, *Pages, Media, and Importing/Exporting Content*

Introducing WordPress 1

How do I make a website? is a question that a lot of people ask in this day and age. Actually, it's probably one of *the* main questions you ask if you're a business owner in the 21st century. But *website making* is not only about business.

These days, dare I say, *everybody* should at least *consider* getting a website of their own. In the past, this was an intimidating concept. The only way you could get a website was to either hire a professional who would build one for you, or learn web technologies and development yourself and then build one on your own. Nowadays, there are *more* options, and particularly if you want to build a website *really quickly* while making sure that it is *top quality* at the same time.

The best option of them all is WordPress—which is the topic of this book. Under the hood, WordPress is an open source web software application that you can use to create and maintain a modern website. At the time of writing, more than 30% of all websites run on WordPress, and the number is only expected to increase in the coming years. In simple terms, with WordPress, anyone can build a beautiful website with minimal effort involved and then make it available to the world in no time. Let's take a look at some of the perks of using WordPress:

- You don't need to hire a team of developers and/or designers
- You don't need to learn advanced PHP
- You don't need to be a pro with computers
- Nevertheless, you can still end up with a high-quality website with almost unlimited extension possibilities

These days, everyone has a good reason to have a website. It's not just large companies anymore. Individuals, families, freelancers, or small/independent businesses can all benefit from a website. However, at the same time, most people don't have the financial resources to hire a web development company or a freelance web developer to create a website for them. This is where WordPress comes into play. WordPress is free, easy to use, and packed with excellent features. Since WordPress is a web application, it does not need to be installed on your home PC or Mac, or any other machine under your control. It can live on a server (kind of a computer) that belongs to a website-hosting company. Originally, WordPress was an application meant to run a blog website. However, it has evolved into a fully featured **content management system** (**CMS**). If you don't know what a blog is, don't worry, we explain everything later in this chapter.

In this book, we'll be going through each important step on your way to understanding how WordPress works and what can be done with it. We'll learn about the basic usage of WordPress, configuration, extending your site with themes and plugins, and much more. But before we can get to all that, we need to start at square one! In this chapter, we'll explore:

- The reasons that will make you choose WordPress to run your website
- The greatest advantages of WordPress
- Online resources for WordPress
- Some of the most useful features in the newest versions of WordPress

Getting into WordPress

WordPress is an open source CMS. **Open source** means that the source code of the system is made available with a license whereby the copyright holder provides the rights to study, change, and distribute the software to anyone and for any purpose (as Wikipedia defines it). CMS means a software application that can run a website (for example, a blog) and allows you to publish, edit, and modify the content. It's a piece of software that lives on the web server (more on what a web server is later on) and makes it easy for you to add and edit posts, themes, comments, and all of your other content. The following is the logo of WordPress:

Even though WordPress was originally a blog engine—used primarily to run blogs—it's now a popular solution among some of the biggest brands on the web and runs their entire websites. Brands such as The New York Times, The Wall Street Journal, Forbes, Reuters, `WIRED.com`, Sony, Toyota, plus some of the most prominent artists (such as Beyoncé or the Rolling Stones) all use WordPress as the base of their web platforms and outlets.

Undoubtedly, WordPress has evolved a lot over the years, and even though a large number of new functionalities have been introduced, WordPress remains one of the easiest-to-use web publishing platforms out there. Originally, it was a fork of an older piece of software named **b2/cafelog**.

WordPress was developed by Matt Mullenweg and Mike Little, but is now maintained and developed by a team of developers that includes Mullenweg.

What WordPress is good for

There are generally three popular types of website for which WordPress is meant to be used:

- A typical website with relatively static content, pages, subpages, and so on
- A blog website, chronologically organized, and frequently updated, categorized, tagged, and archived
- An e-commerce website: a fully functional online store that allows people to buy goods or services, and the website owner to manage orders and fulfill them

However, as experience shows, WordPress is also successfully used to run a wide variety of other sites, such as:

- Corporate business sites
- One-page profile sites
- Portfolio sites
- Membership sites
- Video blogs
- Photo blogs
- Product sites
- Education sites (e-courses) and more

For those of you unfamiliar with blog websites and blogging terminology, let's take a look at the basics.

Starting the journey – what is a blog?

Originally, *blog* was short for *weblog*. According to Wikipedia, the term weblog was first used in 1997, and people started using blogs globally in 1999. The terms *weblog, web blogging,* and *weblogger* were added to the *Oxford English Dictionary* in 2003, though these days most people leave off the *we* part.

Just to give you a more plain-English explanation, a blog is a website that usually contains regular entries made by an author. These entries can be of various types, such as commentary, descriptions of events, photos, videos, personal remarks, tutorials, case studies, long opinion pieces, political ideas, or whatever else you can imagine. They are usually displayed in reverse chronological order, with the most recent additions at the top. Those entries can be organized in a variety of ways, by date, topic, subject, and so on.

One of the main characteristics of a blog is that it's meant to be updated regularly. Unlike a website where the content is static, a blog behaves more like an online diary, wherein the blogger posts regular updates. Hence, blogs are dynamic with ever-changing content. A blog can be updated with new content and the old content can be changed or deleted at any time (although deleting content is not a common practice).

Most blogs focus their content on a particular subject, for example, current events, hobbies, niche topics, and technical expertise. This doesn't mean that blogs are meant to be published only by individuals sharing their personal opinions on given matters. On the contrary, these days, blogs have become a significant part in the online presence for many businesses and even corporations. The modern practice of *content marketing* is now one of the most widely accepted web marketing methods, and its core is based on publishing quality content, often in blog form.

Understanding the common terms

If you are new to the world of blogging (sometimes called the *blogosphere*, which is a fairly popular expression these days), you may want to familiarize yourself with the following common terms.

Post

Each entry in the blog is called a **post**. Every post usually has a number of different parts. Of course, the two most obvious parts are the title and content. The **content** is text, images, links, and so on. Posts can even contain multimedia (for example, videos and audio files). Every post also has a publication timestamp, and most have one or more categories and tags assigned to them. It is these posts, or entries, that are often displayed in reverse chronological order on the main page of the blog. By default, the latest post is displayed first, in order to give the viewer the latest news on a subject.

Categories and tags

Categories and **tags** are ways to organize and find posts within a blog and even across blogs. Categories are like topics, while tags are more like keywords. For example, for a blog about food and cooking, there might be a category called **recipes**, but every post in that category might have different tags (for example, *soup*, *baked*, *vegetarian*, and *dairy-free*).

The purpose and correct usage of tags and categories are one of the widely discussed topics among bloggers. Although there are basic guidelines such as the ones presented here, every blogger develops their own approach after a while, and there are no *written in stone* rules.

Comments

Most blogs allow visitors to post comments on the posts. This gives readers the opportunity to interact with the author of the blog, thus making the whole experience interactive. Often, the author of the blog will respond to comments by posting additional comments with a single click on the reply button, which makes for a continuous public online conversation or dialog.

Comments are said to be one of the most important assets for a blog. The presence of a large number of comments shows how popular and authoritative the blog is.

Themes

A **theme** is the design and layout package that you can choose for your blog. On most blogs, the content (for example, posts) is separate from the visual appearance. This means you can change the visuals of your blog at any time without having to worry about the content being affected. One of the best things about themes is that it takes only minutes to install and start using a new one. Moreover, there are a number of very good free or low-cost themes available online.

That being said, you need to be careful when working with free themes from uncertain developers. Often, they contain encrypted parts and code that can hurt your site and its presence on Google. Always look for user reviews before choosing a theme. Most importantly, the safest bet is getting your free themes only from the official WordPress directory at `https://wordpress.org/themes/`. The themes there have been tested and checked for any suspicious code.

You can learn more about this whole issue at `http://newinternetorder.com/free-wordpress-themes-are-evil/`.

Plugins

WordPress plugins are relatively small pieces of web software that can be installed on any WordPress site. They extend the native functionality to do almost anything that the technology of today allows. Just like WordPress itself, the code within plugins is open source, which means that anyone can build a new plugin if they have the required skill set. Every WordPress website or blog can work with an unlimited number of plugins (although it is not a recommended approach). The most popular functionalities introduced through plugins include spam protection, **search engine optimization** (**SEO**), caching, social media integration, interactive contact forms, and backups.

Widgets

Widgets are a simplified version of plugins. The most common usage of widgets is to have them showcased in the sidebars on your site. Typically, your current theme will provide you with a number of widget areas where you can display widgets (as mentioned, many of these are located in the sidebar). Some of the common usages for widgets is to display content such as categories and tags, recent posts, popular posts, recent comments, links to archived posts, pages, links, search fields, or standard non-formatted text.

Menus

We need to talk some history to explain the meaning of menus in WordPress. Back in the day, WordPress didn't allow much customization in terms of tweaking navigation menus and handpicking the links we wanted to display. This changed in Version 3.0, whereby the new *Custom Menus* feature was introduced. In plain English, it allows you to create completely custom menus (featuring any links of your choice) and then display them in specific areas on your site. To be honest, this feature, even though it sounds basic, is one of the main ones that has turned WordPress into a full-fledged web publishing platform. I promise this will sound much clearer in the upcoming chapters.

Page

It's important to understand the difference between a page and a post. Unlike posts, pages do not depend on timestamps and are not displayed in reverse chronological order. Also, they do not have categories or tags. A page is a piece of content with only a title and content (an example would be *About Me* or *Contact Us*—the two most popular pages on almost any blog). It is likely that the number of pages on your blog remains relatively static, while new posts can be added every day or so.

Home page

A **home page** is simply the main page that visitors see when they visit your website by typing in your domain name or URL address. In the early days of WordPress's existence, a home page wasn't something we used to talk about as a separate kind of page. Originally, a home page was generated automatically from the newest posts—it was a listing of those posts in reverse chronological order. Right now, however, WordPress allows us to build a completely custom home page and display whatever content we wish on it.

Users

As mentioned earlier, WordPress is now a complete web publishing platform. One of its characteristics is that it is capable of working with multiple user accounts, not just a single account belonging to the owner (admin/main author) of the site. There are different types of user accounts available, and they have different credentials and access rights.

WordPress is clearly trying to resemble a traditional publishing house where there are *authors*, *editors*, and other *contributors* all working together. Even though the option to create an unlimited number of user accounts won't be that impressive for anyone planning to manage a site on their own, it can surely be a more-than-essential feature for big, magazine-like websites.

Why choose WordPress?

WordPress is not the only publishing platform out there, but it has an awful lot to offer. In the following sections, I've called attention to WordPress's most outstanding features.

The main benefits of WordPress summarized are:

- WordPress *gives you full control over your website*. You can change/adjust/modify/customize everything, and I mean everything, about your site.
- There are *thousands of themes and plugins* to choose from, enabling you to make your website look and work however you wish. WordPress is extremely extendable. Basically, any additional functionality that you can dream of can be added utilizing a plugin that you or your programmer friends can write.
- The day-to-day work with *the platform is very easy to grasp*. Tasks such as editing content, publishing new articles/posts, or interacting with the audience through comments have no learning curve.
- *WordPress is open source*. There's no price tag on the platform; you can get it for free. This also means that learning how the platform works under the hood, and how to extend it even further, doesn't require anyone's permission.

Who should use WordPress?

Basically, if you need a website, and you want to be able to build it yourself, then WordPress is the platform that will make it possible.

WordPress is the perfect tool, both for beginners just dipping their toes into website building for the first time, and developers working on client websites professionally.

WordPress has been around for quite a while and has been in development the whole time. Developers are working on WordPress constantly to keep it ahead of spammers and hackers, and to *evolve* the application on the basis of the *evolving* needs of its users.

WordPress's very first release, Version 0.70, was launched in May 2003. Since then, it has had more than two dozen major releases, with a number of minor ones in between. Each release came with more features and better security. Each major release comes with a code name honoring a great jazz musician, and this has become a tradition in the WordPress world.

WordPress is not being developed by a lonely programmer in a dark basement room, by the way. On the contrary, there is a large community of people working on it collaboratively by developing, troubleshooting, making suggestions, and testing the application. With such a large group of people involved, the application is likely to continue to evolve and improve without pause.

Getting to know the WordPress family

WordPress, as a platform and as a community of users, has grown in two main areas:

- The first one is gathered around WordPress.org (`https://wordpress.org/`), the native, main website of the WordPress project
- The other is WordPress.com (`https://wordpress.com/`), a commercial platform providing both free and paid blogs to users

Essentially, `WordPress.org` is about developing the platform itself, sharing new plugins, discussing the technical aspects of WordPress, and being all *techie* in general. `WordPress.com` is a commercial website where bloggers can meet with each other and publish their blog content under the `wordpress.com` subdomain (for example, something like `paleorecipeslog.wordpress.com` is a subdomain).

In `Chapter 2`, *Getting Started with WordPress*, we will discuss the differences between hosting your blog on `WordPress.com` versus working with the software you can get from `WordPress.org`.

Digging into WordPress – the features

Here is a list of some of the features that WordPress has to offer (in no particular order):

- Exchangeable designs through WordPress themes, which are also further customizable via *WordPress Customizer*
- Extendable through WordPress plugins

- Unlimited posts and pages
- Unlimited categories and subcategories
- Unlimited tags
- Mobile-friendly and optimized to be viewed on all devices and screen sizes
- Flexible—create any type of website you want
- Scalable—can handle any size of website
- Ability to post via email and mobile devices (there are apps available for all major mobile platforms, including iOS and Android)
- Compliance with the **World Wide Web Consortium** (**W3C**) standards, although it does depend on the theme you're using
- Import of data from other blogs (Moveable Type, b2evolution, Blogger, and others)
- Easy to administer and blog without any previous experience
- Convenient, fully functional, built-in search
- Multilingual with good internationalization, and also works with emojis (including all of the latest Unicode 9.0 emoji characters)
- Secure code
- Ability to password-protect content
- Comments manager and spam protection
- Built-in workflow (write, draft, review, and publish)
- Intelligent text and content editing via a visual editor called Gutenberg
- Multiuser and multiauthor support for user accounts
- Feature-rich *Media Library* for managing photos and other non-text content through a visual and highly usable interface
- Social media integration capabilities
- Dynamic and scalable revision functionality with post (edit) locking
- Built-in embed functionality through shortcodes (compatible with services such as YouTube, Vimeo, Flickr, SoundCloud, and others)
- An admin panel that's accessible via all modern devices, operating systems, and web browsers
- Full accessibility for frontend elements of the website
- User-friendly image editing, plus a drag-and-drop image-importing feature
- Advanced SEO features through plugins and themes
- Integrated REST API infrastructure

Learning more

If you'd like to see detailed lists of all the new features added to WordPress, just take a look into the Codex. You can easily find the subpage for each individual version. Simply take the following web address and replace X and Y with the version number you're looking for.

```
https://codex.wordpress.org/Version_X.Y
```

For example, if you want to learn about WordPress 5.0, go to:

```
https://codex.wordpress.org/Version_5.0
```

Also, you can read a fully explained feature list at https://wordpress.org/about/features/.

Learning more with online WordPress resources

One very useful characteristic of WordPress is that it has a large, active, online community. Everything you will ever need for your WordPress website can most likely be found online, and probably for free. In addition to this, these days we can also find many paid resources and training programs that offer expert advice and training, revolving around many different possible usages of a WordPress site:

- https://codex.wordpress.org/: Here you can find the official documentation for WordPress—we'll talk more about the codex later on in this chapter
- https://themeisle.com/blog/: Offers free guidance on common tasks that can be performed with WordPress
- https://www.wpbeginner.com/: Offers tutorials and resources about WordPress

Staying updated with WordPress news

As WordPress is constantly being developed, it's important to keep yourself up-to-date with the software community's latest activities.

If you visit the dashboard of your own WordPress site regularly, you'll be able to stay up-to-date with WordPress news and software releases. There are widgets on the dashboard that display the latest news and announcements, and an alert always appears when there is a new version of WordPress available for download and installation.

If you prefer to visit the website, then the most important spot to visit or subscribe to is WordPress Releases. Whenever there is a new release, be it a major release, or an interim bug fix, or an upgrade, it will be at `https://wordpress.org/news/category/releases/`.

Also, be sure to stay tuned to the main WordPress blog at `https://wordpress.org/news/`.

Some additional resources worth mentioning are as follows:

- `https://wordpress.org/`: The absolute main hub for WordPress.
- `https://wordpress.com/`: The commercial service for creating blogs and websites.
- `http://jobs.wordpress.net/`: Job listings for anyone searching for employment in areas related to WordPress (or anyone searching for WordPress help).
- `https://wordpress.tv/`: A great source of top-notch WordPress tutorials, how-to advice, case studies, product demonstrations, and WordPress-related conference presentation recordings.
- `https://central.wordcamp.org/`: WordCamp is a conference that focuses on everything WordPress; it takes place a number of times during the year in different locations around the world, and this site is the central point for the conference.

Understanding the Codex

The WordPress **Codex** is the central repository of all the information that the official WordPress team has published to help people work with WordPress.

The Codex has some basic tutorials for getting started with WordPress, such as a detailed step-by-step discussion of the installation, and lists of every template tag and hook. Throughout this book, I'll be providing links to specific pages within the Codex, which will deliver more or advanced information on the topics in this book.

The Codex can be found at `https://codex.wordpress.org/Main_Page`. Refer to the following screenshot:

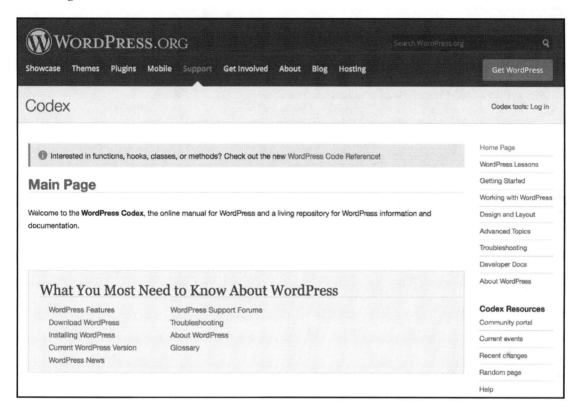

Apart from the Codex, there's also one more resource that will come in handy to new and experienced developers alike. It's called the WordPress *Code Reference*, and it can be found at `https://developer.wordpress.org/reference/`. It delivers a lot of documentation on WordPress's functions, classes, methods, and hooks.

Getting support from other users

The online WordPress community asks questions and responds with solutions on the WordPress forum at `https://wordpress.org/support/`. It's an excellent place to go if you can't find the answer to a problem in the codex. If you have a question, then probably someone else has had it as well, and WordPress experts spend time in the forum answering them and providing solutions.

Using theme and plugin directories

There are official directories for themes and plugins on `WordPress.org`. Though not every theme and plugin is available there, the ones that are, have been vetted by the community and the review teams. Anything you download from these directories is likely to be relatively bug-free. Plugins and themes that you get from other sources can have malicious code, so be careful. You can also see what the community thinks of these downloads by looking at ratings, comments and popularity metrics:

- You can find the **Theme Directory** at `https://wordpress.org/themes/`
- The **Plugin Directory** is located at `https://wordpress.org/plugins/`

Following is the screenshot for the WordPress **Theme Directory**:

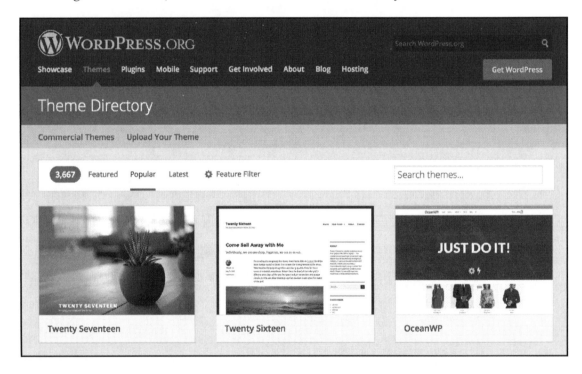

Summary

Having a website of your own is essential these days, no matter if you are an individual or a small business, and no matter if you are blogging regularly or just want some accurate static content up on the internet. In this chapter, we reviewed basic information about WordPress, blogging, and common blog terms for those of you who are new to the concept.

WordPress is an excellent platform that can run your website (blog or otherwise). It's packed with top-of-the-line features and is so flexible that it can really do anything you want, and it has a wealth of online resources. Additionally, it's easy to use, and you need no special skills or prior experience to work with it. Last but not least, it is 100% free!

In the next chapter, we will explore the choices and steps involved in installing WordPress and getting started. We'll cover how to install WordPress in more than a couple of ways, how to find your way around the WordPress admin panel, and how to configure your site's basic details.

Getting Started with WordPress

2

his chapter will guide you through the process of setting up WordPress and customizing its essential features. You can choose between a couple of options regarding where your WordPress website will live. WordPress is a relatively small package of software (less than 10 MB) as well as being easy to install and administer.

Here's what's important:

- WordPress is available in easily downloadable formats at `https://wordpress.org/download/`
- WordPress is a free, open source application and is released under GNU **General Public License (GPL)**, `https://en.wikipedia.org/wiki/GNU_General_Public_License`

This means that anyone who produces a modified version of the software is required to maintain the same freedom that the GPL provides, and then people buying or using the software can also modify and redistribute it. Thus, WordPress and other software released under the GPL are maintained as open source.

In this chapter, you will learn how to do the following:

- Set up WordPress on an external web host
- Install WordPress manually—both on an external host and also locally for development and testing
- Perform basic setup tasks in the WordPress admin panel (the `wp-admin`)

These are your absolute WordPress fundamentals. Learning what's in this chapter will give you a good start in the world of WordPress.

Building your WordPress website – start here

The first decision you have to make is where your blog is going to live. You have two basic options when creating your site:

- Either go to `WordPress.com` and sign up for a free (or paid) website (that way, you get the website installed for you)
- Or, go to WordPress.org and use the open-source version of WordPress—by installing it on your own server or a server of a third-party hosting firm

Let's look at some of the advantages and disadvantages of each of these two options.

The two worlds of WordPress – the difference between WordPress.com and WordPress.org

This aspect of the WordPress ecosystem is a bit confusing, but there are basically two versions of WordPress available out there. To make this simpler, let me just use the website addresses where you can find them:

- WordPress.com (`https://wordpress.com/`)
- WordPress.org (`https://wordpress.org/`)

Surprisingly, those two websites don't lead to the same place. In fact, they lead to two completely different places:

- WordPress.com is a commercial website-building solution. You can go there, sign up for an account, and then configure your website based on the available settings and designs.
- WordPress.org is an open source website software. To use it, you first need to get access to a web server—either rent it out from a hosting company or set up a server on a local machine—and then you can install WordPress on it.

This book is purely about the WordPress software that can be obtained from WordPress.org. We do not cover WordPress.com much, since it is a commercial service that's not as versatile.

Pros and cons

Even though WordPress.org is the topic of this book, there are still valid reasons why some users might be interested in WordPress.com. The main advantage of using WordPress.com (https://wordpress.com/) is that, it's them who take care of all the technical details for you. You're not responsible for anything else but the management of your content. A major disadvantage is that you don't have full control over your website. The other advantages and disadvantages are as follows:

- WordPress.com will not let you upload or edit your own theme, though it will let you (for a fee) edit the Cascading Style Sheets (CSS) of the themes that are already there.
- WordPress.com will not let you upload or manage plugins at all. Some plugins are installed by default (most notably Akismet, for spam blocking, and also plugins supporting Google Sitemaps, caching, carousel slideshows, image galleries, polls, site stats, and some social media buttons), but you can neither uninstall them nor install others. Additional features are available for a fee.
- A major advantage of working with the software from WordPress.org is that *you have control over everything*. You can add and edit themes, add and remove plugins, and even edit the WordPress application files yourself if you wish to (however, don't do this unless you're confident about your WordPress skills).
- The disadvantage of WordPress.org is that you'll have to keep the WordPress software up to date on your own, and in some cases install it by yourself as well, but that's relatively simple, and we'll cover it in this chapter.

Which one to use

The following table is a brief overview of the essential differences between using WordPress.com versus downloading a package from WordPress.org and then installing it on your own server:

	WordPress.com (online platform/service)	WordPress.org (open source software)
Installation	No need to install anything; just sign up.	Install WordPress yourself, either manually or via your host's control panel.
Themes	Use the themes made available by WordPress.com (https://wordpress.com/).	Use any theme available anywhere, written by anyone (even by yourself).
Plugins	No ability to add third-party plugins.	Use any plugin available anywhere, written by anyone (even by yourself).
Upgrades	WordPress.com provides automatic upgrades.	You have to upgrade it yourself when upgrades are available.
Widgets	Widget availability depends on the available themes.	You can widgetize any theme yourself.
Maintenance	You don't have to do any maintenance.	You're responsible for the maintenance of your site.
Advertising	No advertising of your own allowed. However, WordPress.com itself sometimes runs ads on your site.	You can advertise anything and in any amount you like.
Ownership	Even though the content belongs to you, WordPress.com can take down your blog at any moment if they consider it to be inappropriate.	You have complete control over your site, and no one can force you to take it down.
Domain	Your site is available as a subdomain under .wordpress.com by default, but you can also upgrade to a paid package and use your own, manually registered domain name.	You can use any manually registered domain name.

Overall, WordPress.org is a much better choice for those who want to learn how the WordPress platform works and how to use it to build optimized and versatile websites. WordPress.com might be a better solution for those who simply need a website fast.

Getting and installing WordPress

We're going to cover how to install WordPress in three different ways.

Installing WordPress through a web host

In most scenarios, users will want to install and then use WordPress on a live website—one that's publicly visible. The easiest way to do that is to go to one of the popular hosting companies, rent some server space from them, and then have WordPress installed on that server. Even though this might sound intimidating at first, the process is actually very simple, and in most cases, the hosting company takes care of all the technical steps.

The main advantage of this approach is that you're effectively freed from having to worry about server configurations, and instead can simply start working with your WordPress website very quickly. The disadvantage—if we can call it that—is that you don't get the educational value from installing WordPress by hand.

How to choose a web host for WordPress

There are many hosting companies that label themselves *for WordPress* in some capacity. Depending on the budget you have at hand, you can get an optimized hosting setup for as little as $3-4 a month. At the other end of the spectrum, there are also advanced setups at $100 a month or more. When picking a company for your needs, consider the following:

- Your budget—as mentioned in the preceding paragraph
- The number of sites you want to host at the same time—probably just one
- How much traffic you're expecting on the site—probably less than 5,000 visitors a month if you're just starting out
- The reputation of the company that you want to go with - this can be checked via sites like ReviewSignal (`https://reviewsignal.com/webhosting`)

Getting through the installation process

To show you how the installation process is done, we need to pick a host that we're going to use as our example. Looking at the scores at ReviewSignal, SiteGround seems to be at the top of the list, having the best user ratings among shared hosting platforms. We're going to pick that one for our example. Please keep in mind that this works similarly with most hosts, so you shouldn't see significant differences if you choose a different host.

To get started, go to `https://www.siteground.com/wordpress-hosting.htm`:

1. Once there, you can click on the sign-up button below the cheapest plan that SiteGround offers, as seen in the next screenshot:

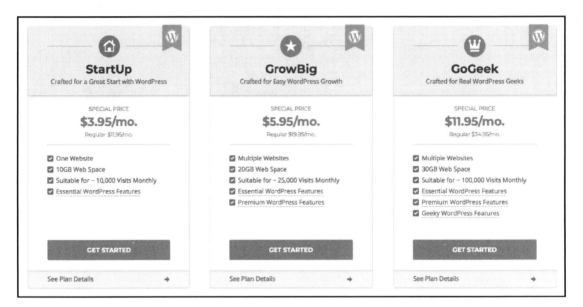

2. In the next step, you will be able to register a new domain name for your site or connect an existing domain name if you have one:

3. The next step is all about inputting your personal data and finalizing the purchase. A couple of things you might want to pay special attention to—all visible in the next screenshot—is your server location and some extras that SiteGround offers you.

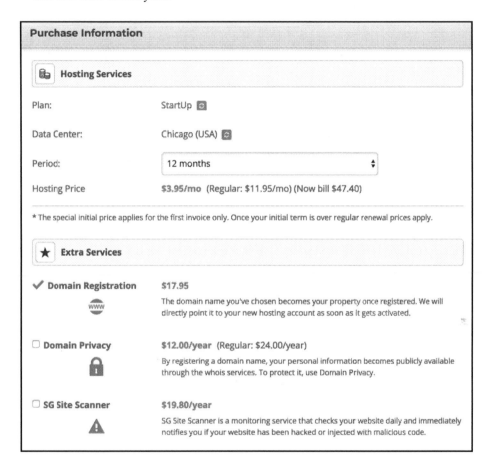

- As for the server location, it's best to pick a location that's the closest to you.
- As for the extras, it's up to you if you need any of them—they are not mandatory.

Once you finalize this setup, you will have a new hosting account ready to go. Now the only thing that's left is to have WordPress installed on that account. What's good about SiteGround is that they will take care of the entire installation for you. When you first log in to your user panel at SiteGround, you will see a prompt asking you if you need any of the popular website platforms installed—with WordPress being one of the options.

The only thing you need to do here is provide SiteGround with your desired login details for WordPress and click the **Confirm** button. That is all. After this step, you will see a new instance of WordPress in your SiteGround user panel. If you click on **Go to Admin Panel**, you will be redirected to the main WordPress dashboard:

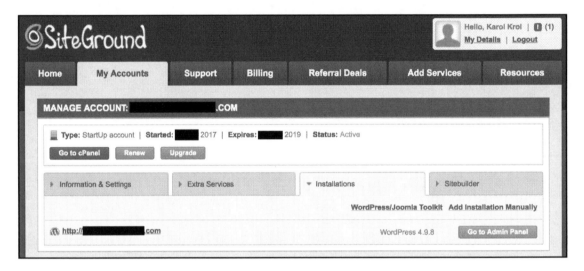

Installing WordPress manually

WordPress can be installed in a variety of different ways, and if you don't want to use the *via a host* method described earlier, you will probably be interested in installing WordPress manually.

Manual installations can be useful for a number of reasons. First of all, you might want to use WordPress on a local server. Secondly, even if you're on a remote server, that server might not have any auto-install features available. This is where the manual installation comes into play.

Preparing the environment

A good first step is to make sure you have an environment setup that is ready for WordPress. This means you need to ensure that the server meets the minimum requirements and that your database is ready. For WordPress to work, your web host must provide you with a server that fulfills the following requirements:

- Support for PHP version 5.2.4 or greater (PHP 7.2+ is recommended)
- Provision of a MySQL database (full access) of version 5.6 or greater (alternatively, MariaDB version 10.0 or greater)

These minimum requirements tend to change occasionally. The most current requirements can always be found at https://wordpress.org/about/requirements/.

You can determine whether your host meets these two requirements by contacting the support team at your web host. If it does, you're ready to move on to the next step.

Installing WordPress locally

In order to test WordPress out, you don't actually need access to a live web server. You can do your tests on a local server as well and then only deploy your site to the public if need be. The most common way of working with local WordPress is by installing it on a XAMPP server. XAMPP is available for Windows, Mac, and Linux, plus it is free. You can get it from https://www.apachefriends.org/index.html.

XAMPP's official website offers some guides on how to set up the server, but if you need a more step-by-step tutorial, please refer to https://themeisle.com/blog/install-xampp-and-wordpress-locally/.

Downloading WordPress

Once you have checked your environment, you need to download WordPress from https://wordpress.org/download/. There's a big blue download button there. It's hard to miss. What you get once you click it is a .zip archive of the most recent version of the WordPress software. Extracting that archive onto your desktop will give you a directory called wordpress. In itself, that directory isn't very useful as a stand-alone thing. In order to make it work, you somehow need to get it onto your web server. This will be covered in the next subsections in this chapter.

If you're working on local server setup, all you have to do is copy that WordPress directory to wherever your local server operates from. If you're working on a remote server, you'll have to use third-party tools to upload WordPress there. I'll show you how to do that next.

Uploading the files

We need to upload all the files of WordPress to our web server using any **File Transfer Protocol (FTP)** client. There are several FTP clients available on the internet that are either freeware (no cost) or require a small fee. If you don't already have an FTP client, try one of the following:

- **Filezilla**: https://filezilla-project.org/download.php?type=client (for Mac, Windows, or Linux)
- **Fetch**: https://fetchsoftworks.com/ (for Mac only)
- **SmartFTP**: https://www.smartftp.com/ (for Windows only)

A note about security

Whenever possible, you should use **secure FTP (sFTP)** rather than regular FTP. If you're using sFTP, all of the data sent and received is encrypted. With FTP, data is sent in plain text and can easily be nabbed by hackers. Check both your FTP software and your hosting options and select sFTP if it's available.

Here's the process of installing WordPress via FTP:

1. Using your FTP client, connect to the FTP server using the server address, username, and password provided to you by your host. (If you're not sure what those are, you can always contact your web host support and ask a support agent for these details.)

2. Next, open the folder where you want WordPress to live. You may want to install WordPress in your root folder, which will mean that visitors will see your WordPress website's home page when they go to your main URL - for example, `http://yoursite.com`. Alternatively, you may want to install WordPress in a subfolder, for example, `http://yoursite.com/blog/`. Refer to the following screenshot:

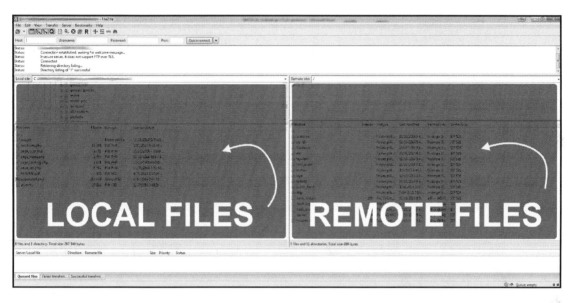

3. On the left side, you will see the files from your local folder, and on the right side, you will see your remote folder. (Note that the FTP client you are using may have a slightly different layout, but this is a general idea.)

4. Now select all of the WordPress files on your local machine from the left pane, and drag them onto the right pane. You can watch as your FTP client uploads the files one at a time and they appear on the right panel. This may take a few minutes, so be patient.

5. If you're installing WordPress on your local server, just be sure to place the WordPress files in the correct `webroot` directory on your computer.

Once all of the files have been uploaded, you're ready to proceed with the installation.

Finalizing WordPress's on-screen setup

At this point, it's time to proceed with the famous 5-minute installation of WordPress. (The fact that WordPress can be installed in 5 minutes or less is widely advertised on the official WordPress website.)

1. If you access the main website URL of your new WordPress site via a web browser, you will see a short introductory message instructing you to choose the language that you want to perform the installation in:

2. After this, you will be presented with another screen informing you of all the required details that you'll need in order to complete the installation successfully. Currently, those details are the following:

   - **Database name**: For example, this can be `wptestblog`.

   - **Database username**: For example, this can be `localdbuser`.

   - **Database password**: For example, `62dcx%^_0hnm`—the more complex the password, the better.

   - **Database host**: This is the host address of your web server's database. If you're running the server locally, this will be `localhost`. If you're trying to run WordPress on a third-party web host, this is the address of the database server of that host.

The big question, therefore, is where to get all of this information from. The answer is your web host. Most of the large web hosts offer you a way to create your own databases via an online control panel, with usernames and passwords of your choice. If you're not sure how to do this, just email or call your hosting provider for assistance. Professional support teams will be glad to help you with this.

3. Once you have those four parameters, you can press the **Let's go!** button and proceed to the next step of the installation. The following is a screenshot of the main setup form:

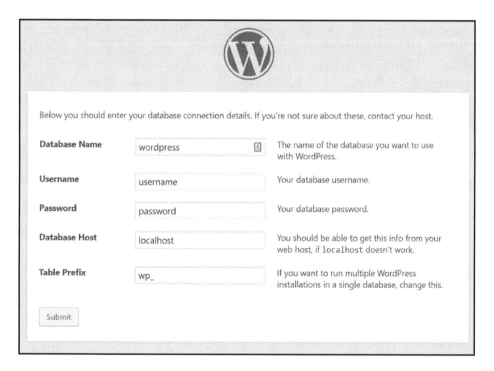

As you can see, the details are the same as those shown in an earlier screenshot. Of course, your details will be different. Also, another important point to note is that there's an additional field labeled **Table Prefix**. This is the default prefix that every table in your database will have before its name. The default value in that field is wp_. It is recommended that you change this to any two- or three-letter word of your choice and end it with an underscore (_), just as a safety precaution against standard database attacks on known WordPress tables.

4. After clicking on the **Submit** button, you will be redirected to the final confirmation page. All you have to do here is click on the **Run the install** button. The best indication that the online installation is going well is the presence of the following screen:

5. This is the final setup page. Here, you set up the core details of your new site. Now, fill out the installation form (you will be able to change all of these later, so don't be too worried about getting locked into your choices):

   - **Site Title**: Fill in the name of your blog (it can be something simple, such as *Daily Cooking*).
   - **Username**: It's in your best interest to choose a username that's not obvious. For instance, if you go with *admin*, it will be very easy to guess for someone who might want to hack into your blog. Also worth pointing out is the fact that this account is the administrator account, which has the most privileges and access rights to all areas of the site. Opt for something difficult to guess, such as *Site-Master-45* and don't worry, silly is good.
   - **Password**: Choose a secure password, one that has both upper and lowercase letters, a number or two, and even a few punctuation marks. WordPress suggests some options for you here.
   - **Your Email**: Double-check that this is correct. This is the email address WordPress will use to contact you about the blog, comments, and so on. If you do not get an email from your WordPress site shortly after installing it, check your spam folder.
   - **Search Engine Visibility**: This is the final checkbox, yet possibly one of the most important settings on this list. If you leave it unchecked (recommended), your site is going to be accessible through Google and other search engines. Checking it means banning your site from the search engines.

6. Now, click on **Install WordPress**.

You're done with the installation! WordPress will now greet you with the main login page - this is where you can access the main admin panel of the website (also known as the `wp-admin`). Alternatively, you can also enter the admin panel by pointing your browser to `http://yoursite.com/wp-admin`. If you're not already logged in, this URL will redirect you to the login page.

Learning more

If you'd like to see an even more detailed step-by-step guide for manual installation, take a look at this page in the WordPress codex: `https://codex.wordpress.org/Installing_WordPress`.

Furthermore, if you visit `https://codex.wordpress.org/Getting_Started_with_WordPress#Installation`, you will find additional installation instructions as well as specifics on changing file permissions, using FTP, importing from other blogging engines, and more.

Installing WordPress through an auto-installer script

Some web hosts provide their customers with access to a range of auto-installer scripts for various web platforms, including WordPress. Most of these auto-installers have quite similar functionalities, and the actual process of installing a new WordPress site is similar as well. Here, we're going to focus on one of these scripts, **Softaculous** (`https://www.softaculous.com/`).

 This is yet another way of installing a WordPress site, and we're covering it here to make this book as complete as it can be. However, if you've already managed to install your site using the methods described earlier, then this section won't be of any use to you at this point.

Softaculous is the preferred method of WordPress installation for many professional developers and bloggers. In some cases, it's the fastest method when dealing with a completely new hosting account maintained by a new web host. Softaculous is available on hosting accounts running on many management platforms, such as *cPanel*, *Plesk*, *DirectAdmin*, *InterWorx*, and *H-Sphere*. Most probably, your hosting account will be using one of these platforms. The following screenshot shows cPanel, which is the most popular platform of its kind:

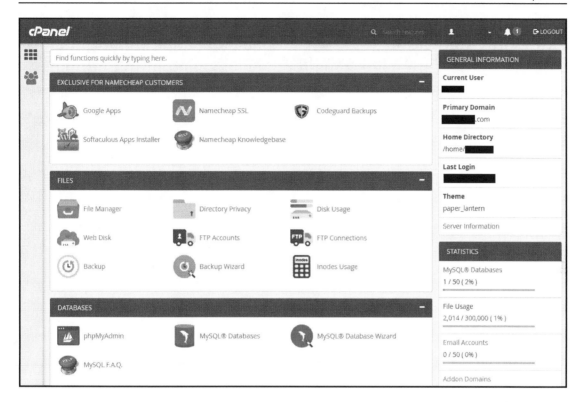

Although different platforms have different user interfaces, the core functionalities from a user's point of view remain mostly the same. To access Softaculous, just scroll down until you see the main section (or icon) labeled Softaculous. Once there, you can see the WordPress icon among the others:

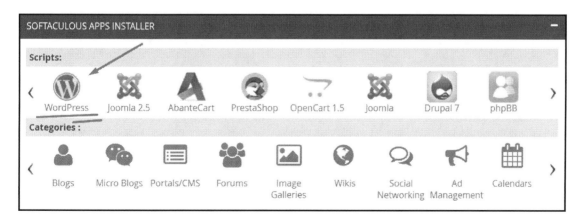

The whole idea of using this script is to make things quicker and more hassle-free so that you don't have to take care of creating databases manually or of setting configuration files. Softaculous will handle all of this for you. The following is the site creation form:

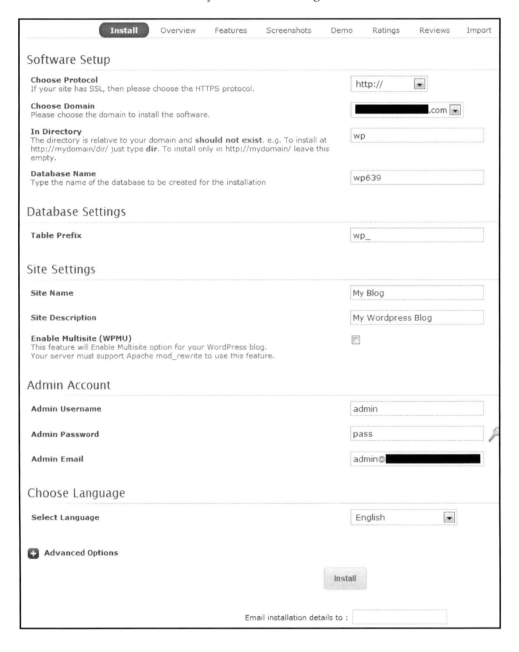

Keep in mind that those interfaces tend to change from time to time, so depending on when you read this book, your Softaculous panel may look different. Don't worry though, as it surely will be similarly understandable. Here's a breakdown of all the fields you can expect to see and what details to put in them:

- **Choose Protocol**: You can stick with the default value of `http://` or change to `https://`, if available.
- **Choose Domain**: If you have more than one domain assigned to your hosting account, then you get to choose which one you want to use here. For single-domain accounts (most likely the case), this drop-down field has only one option.
- **In Directory**: If you want to install your WordPress site under a subdirectory, then input its name here (just the name). If you want to install the site in the main directory (`http://yoursite.com/`), then make sure the field is blank.
- **Database Name**: You can confidently go with the default value.
- **Table Prefix**: As discussed earlier in this chapter, you can change this to something unique (in my case, it's `wp_`).
- **Site Name**: This is the name of your site (in the present case, `My Blog`).
- **Site Description**: This is the tagline (in the present case, **My WordPress Blog**).
- **Enable Multisite (WPMU)**: Leave this unchecked unless you're an advanced user planning to launch a multisite installation.
- **Admin Username**, **Admin Password**, and **Admin Email**: These are the details of your admin account, similar to the ones we had to provide during the manual WordPress installation.
- **Select Language**: WordPress has many localized versions of the platform, not just English, and you can choose one here.

Clicking on the **Install** button starts the installation process. The process itself requires no supervision, and you will be able to access your site as soon as it finishes after roughly 1 or 2 minutes. You can check whether the installation has been successful through the standard `http://yoursite.com/` and `http://yoursite.com/wp-admin/` URLs. In other words, this is the end of the installation process through Softaculous. As you can see, it's much simpler and quicker than manual installation. Furthermore, Softaculous always installs the most recent version of WordPress, so you don't have to worry about getting something out of date.

 You can also encounter other auto-installer scripts, which are similar to Softaculous, such as *Fantastico, Installatron, MOJO,* and *SimpleScripts*.

The wp-admin panel

WordPress installs a powerful and flexible administration area where you can manage all of your website content and so much more. Throughout the book, this will be referred to in shorthand as the **wp-admin**, or **WP Admin**, or the **WordPress dashboard** in some cases.

Now that you've successfully installed WordPress, it's time for our first look at the wp-admin. There are some immediate basic changes that are recommended to make sure your installation is set up properly.

You can always get to the wp-admin by visiting http://yoursite.com/wp-admin/ (this URL is also the reason why we're calling it the wp-admin). If it's your first time there, you'll be redirected to the login page. In the future, WordPress will check whether you're already logged in and if so, you'll skip the login page.

To log in, just enter the username and password you chose during the installation. Then, click on **Log In**.

Whenever you log in, you'll be taken directly to the **Dashboard** section of the wp-admin. The following is a screenshot of the wp-admin that you will see immediately after logging in:

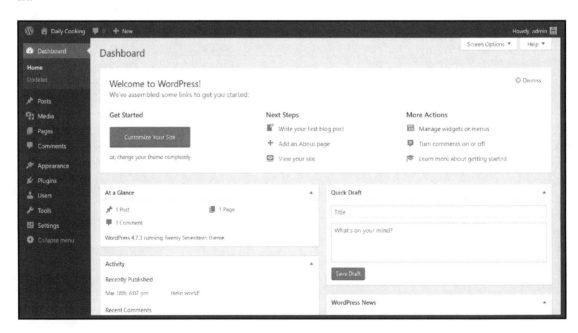

You'll see a lot of information and options there, which we will explore throughout this book. For now, we will focus on the items that we need to consider right after a successful installation. First, let's take a brief look into the `wp-admin` and the main **Dashboard** section. The very top bar there, referred to as the *top bar* or *admin bar*, is mostly dark gray and contains the following:

- A rollover drop-down menu, triggered by hovering over the WordPress logo in the top-left corner, featuring a set of links to **About WordPress** (some details about the current installation of WordPress), **WordPress.org**, **Documentation**, **Support Forums**, and **Feedback**
- A link to the front page of your WordPress website (in this example, the title of the whole site is *Daily Cooking*), the clickable *house* icon
- An updates and activity section containing either links to the newest comments or pending updates
- A rollover drop-down menu with handy links to **New Post**, **New Media**, **New Page**, and **New User**, triggered by hovering over the *plus* icon
- Lastly, on the far right, your user-linked to your profile, which is yet another drop-down menu containing a link labeled **Edit My Profile** and, finally, the **Log Out** link

You'll also notice the **Screen Options** tab, which appears on many screens within the `wp-admin`. If you click on it, it will slide down a checklist of items on the page to show or hide. This will be different on each page. I encourage you to play around with this element by checking and unchecking the items, as you discover whether you need them or not:

Right next to the **Screen Options** tab, you will find the **Help** tab. Just like the **Screen Options** tab, this one appears on many screens within the `wp-admin`. Whenever you're in doubt regarding a specific screen, you can always check the **Help** tab for instructions. Accessing the **Help** tab is always quicker and, in most cases, more effective than searching for solutions online.

On the left side of the screen is the main menu:

You can click on any word in the main menu to be taken to the dedicated page for that section, or you can hover your cursor over a given link to see all of the possible subsections you can visit. For example, if you hover your cursor over **Settings**, you'll see the subpages for the **Settings** section, and at that point, you can click on either of the subpages or the main **Settings** link itself:

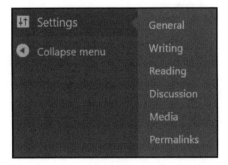

The top menu and the main menu exist on every page within the `wp-admin`. The main section on the right contains information for the current page you're on. In this case, we're in the **Dashboard** section. It contains boxes that have information about your blog, and about WordPress in general.

In the new versions of WordPress, when you log in for the first time, you're presented with a welcome message, similar to the one that follows:

In short, it's the welcome panel that allows you to access some of the crucial sections of the `wp-admin` with just one click. Once you click on the **Dismiss** link, the panel will no longer be displayed after login. In its current version, the panel allows you to do the following (going from top left to bottom right):

- Customize the current theme, but only if the theme provides some customization features (not all themes do)
- Change the current theme to a new one
- Edit the front page
- Create new pages
- Write your first blog post
- View your site
- Manage menus and widgets
- Turn comments on or off (by default, they are on)
- Learn more about how to get started with WordPress, which is an external link pointing to `https://codex.wordpress.org/First_Steps_With_WordPress`

In this and the following chapters, we will get to know all of the crucial methods of managing a WordPress site, and once we gain some experience, with time, this welcome panel can make our everyday work much quicker. Therefore, let's jump right into the general site settings section.

In this book, all instructions regarding which page within the `wp-admin` to navigate to are indicated by phrases such as *navigate to Settings | General* or *navigate to Posts | Add New*. This always describes the path you should take to get there via the main menu.

Changing general blog information

You may need to change or add some general blog information after a successful installation (such as the blog title or a one-sentence description) to get your website set up and running with the correct information. To get started with this, navigate to **Settings** in the main menu:

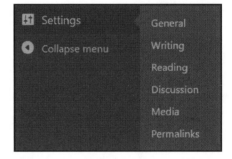

There are many options you can set here, most of which are self-explanatory. We'll look at the most important ones. Obviously, you can change your blog's title. Mine is called **Daily Cooking**, for example. You can also change the blog description, which is used in most themes as a subtitle for the blog, like the subtitle of a book. The default description is *Just another WordPress site*. You'll probably want to change that. Let's change ours to `Exploring cooking every day of the week`:

General Settings

Site Title	Daily Cooking
Tagline	Exploring cooking every day of the week
	In a few words, explain what this site is about.
WordPress Address (URL)	https://YOURSITE.com
Site Address (URL)	https://YOURSITE.com
	Enter the address here if you want your site home page to be different from your WordPress installation directory.
Email Address	
	This address is used for admin purposes. If you change this we will send you an email at your new address to confirm it. The new address will not become active until confirmed.
Membership	☐ Anyone can register
New User Default Role	Subscriber ⬍
Site Language	English (United States) ⬍
Timezone	UTC+0 ⬍
	Choose either a city in the same timezone as you or a UTC timezone offset.
	Universal time (UTC) is 2019-02-18 16:43:38 .

One of the things you probably want to take a look at on this page is the **Timezone** option. Whether you have a blog (with timestamps on every post) or not, it's important that WordPress knows what time zone you're in. Particularly when you want to schedule a page or post for the future, show users accurate time stamps, or even just make sure that email notifications are correctly timestamped. Additionally, if you're planning to publish content internationally, meaning that your target audience is located in an entirely different location, it's good to set the time zone to represent your target audience and not yourself.

The pull-down menu will show you different UTC settings, along with the biggest cities around the world. Just choose a city in your favored time zone. After you save the changes, the time that appears further down the page (next to **Time Format**) will change to the time you chose, so that you can check and make sure it's correct.

Another feature worth considering on this page is whether or not you want to allow user registration on your site. For most sites, this is not particularly useful, but if you're planning to make the site community-driven or utilize some form of crowdsourcing, then this might be worth considering. In that case, it's not advisable to give new users a user role higher than **Subscriber** (the default value).

When you're done making changes to this page, be sure to click on the **Save Changes** button at the bottom of the page.

Finally, there's only one more component you should adjust in your new site's settings before publishing any content: the permalinks. As WordPress defines them, *permalinks* are the permanent URLs to your individual pages, blog posts, categories, and tags. By default, WordPress links to your new posts using a highly unoptimized URL structure. For instance, if you create a post titled *How to Cook the Best Meal Ever*, WordPress will link it as `http://yoursite.com/?p=123` (or something similar). The main problem with this structure is that it doesn't indicate what the page is about. Neither your visitors nor Google will be able to make a guess. In the case of Google, such a structure can also significantly impact your future search engine rankings. Therefore, to set a more optimized structure, you can go to **Settings** | **Permalinks**. Here are the available settings:

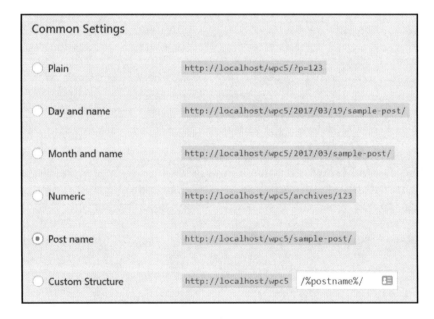

The best setting from a visitor's point of view, as well as from Google's, is the one labeled **Post name**. Going back to the example with the *How to Cook the Best Meal Ever* post, if you set the permalinks to **Post name**, the URL of this post will be `http://yoursite.com/how-to-cook-the-best-meal-ever/`, which is a lot clearer and predictable. You can always review the official information on permalinks whenever you wish at `https://codex.wordpress.org/Using_Permalinks`.

Further down the page, there are also optional settings for **Category base** and **Tag base**. By default, **Category base** is set to `category`. For example, if you have a category called *recipes* then you can view all posts under this category at `http://yoursite.com/category/recipes`.

Some site owners prefer to change this to something more user-friendly, for example, `topics`. Even though this conveys the exact same message, it can be much easier to grasp for visitors who are not that familiar with the standards of web content publishing. In the end, your category base is solely down to your discretion. **Tag base**, on the other hand, rarely needs any adjustments.

Retrieving a lost password

If you have lost your password and can't get into your `wp-admin` panel, you can easily retrieve it by clicking on the **Lost your password?** link on the login page. A newly generated password will be emailed to you at the email address you provided during the installation process. This is why you need to be sure that you enter a valid email address. Otherwise, you will not be able to retrieve your password.

Getting a Gravatar

One final point that's worth discussing in this chapter is the matter of WordPress avatars. Although WordPress provides a number of possibilities in this area, the most popular one revolves around an external service, **Globally Recognized Avatar** (**Gravatar**). Gravatar started as a tool meant to provide people with the capability of using the same profile picture (avatar) across the entire web.

What this means in plain English is that whenever you sign up for a web service, and if the service is Gravatar-compatible, so to speak, then it will fetch your profile picture from Gravatar automatically, instead of forcing you to upload it manually from your computer. Apart from the profile picture, Gravatar also gives you a personal online profile that anyone can see whenever they click on your (Gravatar) profile picture or something called Hovercard. Now, what does all this have to do with WordPress, right? Well, WordPress is one of those services and tools that widely support Gravatar in all possible areas of the platform. For example, if you create a new blog and use an admin email address that's hooked up to Gravatar, your profile picture in WordPress will immediately be replaced with the one provided by Gravatar. Moreover, if you ever comment on any WordPress blog with a Gravatar email address, your profile picture will be set as the avatar for the comment itself.

To set your own Gravatar, just go to `https://en.gravatar.com/` and click on the **Create Your Own Gravatar** button. You'll be presented with a sign-up form for Gravatar. Since Gravatar is part of WordPress.com, you are able to log in if you already have a WordPress.com account. If not, you can create a new one. The fields are quite standard, with you being prompted to enter your email address and your preferred username and password.

Once you've completed the sign-up process, you can finally set your Gravatar. On the main **Manage Gravatars** page (accessible via the top menu), there's a link labeled **Add a new image**—this is where you can upload a Gravatar. The good thing about Gravatar is that you can choose where you want to get the picture from. You can either upload it from your computer, get it from some other place on the web (for example, from a direct link to your Facebook profile image), or use a picture that you've uploaded as your Gravatar previously.

In the next step, Gravatar allows you to crop and adjust your image. When you're finally happy with the result, you can click the big button and proceed to the rating settings of your image. Every Gravatar can be classified as **G-rated**, **PG-rated**, **R-rated**, or **X-rated**. The fact is that if you select anything other than **G-rated**, your Gravatar won't be displayed on all sites. Thus, it's a good practice to upload only appropriate images. When you're done with this step, from now on, your Gravatar is set up and ready to use. Gravatar also enables you to hook up more than one email address to a single account, as well as use more than one image. This is actually a great feature because you can manage each of your email addresses and every form of your online presence with just one Gravatar account.

Now, you can go back to your WordPress blog and check whether your new Gravatar has appeared in the profile section within the `wp-admin` (provided that you've used the same email address for the account).

Summary

You have learned a lot in this chapter. You now know how to install WordPress on a remote as well as a local server, and then change the basic settings of your website. You also have a basic understanding of how to handle your online image or brand via Gravatar.

In the next chapter, you will learn how to create your first blog posts and other types of content, how to work with comments and moderate discussions, plus other crucial aspects of blog/website management.

3
Creating Blog Content

Now that your WordPress installation is up and running, you are ready to start creating content. Learning how to do this effectively will help you resonate with your audience better and give them content that's optimized and easy to consume. In this chapter, you will learn the following topics:

- How the WordPress admin dashboard works (also commonly referred to as wp-admin) and how to find your way around it
- How to write a new blog post
- How to control all the information associated with a blog post, not just the title and content, but also images and media
- How to work with comments—what they are for and how to manage them
- How to keep your content organized and searchable using tags and categories

WordPress admin conventions

In the wp-admin, you have the ability to manage a number of different types of content and ways of sorting content, including posts, categories, pages, links, media uploads, and more. WordPress uses a similar format for various screens. Let's explore them here.

Lists of items

Every type of content that can be managed in WordPress has a separate dedicated screen that lists all of the individual content items. Since this chapter is about creating posts, let's see an example of what a list of posts would look like:

As you can see, the name of the content type is at the top (in this case, it's **Posts**). The list of the items also has columns with various other info:

- Each item on the list shows its **Title**. You can always click on an item title to edit it.
- If you hover your mouse over a specific row, as I hovered over **Hello world!** in the preceding screenshot, you will see four additional links. The first three are always the same (**Edit**, **Quick Edit**, and **Trash**), while the fourth varies between **View** and **Preview**, depending on whether we're dealing with an already published post or one that's pending. The **Edit**, **Trash**, and **View/Preview** links are pretty self-explanatory, but the **Quick Edit** link deserves an additional word. When you click on it, you will see a panel allowing you to perform some simplified editing (just the basic details and parameters, with no actual content editing):

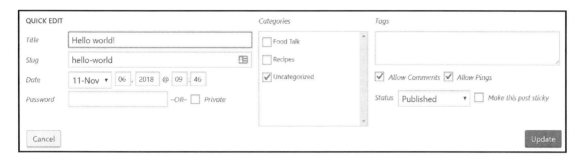

- You can make changes and then click on **Update**, or click on **Cancel** if you've changed your mind.
- The area above the list of posts lets you choose whether to view **All** (posts), **Published** (posts), and also **Drafts**, **Pending**, and **Trash**. At the moment, I have only **All**, **Drafts**, and **Published** posts on my list. Over time, however, the list is bound to get populated some more, as we're going to continue writing new posts (and the same goes for your own site).
- Just below those links is the **Bulk Actions** menu and its corresponding **Apply** button. Choose one or more posts by clicking on their checkboxes (or check the top checkbox to select every item). Then, choose **Edit** or **Move to Trash** from the **Bulk Actions** menu, and, after clicking on **Apply**, you'll be able to bulk delete or bulk edit those posts. Additionally, further down the road, so to speak, when you install some third-party plugins, you'll notice that this **Bulk Actions** menu might contain more options on top of the standard two—editing and deleting.
- The **Filters** menu lets you choose options from the **Date** and **Categories** pull-down lists, and then clicks on the **Filter** button to only show items that meet those criteria.
- The search field along with the **Search Posts** button provides yet another way of filtering through your posts, to find the specific one you're looking for. This might not seem like a particularly useful feature at first, but once you have more than, say, 200 posts published on the site, finding individual entries becomes quite a challenge.
- At the very top is the **Screen Options** dropdown. This tab, which appears on every screen on the WordPress dashboard, will allow you to hide or show particular columns, and choose the number of items to show per page.

Now, let's move on to the main topic of this chapter—posting content.

Posting on your blog

The central activity you'll be doing with your blog is adding posts. A post is like an article in a magazine; it needs a title, body content, and an author (in this case though, WordPress allows multiple authors to contribute to a blog). A blog post also has a lot of other information attached to it, such as a date, excerpt, tags, and categories. In this section, you will learn how to create a new post and what kind of information to attach to it.

Adding a simple post

Whenever you want to add content or carry out maintenance on your WordPress website, you have to start by logging in to the **WordPress administration panel** (wp-admin) of your site. To get to the admin panel, open https://yoursite.com/wp-admin in your web browser.

 Remember that if you have installed WordPress in a subdirectory (for example, blog), then your URL has to include that subdirectory (for example, https://yoursite.com/blog/wp-admin).

From here, there are two ways to get to the screen that will allow you to add a new post:

- Go to **Posts** | **Add New** from the main sidebar menu of the WordPress dashboard
- Click on the **+ New** button in the top bar of the WordPress dashboard and then on **Post** (refer to the following screenshot):

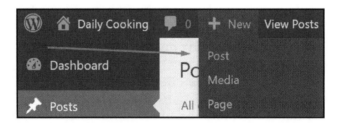

Once you get to the post creation panel, you'll see the main content editor. The next section explains how to use it.

Working in the block-based content editor

The block-based content editor is the latest and greatest addition to WordPress. The project started its life under the name of **Gutenberg** and was in development for around two years before it was finally included in WordPress 5 as the primary content-editing tool:

What you can see in the preceding screenshot is the main view of the block-based content editor. Also notice the helpful onboarding tips that provide you with assistance during your initial encounter with the new editor.

So why is it called the *block-based* editor? Because of the way the editor handles content and manages their structure. The content that you have within your posts or pages is divided into individual blocks, one below the other, all arranged neatly on a (digital) canvas.

Before block-based editing, WordPress used a traditional what-you-see-is-what-you-get editor. It used a classic paragraph-based structure—an approach very similar to how you'd build a Google or a Word document. However, such a traditional structure isn't always suited to handle the modern content requirements of the web. In other words, it makes it hard to build elaborate, visually pleasing blog posts or pages and present them effectively on different devices.

Block-based editing makes more sense since each block of content can be treated individually and handled differently depending on the device used to view the content. Moreover, it's easier to rearrange blocks than it is paragraphs.

So what can *a block* actually be? Think about everything that can be put on a web page. This includes the following:

- Blocks of text
- Images
- Videos
- Quotes
- Headings
- Tables
- Buttons
- Embeds from third-party websites (such as YouTube or Facebook)
- And much more

The following section of the chapter describes how to use the block-based editor to create your first blog post.

Understanding the editor interface

The editor (**Posts** | **Add New**) consists of three main sections, as seen in the following screenshot:

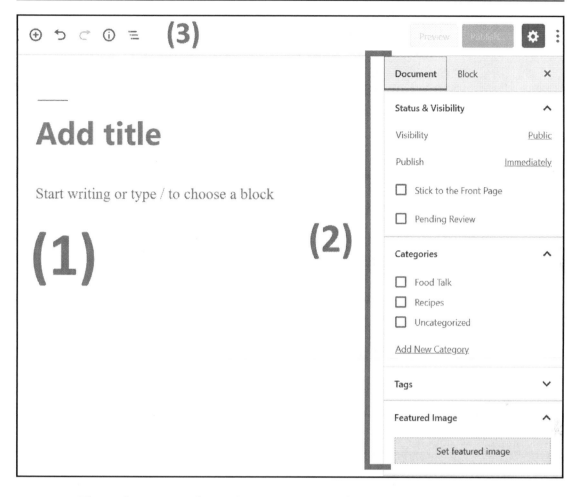

1. **The main canvas**: This is the main content-editing section where you'll be doing most of your work
2. **The settings sidebar**: This allows you to get more in-depth and fine-tune the whole document as well as the individual blocks of content
3. **The top menu bar**: This is where you can handle various administrative tasks

Here is a closer view of what's available in the top bar:

We'll review the symbols from the left:

- The **+** icon allows you to add a new block to the document.
- The next two are the undo and redo buttons.
- The **i** icon gives you some information on the content structure of the document (including the number of words, headings, paragraphs, and blocks).
- The icon with three horizontal bars allows you to navigate between the blocks that are already on the page when editing content; it provides you with shortcut links.
- Then, on the right-hand side, you have the **Preview** and the **Publish** buttons.
- Next to them is the *gear* icon—this toggles the settings sidebar on and off.
- Lastly, there's the icon with three vertical dots. This one lets you enable additional on-screen elements that can make your work with the document more straightforward (for example, you can enter the distraction-free mode, focus on one block at a time, view the keyboard shortcuts, and more).

I encourage you to experiment with what's available here on your own.

Creating your first blog post

Now that we know what's going on with the block-based editor interface, it's time to start working on our first blog post!

1. To begin, enter a title for your blog post where it says **Add title**:

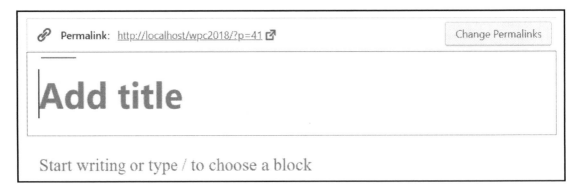

2. When you have done that, move your mouse cursor one line and start typing your post:

As you start typing, you'll immediately see that there are various editing tools available now. You can align your text to the left, right, and center. You can use bold or italics, and even add links to your content. To add a bullet list, just press the *Enter* key on your keyboard and then start the next line with a hyphen (-). It will be converted to a list item automatically.

3. To remove a block or perform some other action on it, you can click on the three dots next to the formatting options:

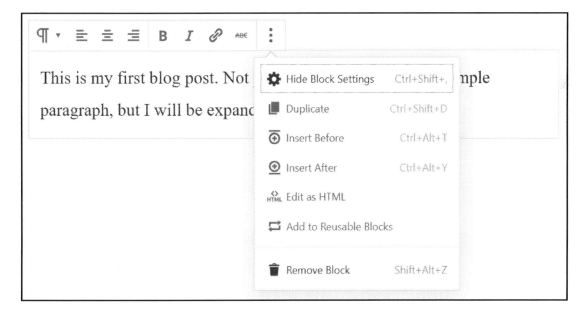

4. Apart from that, as you're editing any block, you can see the specific options available for that block in the settings sidebar on the right. For example, for the paragraph block, you can adjust the font, add a drop cap, change the text color, and perform a couple of advanced modifications, everything as seen in the following screenshot:

With our first paragraph of text on the page, now let's add an image.

5. To do that, click on the + icon in the top-left corner of the screen. From the drop-down menu, select **Image**:

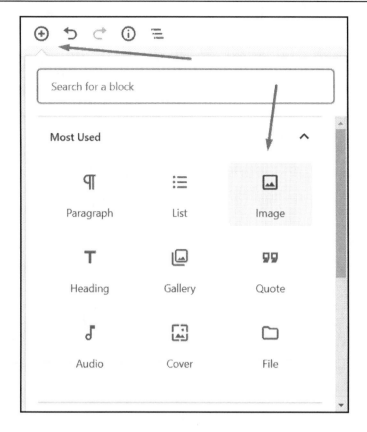

6. You will see a new image block added to the page:

7. That image block allows you to **Upload** a new image, select it from the **Media Library**, or **insert from a URL**. The most common way is to upload a new image from your computer. With that done, you'll see that there are some quite useful options available for images as well. Among other things, you can change the alignment of the image, change its size, add a caption, add a link on the image, and more. Refer to the following screenshot:

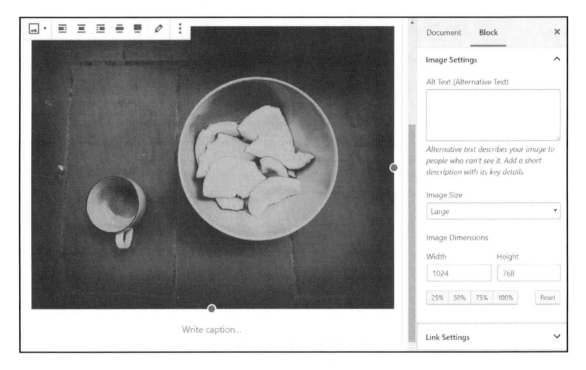

8. Continuing the same approach, we can add all sorts of other blocks onto the canvas, and thus end up with quite a compelling blog post. For example, as an experiment, I created the following blog post:

Daily Cooking

Recipes ∨   This Is the Full Width Page   Home

___

My First Blog Post

👤 Karol   🕓 December 3, 2018   💬 Leave a comment   ✏ Edit

This is my first blog post. Not particularly exciting, just a simple paragraph, but I will be expanding it soon.

That was a nice image, wasn't it?

- it's big
- it's colorful
- it's tasty!

> ## *In the middle of difficulty lies opportunity.*
>
> Albert Einstein

👤 Karol   🕓 December 3, 2018   📁 Uncategorized   ✏ Edit

It consists of the following:

- A standard text paragraph
- An image set to wide
- One more text paragraph
- A bullet list
- A pull quote

Now that we have some "building blocks" in place, we'll see how we can work with them to refine our post.

Aligning blocks and building a post layout

One of the best things about the block-based editor is its versatility and functionality. It's really easy to move things around and fine-tune your blog post up to a point where it looks just perfect.

Adding content blocks one beneath the other—as we've done in the previous step—is just one side of the coin. What's equally impressive is that you can drag and drop the blocks to rearrange them, or use the arrow buttons to move a given block up or down:

What you see in the preceding screenshot are three icons. They appear as you hover your cursor over a block:

- The up and down arrows move the current block one position up or down—this provides a great way to switch text and images around, or do any other simple adjustments to the post's layout.
- The one button in the middle—the grid of six dots—allows you to use drag-and-drop; just grab onto that icon with your mouse and drag the block wherever you want it in the sequence of blocks that are currently part of the post.

One more thing you can do is add new blocks directly below or above another block that's already on the canvas. To do that, hover your cursor close to the top or bottom border of a given block. A new + icon will appear, as seen in the following screenshot. Click that + icon to add a new block exactly where you need it:

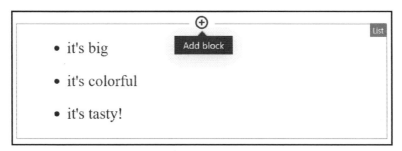

When you're ready and you like how your post looks, it's time to publish it. To do that, click the blue **Publish** button in the top-right corner. When you do that, you'll see one final confirmation screen (we will review the other options on this screen in the next section). Click the **Publish** button again, and your post will go live:

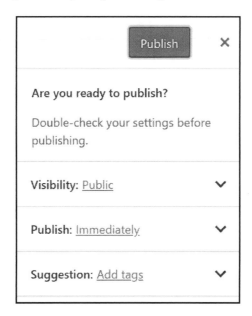

When the process completes, you'll see yourself still on the same screen, but now, the following message will have appeared telling you that your post has been published and that you can see it by clicking on the **View Post** link:

If you view the front page of your site, you'll see that your new post has been added at the top.

Common post options

Now that we've reviewed the basics of creating a post, let's look at some of the other options available when adding a new post or editing an existing one. In this section, we'll look at the most commonly used options and, in the next section, we'll look at the more advanced ones.

Categories and tags

Categories and tags are two types of information that you can add to a blog post. We use them to organize the information in your blog by topic and content (rather than just by date) and to help visitors find what they are looking for on your blog:

- **Categories** are primarily used for structural organizing. They can be hierarchical, meaning a category can be a parent of another category. A relatively busy blog will probably have at least 10 categories, but probably no more than 15 or 20. Each post in such a blog is likely to have between one and four categories assigned to it. Of course, the numbers mentioned are just suggestions; you can create and assign as many categories as you like. For example, a blog about food and cooking might have these categories: **Recipes**, **Food Talk**, **In The Media**, **Ingredients**, and **Restaurants**. The way you structure your categories is entirely up to you as well. There are no real rules regarding this in the WordPress world, just guidelines like these.

- **Tags** are primarily used as shorthand for describing the topics covered in a particular blog post. A relatively busy blog will have anywhere from 15 to even 100 tags in use. Each post in that blog is likely to have three to 10 tags assigned to it. For example, a post on a food blog about a recipe for butternut squash soup may have these tags: *soup, vegetarian, autumn, hot*, and *easy*. Again, you can create and assign as many tags as you like.

To demonstrate how this all works, let's add a new post to the blog. After giving it a title and some content, let's proceed to assign some new tags. To add tags, look at the settings sidebar in the block-based editor and switch the tab to **Document**. From there, click on the **Tags** toggle to enable it, as seen in the following screenshot:

Adding **Tags** couldn't be easier; just type your list of tags into the empty box. Separate them with commas to define where one tag ends and another begins. The tags will be assigned automatically as you type them in. If you want to remove a tag, click on the **x** icon next to it, as demonstrated in the following screenshot:

Each tag you assign using this method will be added to your blog's catalog of tags. The next time you'll start typing in the same tag, WordPress will autosuggest it.

Categories work a bit differently to tags. Once you get your blog going, you'll usually just check the boxes next to existing categories in the **Categories** section of the settings sidebar. When you're just getting started with your first categories, however, you need to create them by hand. To add a new category, look at the same settings sidebar in the block-based editor, switch the tab to **Document**, and then click on the **Categories** toggle to enable it:

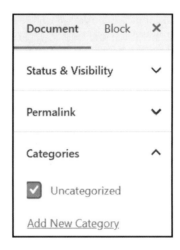

Click on the **Add New Category** link. Type your category into the text field, and click on the **Add New Category** button. Your new category will show up on the list, already checked, just like in the following screenshot:

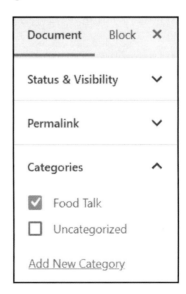

Categories and tags don't just help organize the posts on your blog. They serve an additional important purpose: search engine optimization. To increase the likelihood of your posts showing up for relevant online searches, thereby increasing the visits and views to your website, selecting the right categories and tags will help immensely.

Images in your posts

WordPress makes it easy to add an image to your post, control default image sizes, make minor edits to that image, and designate a *featured* image for your post.

Adding an image to a post

Earlier in this chapter, we learned how to add a simple image to a blog post. Let's now expand on that a bit more.

There are two main methods of adding an image to a blog post (of which we already know the first one):

- Either click on the + button in the top bar of the block-based editor,
- Or click on the image icon that's on the right-hand side of the last empty content block on the canvas, as seen in the following screenshot:

At this point, all you need to do in order to add an image to a post is either select it from the **Media Library**, **Upload** from your computer, or **insert from URL**. There are corresponding buttons for each of these methods. Additionally, you can drag and drop an image straight from your desktop.

Once your image finishes uploading, you'll see it added onto the post's canvas. At this stage, you can customize it some more by taking advantage of the options available in the image's pop-up menu, as seen in the following screenshot:

Starting from the left, we have the following:

- Change block type. This button lets you transform your image block to a gallery block, cover block, file block, or media and text block. Essentially, this feature is meant to show you other similar block types that might be more suited for the type of content you want to add. I encourage you to experiment with those to see what's possible.
- The next section of five icons is for tuning the image's alignment. The options available are align left, center, right, wide, and full width. While left, right, and center are pretty self-explanatory, the appearance *of* wide *and* full *width* depends on the theme you're currently using. Go ahead and experiment with those options to see what the effect is.
- The pencil icon allows for more in-depth editing of your image. Upon clicking it, you'll see the following screen:

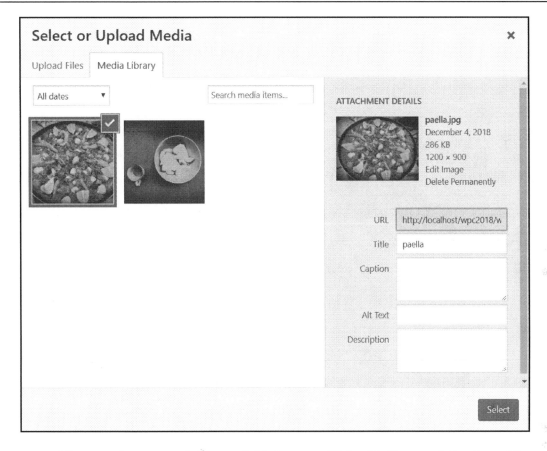

The more important fields available here are **Title**, **Alt Text**, and **Caption**. **Alt Text** is a phrase that's going to appear instead of the image in case the file goes missing, or any other problems present themselves. **Caption** is a short description that you want to have displayed beneath the image itself.

- The last icon—the three vertical dots—is an icon that appears with all other content blocks as well, and it's not unique to the image block. It gives you additional options for what you can do with the block:

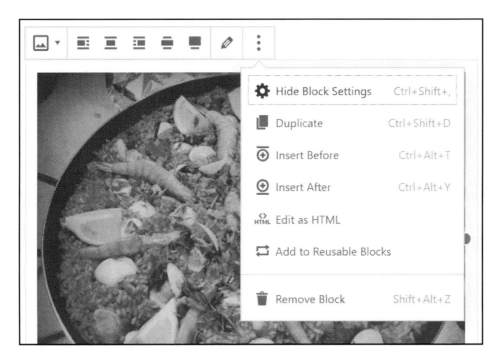

Additionally, if you want to, you can also write the caption for your image beneath the image itself, via a standard input box:

Remember that in order to save all the changes, you must save the post itself, either by clicking on the main **Publish...** button (but this will mean the changes get saved and go live too) or the **Save Draft** link that's next to it.

Designating a featured image

Another cool thing about WordPress—if we didn't have enough of those already—is that you can choose any single image as the featured image for a given blog post. For that purpose, you want to pick an image that represents the post well.

Some themes will make use of the featured images and display them prominently, while some will not. The default theme, the one we've been using, **Twenty Nineteen**, uses the featured image to create a great-looking, full-width bar right above the main content of the post. Depending on the theme you're using, its behavior with featured images can vary; but in general, every modern theme supports them in one way or another.

In order to set a featured image, once again look at the options available in the settings sidebar of the block-based editor. Upon switching to the **Document** tab, scroll down to the **Featured Image** section. There's a single button there labeled **Set featured image**:

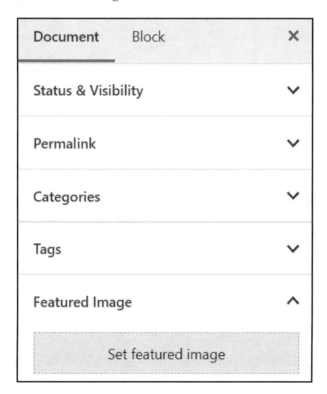

When you click on it, you'll see a pop-up window, very similar to the one we used when adding images to a blog post. Here, you can either upload an entirely new image or select an existing image by clicking on it. All you have to do now is click on the **Select** button in the bottom-right corner. With that done, you'll see the image appear in the **Featured Image** section of the settings sidebar. However, seeing it there is just for your confirmation that the image was indeed appropriately assigned.

To see it in its full glory, you'll need to navigate to the frontend of your site and see the post in question like a reader would. Look at the following screenshot:

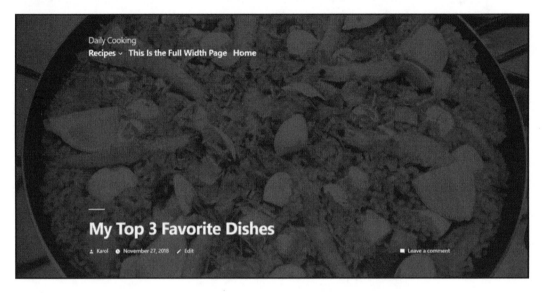

This a great example of a featured image in a live post. Remember, the impact of the featured image will be dictated by the theme of your blog.

Controlling default image sizes

Whenever you upload an image, WordPress provided three options for resizing of the image (aside from retaining its original size): **Thumbnail size**, **Medium size**, and **Large size**. You can set the pixel dimensions of these options by going into **Settings | Media** from the main sidebar menu of the WordPress dashboard. This will take you to the **Media Settings** page:

Media Settings

Image sizes

The sizes listed below determine the maximum dimensions in pixels to use when adding an image to the Media Library.

Thumbnail size	Width	150
	Height	150
	☑ Crop thumbnail to exact dimensions (normally thumbnails are proportional)	
Medium size	Max Width	300
	Max Height	300
Large size	Max Width	1024
	Max Height	1024

Uploading Files

☑ Organize my uploads into month- and year-based folders

Save Changes

Here, you can specify the size of the uploaded images for the three resizing options we just discussed.

If you change the dimensions on this page and click on the **Save Changes** button, only the images you upload in the future will be affected. The images you've already uploaded to the site will stay at their original/previous thumbnail, medium, and large versions.

It's a good idea to decide what you want your three media sizes to be early on in your site's lifespan, so you can set them and have them applied to all images, right from the outset.

Editing an uploaded image

Every image that has been previously uploaded to WordPress can be edited. In order to do that, go to the **Media Library** by clicking on the **Media** button in the main sidebar. What you'll see is a new kind of listing, introduced in one of the latest versions of WordPress.

Instead of a traditional list, what you get to work with now is a grid-based archive that gives each piece of media much better visibility. Right now, we only have one image in the library (see screenshot); but as you continue working with your site, the list will become much more impressive.

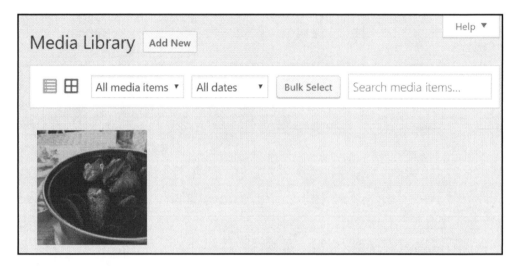

When you click on any of the images and then on the **Edit Image** button at the bottom of the pop-up window that's going to appear, you'll enter the **Attachment Details** screen. Here, you can perform a number of operations to make your image just perfect.

As it turns out, WordPress does a sufficiently good job of simple image tune-up so that you don't really need expensive software such as Adobe Photoshop for this. Among the possibilities, you'll find the option of cropping, rotating, scaling, and flipping vertically and horizontally (as shown):

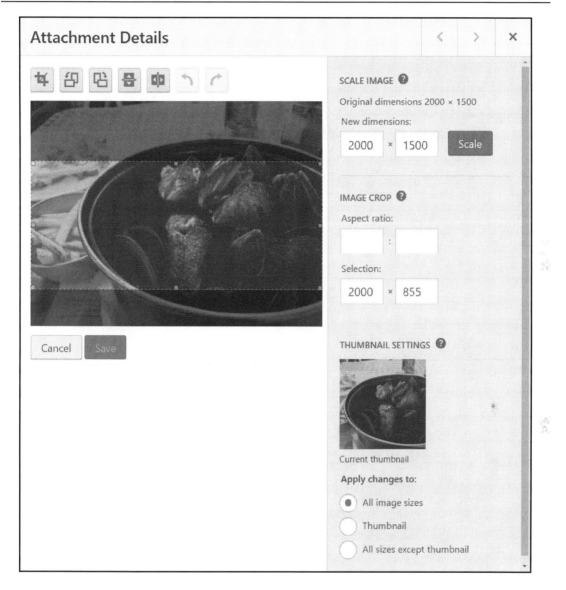

For example, you can use your mouse to draw a box, as I have done in the preceding screenshot. On the right, in the box labeled **Image CROP**, you'll see the pixel dimensions of your selection. Click on the crop icon (top left), then the **Thumbnail** radio button (on the right), and then **Save** (just after your photo). You now have a new thumbnail!

Of course, you can adjust any other version of your image just by making a different selection before hitting the **Save** button. Play around a little until you become familiar with the details.

Videos and other media in your posts

These days, the newest versions of WordPress are capable of not only including images in our blog posts but other types of media too, such as audio files and videos.

Adding videos to blog posts

Luckily for us, the process of adding a video to a standard blog post or page has been made more than easy. Let's discuss this step by step.

We'will create a whole new post for this. Let's use the title *Great Baby Back Ribs Recipe*. Creating the post itself is pretty basic.

1. Navigate to **Posts** | **Add New**. You'll see a screen that we've already covered earlier in this chapter.

2. Let's put some example content in place, and try including a video right away. All we need to do is copy and paste the URL of the video that we'd like to include in the content; just a standard copy-and-paste operation, and nothing else.

 When copying the URL of the video, it's important to make sure that the link is copied as is in raw text form (not hyperlinked anywhere: that is, not clickable).

The example I'm going to use here is the video at `http://www.youtube.com/watch?v=hDyHbTxTL-A`. As you would have guessed, it's a nice video recipe for some baby back ribs! So, in order to include this video in a blog post, all I need to do is take its URL and just paste it in. Here is the raw text content of the new post that I'm working on now:

```
Here's a great video recipe for some killer baby back ribs:
http://www.youtube.com/watch?v=hDyHbTxTL-A
```

However, something you'll notice right away as you're adding the video URL is that it's going to be turned into a live video block automatically. This will happen both on the front page of the website and even on the **Edit Post** screen itself. Refer to the following screenshot:

Here's a great video recipe for some killer baby back ribs:

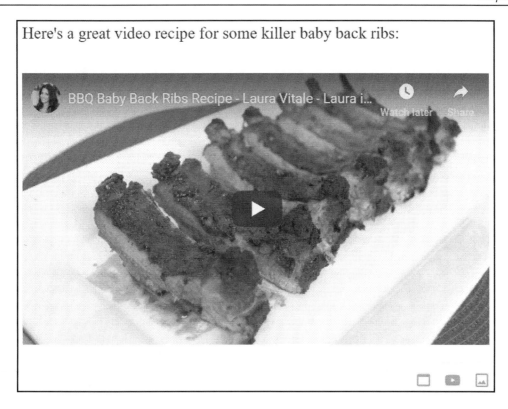

3. To give the post some more unique presence, let's add a new category, **Recipes**, and assign a new tag, **video**. After that, all we need to do is publish the post normally.

The process described here explains how to embed YouTube videos and make them a part of your blog posts, but the same goes for other popular platforms too, such as Vimeo, TED, Hulu, and WordPress.tv. To get the full list of supported platforms, please visit `https://codex.wordpress.org/Embeds`.

One more method of adding videos to blog posts is uploading the raw video files manually (instead of using a third-party platform such as YouTube). Even though this is possible in WordPress, it's not a recommended solution. Video files are always quite large in size, and having them hosted on your standard web server can become very expensive (bandwidth costs) should the video become popular and end up being viewed by thousands of people. It's a lot more efficient and user-friendly to just upload your video to YouTube or a similar platform, and then have it embedded on your site, like we just did.

Adding audio to blog posts

WordPress also makes adding audio to your blog posts just as easy as adding video. To demonstrate this, I'm going to create an entirely new post and call it, **Risotto Podcast**. In it, I'm going to share an episode of a popular cooking-related podcast. I have two ways of doing that:

- Much like with videos, if I have a direct URL of the audio file, I can copy and paste it straight into the post.
- If what I have instead is the actual audio file on my desktop, I can upload it using the **Audio** block of the block-based editor. Here's what that block looks like once added to the post:

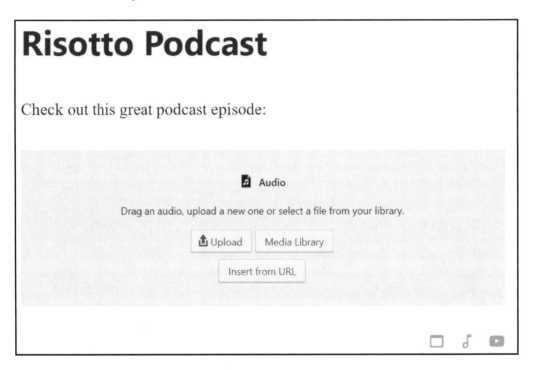

All I need to do now is select the audio file from my desktop. Once the upload finishes, WordPress will display a live audio player right there on the canvas:

Apart from uploading your audio files directly, you can also embed them from third-party platforms. WordPress supports embeds from SoundCloud, Spotify, Rdio, and a bunch of other services. Again, to get the full list of supported platforms, feel free to visit `https://codex.wordpress.org/Embeds`.

Limited editing possibilities

Unlike with images, WordPress doesn't really give us any editing possibilities when it comes to audio and video. It's understandable that images can be manipulated in a lot of ways, for example, they can be rotated, cropped, and scaled. However, there's no such possibility with videos in WordPress. Once a video file or audio file is uploaded, we can't alter it in any way. We can only take it and display it on our sites as is.

Using the block-based editor versus the code editor

As we've discussed, WordPress comes with a new block-based editor that's meant to make creating web pages easier for most users, even if they have no prior experience with website management. However, if you are comfortable with coding and HTML, you might want to take a peek into the code editor that's available in WordPress as well. This can be particularly useful if you want to add special content or styling that's not otherwise possible to achieve using the block-based editor.

To switch from the visual editor to the code editor, click on the three dots that are in the top-right corner of the screen when editing a post, and then click on **Code Editor**. Refer to the following screenshot:

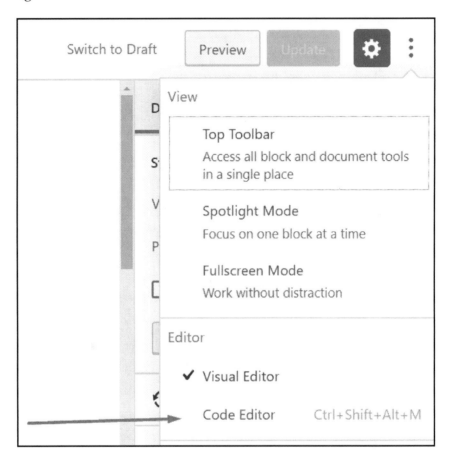

You'll see the post you're currently editing in all its raw HTML glory. Just to give you an example, here's what one of the initial posts created for this book looks like when viewed in the **Code Editor**:

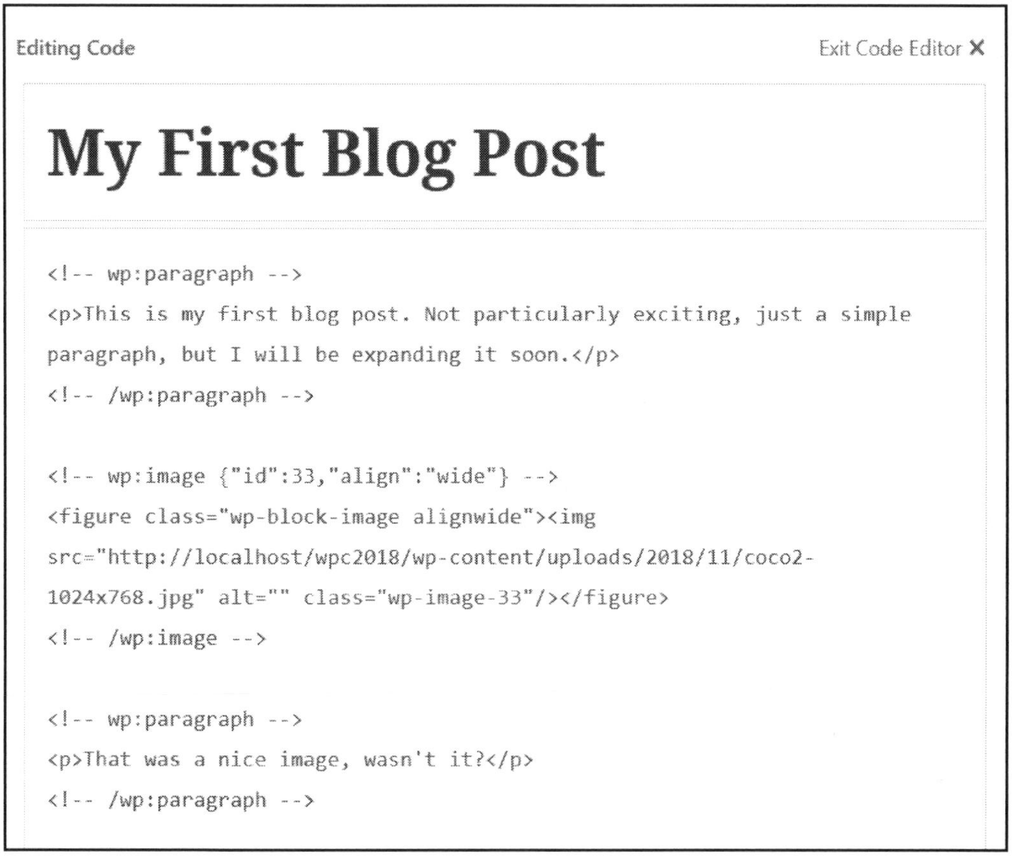

Editing Code   Exit Code Editor ✖

My First Blog Post

```
<!-- wp:paragraph -->
<p>This is my first blog post. Not particularly exciting, just a simple
paragraph, but I will be expanding it soon.</p>
<!-- /wp:paragraph -->

<!-- wp:image {"id":33,"align":"wide"} -->
<figure class="wp-block-image alignwide"><img
src="http://localhost/wpc2018/wp-content/uploads/2018/11/coco2-
1024x768.jpg" alt="" class="wp-image-33"/></figure>
<!-- /wp:image -->

<!-- wp:paragraph -->
<p>That was a nice image, wasn't it?</p>
<!-- /wp:paragraph -->
```

Although this panel lets you do whatever you wish, you also need to be careful not to break the HTML structure of the document. For this reason, it's perhaps not a good idea to get into these sorts of modifications until you get a basic understanding of how an HTML document is structured.

Lead and body

One of the many interesting publishing features WordPress has to offer is the concept of the lead and the body of the post. This may sound like a strange thing, but it's actually quite simple.

When you're publishing a new post, you don't necessarily want to display its whole content right away on the front page. A much more user-friendly approach is to display only the *lead*, and then display the complete post under its individual URL.

Achieving this in WordPress is very simple. All you need to do is use the **More** block available in the block-based editor. Simply add it onto the canvas and then drag and drop it somewhere near the top of the post—preferably right after the first paragraph. See the following screenshot for reference:

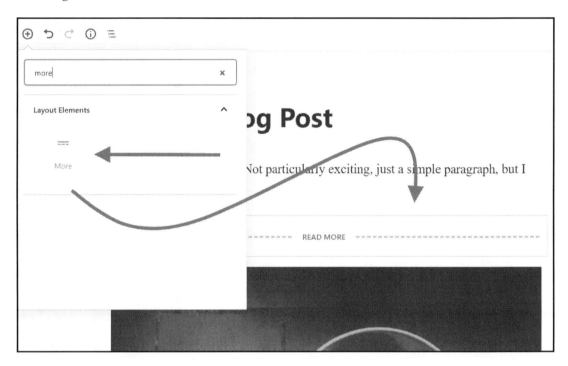

On the front page, most WordPress themes display such posts by presenting the lead along with a continue reading link, and then the whole post (both the lead and the remainder of the post) is displayed under the post's individual URL.

Drafts, pending articles, and timestamps

There are three additional items I'd like to cover in this section: Drafts, Pending articles, and Timestamps.

Drafts

WordPress gives you the option to save a draft of your post. The term is quite explanatory. It means you don't have to publish your post right away, but you can still retain your progress and pick up right where you left off.

If you're working on a new post, the good news is that WordPress will save your progress automatically. Generally speaking, if you can see the **Saved** badge in the top-right corner of the editing panel (next screenshot), then it means that all your progress up to this point has been saved:

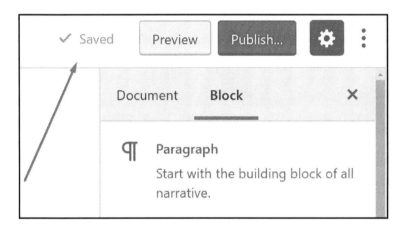

You can safely navigate away from the page and not worry about anything getting lost. If there's no **Saved** badge, then there will be a link labeled **Save Draft** in its place. You can click on it to save your progress manually.

Pending articles

Pending articles is a functionality that's going to be a lot more helpful to users working on multi-author blogs. In a bigger publishing structure, there are multiple individuals responsible for different areas of the publishing process. WordPress, being a quality tool, supports such a structure by providing a way to save articles as **Pending Review**. In an editor-author relationship, if an editor sees a post labeled **Pending Review**, they know that they should have a look at it and prepare it for publication.

When working on a post, switch to the **Document** tab in the settings sidebar and then check the box where it says **Pending Review**. Next, click on the link labeled **Save as Pending** that is going to appear next to the **Preview** button. Refer to the following screenshot:

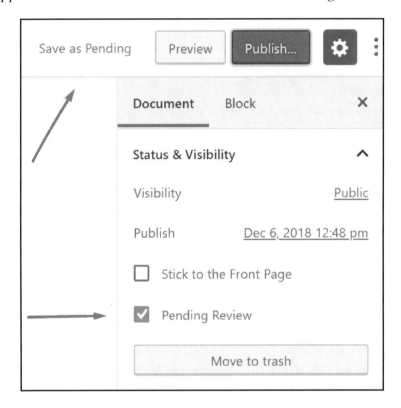

With that done, you have a shiny new article that is now pending review.

Timestamps

WordPress also lets you alter the timestamp of any given post. This is useful if you are writing a post today that you wish could have been published yesterday, or if you're writing a post in advance and don't want it to show up until the right day.

By default, the timestamp will be set to the present time. To change that, click on the main **Publish** button and then do the necessary changes in the box responsible for handling the publication date. Refer to the following screenshot:

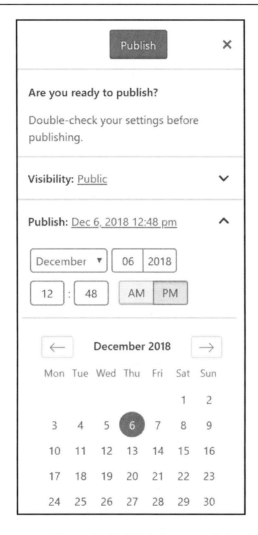

Once you set the date you want, the main **Publish** button might change its label to **Schedule** (if you're scheduling a post to be published at a later date). Click that button to save your changes.

Advanced post options

By now, you have a handle on the most common and simple options for posts, and you may be wondering about some of the other things worth doing when working on a blog post. We'll cover them all in this part of the chapter.

Excerpt

Excerpts can be shown in various places throughout your website. The exact ways in which they're used depends on the theme that you have active on the site. Most commonly, themes will display a post's excerpt in place of the lead (described earlier in this chapter), which is taken from the body of the post. Effectively, excerpts provide you with yet another way to summarize the content of your post and use that text instead of what's taken automatically from the body of the post itself.

To edit a post's excerpt, switch to the **Document** tab of the settings sidebar and scroll down to the **Excerpt** section (as can be seen in the following screenshot). There, you can write a short excerpt, usually best kept to a single paragraph of not more than three lines:

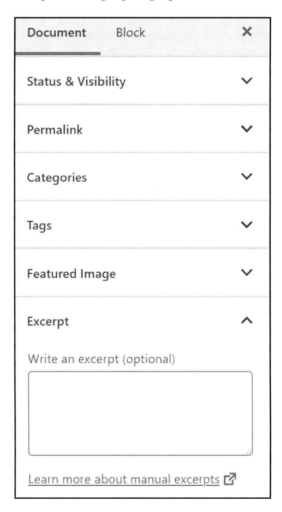

With that being said, it's worth pointing out that entering the excerpt is optional. However, it is advisable that you do take advantage of this possibility. Excerpts can introduce big readability improvements to your site, and make your content easier to grasp for the reader—provided that your current theme does use excerpts in one way or another. In some cases, excerpts also give your site additional SEO benefits—provided that your theme displays them in places where Google and the other search engines can see them.

Discussion

Another useful section that you can find inside the **Document** tab of the settings sidebar is **Discussion**. It is where you can set how you want to handle community interaction for the post you're currently working on.

There are two checkboxes available: one for allowing comments and the other for trackbacks and pingbacks. Both these checkboxes will probably be checked by default. You have to uncheck them if you want to turn off the comments or trackbacks and pingbacks for the post:

If you uncheck the **Allow Comments** box, visitors will not be able to comment on that given blog post. If you uncheck the **Allow Pingbacks & Trackbacks** box, something a bit more complicated happens, and you won't see its effect right away. With that box unchecked, when other people mention and link to your blog post from their own websites, your blog won't recognize that fact. If the box stays checked, other people's pingbacks (mentions) will show up under your post along with the other comments.

If you want either or both of these boxes to be unchecked by default, go to **Settings**, and then **Discussion** from the main left sidebar of the WordPress dashboard. You can uncheck either, or both, of the boxes labeled allow link notifications from other blogs (pingbacks and trackbacks) on new articles and allow people to post comments on new articles.

Originally, the trackback and pingback functionality was meant to provide you with a way to communicate with other websites—to let them know that you've published a post mentioning them, or vice versa, in one way or the other (usually through a link). Nowadays, however, trackbacks and pingbacks are becoming somewhat out of date and most bloggers don't even bother to check the trackbacks/pingbacks that they're receiving. For what it's worth, you can probably safely ignore trackbacks and pingbacks entirely. The decision of to whether or not to support them on your site is entirely up to you.

If you want to learn more about trackbacks and pingbacks, you can go to the codex at `https://codex.wordpress.org/Introduction_to_Blogging#Trackbacks` and `https://codex.wordpress.org/Introduction_to_Blogging#Pingbacks`.

Working with post revisions

Apart from many content-formatting features, WordPress also allows some basic version control for your posts. What this means is that WordPress keeps every subversion of all your posts. Or in plain English, every time you press the **Update** button, instead of overwriting the previous version of the post, WordPress creates a completely new one and still stores the old version safely in the database.

Although this feature doesn't seem like the most useful one at first, it's actually very important for sites where the content is managed by more than one person. In such a scenario, it's easy to get the newest versions of the posts mixed up, so it's always good to have the possibility to return to the previous one.

Once again, we're going to find the revisions by looking into the **Document** tab of the settings sidebar. There's a section labeled **Revisions** there, along with a number corresponding to how many actual revisions there are for the post you're currently editing:

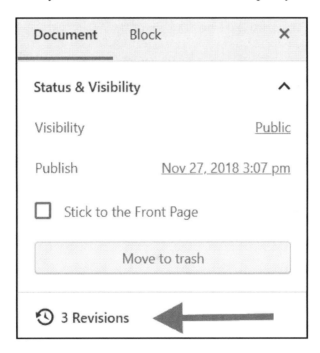

If you click on this label, you will be taken to a page where you can compare individual revisions, and then restore the one you want to work with from now on. The interface provides the main slider that can be used to select individual revisions of the post. This is visible in the following screenshot:

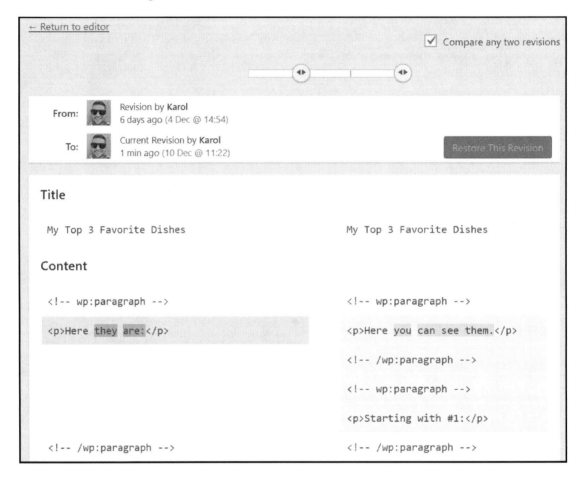

The revision functionality has two main versions:

- The first one is when the **Compare any two revisions** box isn't checked, and it lets you compare the revision that's currently selected (on the slider) to the revision directly preceding it.

- The second version is when the **Compare any two revisions** box is checked. In this case, you can select the revisions you want to compare individually, which essentially allows you to compare any two revisions, just like the box suggests. The revision on the left is always the *previous* revision, while the one on the right is the next or *current* one (visible in the preceding screenshot). Every paragraph where a difference is established will be highlighted in red and green, and every individual difference will have additional highlighting. Clicking on the **Restore This Revision** button will restore the revision on the right, and you will be brought back to the post-editing screen automatically.

If you feel that revisions won't be of any particular use to your site, then you can simply choose to not pay attention to the **Revisions** box. When you work with your content normally, not worrying about the revisions, WordPress will always display the most recent versions of your posts by default.

Changing the author of the post

This is a very basic, yet useful, feature in WordPress. Every post and page in WordPress has an author, which is quite obvious in itself. However, if you want, you can change the assigned author of any given entry. In order to do it, look at the **Document** tab of the settings sidebar, and locate the **Author** label. There's a drop-down menu next to it that lists every user account on your site. Just select a new author, and click on the main **Update** button to save the changes:

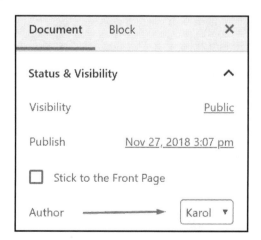

Note: If you only have one user on your site, then the box won't even be visible.

Protecting content

WordPress gives you the option to hide posts. You can hide a post from everyone but yourself by marking it **Private** (although the user roles of admin and editor will still see it), or you can hide it from everyone, apart from the people with whom you share a password, by marking it **Password Protected**.

To implement this, look at the **Document** tab of the settings sidebar, and locate the **Visibility** label. Next to it, there's a link that says **Public**. Once you click on it, you'll see the available options:

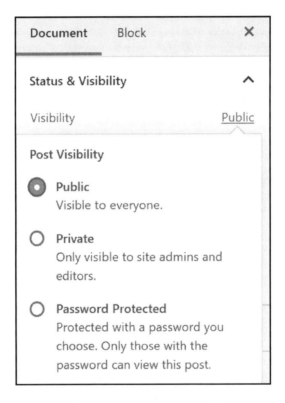

If you click on the **Private** radio button, the post will not show up on the blog at all, unless it's viewed by someone with the role of admin or editor. If you click on the **Password Protected** radio button, you'll get a box where you can type in a password. Visitors to your blog will see the post title along with a note that they have to type in the password to read the rest of the post.

Pretty post permalink

We've already talked about tuning the permalinks settings of your site in `Chapter 2, Getting Started with WordPress`. Now is a good moment to expand on this knowledge and discuss a little something called the *post permalink*, or *slug*.

One of the most accurate definitions of what a post slug is comes from the WordPress Codex itself. The resource provided at `https://codex.wordpress.org/Glossary#Post_Slug` teaches us that the post slug is made from a few lowercase words separated by dashes, describing a post and usually derived from the post title to create a user-friendly permalink.

In other words, the post slug is what comes after your domain name in the post's URL. For example, my post about my top three favorite dishes uses this URL: `http://localhost/my-top-3-favorite-dishes/`, where the last part —`my-top-3-favorite-dishes`, is the slug. Just like the official definition says, WordPress chooses the slug by taking my post title, making it all lowercase, removing all punctuation, and replacing spaces with dashes. If I'd prefer it to be something else, such as `3-favorite-dishes`, I can change it by going to the **Document** tab of the settings sidebar and looking for the section labeled **Permalink**:

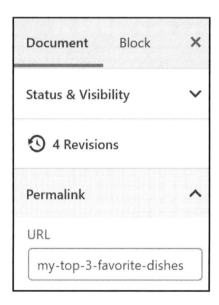

Readable URLs are something that Google Search loves, so using them helps to optimize your site for the search engines. It also helps users to figure out what a post is about before clicking on the URL.

Discussion on your blog – comments

Comments are an important element for most blogs. While only you and your authors can write new posts for your blog, your visitors can add comments under those posts. This can fuel a sense of community within a blog, allow people to give you feedback on your writing, and give your visitors a way to help or talk to other visitors.

Adding a comment

If you look at the front page of your blog, you'll notice that every post has a link that says **Leave a comment** (provided that you didn't disable comments entirely). Clicking on that link will take you to the bottom of the post page, which is where comments can be added.

If you're logged into the WordPress dashboard, you'll see your name and a space to write your comment. If you're not logged in, you'll see a comment form that any other visitor will see. This form includes fields to fill in a name, email, website, and, of course, a big box for the comment itself:

Leave a comment

Your email address will not be published. Required fields are marked *

Comment

Name *   Email *

Website

Post Comment

Once you type in the required information and click on the **Post Comment** button, the comment will be entered into the WordPress database. How soon it shows up on the site depends on your discussion settings.

Discussion settings

In the preceding screenshot, notice that the **Name*** and **Email*** fields are both marked as required (*). As the owner of the blog/site, you can change the requirements for comments. This can be done when you go to **Settings | Discussion** in the WordPress dashboard.

Submission, notification, and moderation settings

Let's focus on the checkboxes on the **Settings | Discussion** page that relate to submission, notification, and moderation. The boxes that are checked on this page will determine how much moderation and checking a comment has to go through before it gets posted on the blog.

First, let's look at the settings that have to do with moderation visible under **Before a comment appears**. These two options have to do with the circumstances that allow comments to appear on the site:

Before a comment appears	☐ Comment must be manually approved
	☑ Comment author must have a previously approved comment

- **Comment must be manually approved**: If this box is checked, every comment has to be manually approved by you before it appears on the site.
- **Comment author must have a previously approved comment**: If you uncheck the box above this, but check this one, then you've relaxed your settings a little bit. This means that if the person commenting has commented before and had his or her comment approved, then the person's future comments don't have to be verified by you—they'll just appear on the website immediately. The person just has to enter the same name and email as the one in the previously approved comment.

Next, let's look at the settings for comment submission that are visible under **Other comment settings**:

Other comment settings	☑ Comment author must fill out name and email
	☐ Users must be registered and logged in to comment
	☐ Automatically close comments on articles older than `14` days
	☐ Show comments cookies opt-in checkbox.
	☑ Enable threaded (nested) comments `5 ▾` levels deep
	☐ Break comments into pages with `50` top level comments per page and the `last ▾` page displayed by default
	Comments should be displayed with the `older ▾` comments at the top of each page

The first two options control what the user has to do before even being able to type in a comment:

- **Comment author must fill out the name and email**: If you leave this checked, then anyone posting a comment will encounter an error if they try to leave either of the fields blank. This doesn't add a huge amount of security because robots know how to fill out a name and an email and because anyone can put fake information in there. However, it does help your blog readers to keep a track of who is who if a long discussion develops, and it can slightly discourage utterly impulsive commenting. Also, visitors who have a Gravatar account are quite willing to provide their email addresses anyway. That's because using an email address that's connected to Gravatar will result in their profile picture (avatar) being displayed along with the comment, making it much more personal and visible among all the other comments.

- **Users must be registered and logged in to comment**: Most bloggers do not check this box because it means that only visitors who register for the blog can comment. Most bloggers don't want random people registering, and most visitors don't want to be compelled to register to your blog. If you check this box, there's a good chance you'll get no comments. Alternatively, if you're setting up a blog for a closed community of people, this setting might be useful.

- **Automatically close comments on articles older than X days**: Here, you can set any number of days after which the comments on your content will be closed. Although this feature might not seem like a useful one at first, it can actually be valuable to various kinds of news sites or other online publications, where allowing comments on old events makes little sense.

- **Show comments cookies opt-in checkbox**: When checked, the user will see another checkbox under the comment form, saying: *Save my name, email, and website in this browser for the next time I comment.*
- **Enable threaded (nested) comments X levels deep**: This option is enabled by default, and it's yet another way of making your site more readable and user-friendly. Sometimes, commenters want to be able to respond to someone else's comments, simply as part of an ongoing discussion. This is the feature that allows them to do so. Also, it gives you, the author, a great way of interacting with your audience, through direct responses to every comment of theirs.
- **Break comments into pages [...]**: This feature won't be of any value to you unless you're getting more than 200 comments per post. So you can confidently leave it unchecked.

Lastly, let's look at the settings that have to do with notifications. These two options are under the **Email me whenever** header. These options are related to the circumstances of receiving an email notification regarding comment activity:

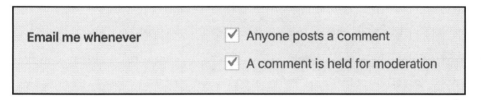

- **Anyone posts a comment**: This is generally a good setting to keep. You'll get an email whenever anyone posts a comment, irrespective of whether it needs to be moderated. This will make it easier for you to follow the discussion on your blog, and to be aware of a comment that is not moderated, and that requires deletion quickly.
- **A comment is held for moderation**: If you're not particularly interested in following every comment on your blog, you can uncheck the **Anyone posts a comment** checkbox, and only leave this one checked. You will only get an email about legitimate-looking comments that appear to need moderation and/or your approval.

When to moderate or blacklist a comment

If you scroll down the page a bit, you'll see the **Comment Moderation** area:

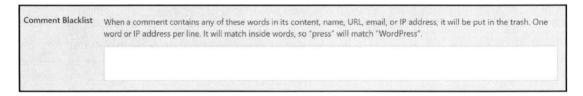

This is an extension of the moderation settings from the top of the page. Note that if you've checked the **Comment must be manually approved** checkbox, you can safely ignore this **Comment Moderation** box. Otherwise, you can use this box to help WordPress figure out which comments are probably okay, and which might be spam or inappropriate for your blog. You can tell WordPress to suspect a comment if it has more than a certain number of links, as spam comments are frequently just a list of URLs.

The larger box is for you to enter suspect words and IP addresses:

- Here, you can type words that are commonly found in spam (you can figure this out by looking through your junk email), or just uncouth words in general.
- The IP addresses would be those of any comments you got in the past from someone who commented inappropriately or added actual spam. Whenever WordPress receives a comment on your blog, it captures the IP address for you so that you'll have them handy.

Scroll down a bit more, and you'll see the **Comment Blacklist** box:

Comment Blacklist   When a comment contains any of these words in its content, name, URL, email, or IP address, it will be put in the trash. One
word or IP address per line. It will match inside words, so "press" will match "WordPress".

Unlike the **Comment Moderation** box we just saw, which tells WordPress how to identify suspect comments, the **Comment Blacklist** box tells WordPress how to identify comments that are almost definitely bad. These comments won't be added to the moderation queue, and you won't get an email about them; they'll be marked as spam right away.

Avatar display settings

The final section on this page is labeled **Avatars**. Just as I mentioned in `Chapter 2`, *Getting Started with WordPress*, an avatar is an image that is a person's personal icon. Avatars in WordPress are provided through Gravatar, a service available at `https://gravatar.com/` that lets you create your personal online profile, which is going to then to be consistently used on other websites across the web. By default, avatars will show up on your blog if you leave the **Avatar Display** box checked, which is visible near the bottom of the discussion settings page.

The second box, **Maximum Rating**, will tell WordPress when it should not show avatars that have been rated as too explicit. Remember the rating we set when uploading a new picture to Gravatar? This setting here is the place where you can choose which pictures you want to allow on your site (selecting the **G** rating is advisable).

The third box, **Default Avatar**, tells WordPress what avatar to use for visitors who do not come with their own image.

Moderating comments

Now that we've thoroughly explored the settings for which comments need to be moderated, let's discuss what you actually need to do in order to moderate comments. *Moderating* means that you look over a comment that is in limbo and decide whether it's insightful enough that it can be published on your blog. If it's good, it gets to appear on the frontend of your website; and if it is bad, it's either marked as spam, or gets deleted and is never seen by anyone but you, and the person who wrote it.

To view comments waiting for moderation, navigate to **Comments** from the main sidebar of the WordPress dashboard. If you have any comments awaiting moderation, there will be a little number in the main menu telling you how many comments are awaiting moderation:

This main **Comments** page is fully featured, just like the **Posts** page. For each comment, you see the following information from left to right:

- Commenter avatar, name, website address (if there was any given), email address (if there was any given), and IP
- Comment text, along with links to approve it so that it shows up on the site (the links appear when you hover your mouse over the comment); you can also mark it as **Spam**, **Trash** it, **Edit** it, **Quick Edit** it, or **Reply** to it
- Comment submission time and date
- The title of the post on which the comment was made (which is also a link to edit that post), a number in parentheses indicating how many approved comments are already there for that post (which is also a link that will filter the comments list so that it shows only the comments for that post), and a link to the post itself (labeled **View Post**)

Comments that are awaiting moderation have a reddish background, like the first comment in the preceding screenshot.

You can click on the **Quick Edit** link under any comment to open its quick-access options. This will allow you to edit the text of the comment and the commenter's name, email, and URL.

You can use the links at the top—**All**, **Pending**, **Approved**, **Spam**, and **Trash**, to filter the list based on those statuses. You can also filter either pings or comments with the **All comment types** pull-down filter menu. You can check one or more comments to apply any of the bulk actions available in the **Bulk Actions** menus at the top and bottom of the list.

Another quick way to get to this page, or to apply an action to a comment, is to use the links in the email that WordPress sends you when a comment is held for moderation (provided you've selected that option in the **Settings** | **Discussion** panel).

Additionally, this listing is where all pingbacks appear for moderation. From a blog owner's point of view, pingbacks look just like any other comments, which means that you can edit them, mark them as spam, or trash them like you normally would with standard comments.

Adding and managing categories

Earlier in this chapter, you learned how to add a category quickly when adding a post. Now, let's talk about how to manage your categories in a bigger way. First, navigate to **Posts** | **Categories**. You'll see the **Categories** page, as follows:

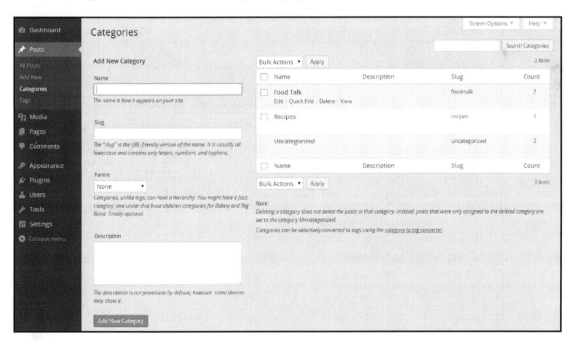

This is a useful page that combines the ability to add, edit, and review all of your categories. As you can see, any category that you've added when working on your blog posts is listed here. You can **Edit**, **Quick Edit**, or **Delete** any category by clicking on the appropriate link in the list.

If you add a category on this page, you can also choose its **Slug**. The slug is the short bit of text that shows up in the URL of your site. If you don't choose a slug, WordPress will create one for you by taking the category name, reducing it to all lowercase, replacing spaces with dashes, and removing any other punctuation mark (similar to what's being done with slugs for posts).

Another thing you can do on this page is to choose a parent category for any category. Some themes support displaying categories hierarchically, but not all do. In a good, modern theme, if you create a custom menu for categories, all child categories will be displayed as submenus.

The ability to create a hierarchy of categories is actually the main technical thing that separates categories from tags. Other than that, both taxonomies are quite similar in construction, although they still have different purposes.

Summary

In this chapter, you learned everything you need to know in order to add content to your blog and then manage that content. You learned about posts, categories, and comments. You discovered tags and excerpts. You also learned about adding and editing images, working with video and audio content, using the new block editor, changing timestamps, customizing excerpts, and the different ways of posting.

Your control over your blog content is complete, and you are well-equipped to set your blog on fire!

In the next chapter, you'll learn about all the other types of content that you can manage with WordPress.

4
Pages, Media, and Importing/Exporting Content

By now, you have the blog part of your website fully under control. However, you've probably noticed that WordPress offers you a lot more than simply posts, comments, tags, and categories.

In this chapter, we will explore and learn to control all the other types of content that WordPress lets you use. You'll be able to create static pages that aren't a part of your ongoing blog, add various types of media to your posts, and create appealing image galleries to display photos and other images.

The following topics will be covered in this chapter:

- Creating and managing your page
- Navigating through your media library
- Importing/exporting content

Pages

At first glance, pages look very similar to posts. Both pages and posts have a title and a content area in which we can write extended text, add images, and so on. However, pages are handled quite differently from posts. First of all, pages don't have categories or tags (pages don't need to be categorized, since on most websites, there are a lot fewer pages than posts). Moreover, posts belong to your blog and are meant to be a part of an ongoing, expanding publication revolving around specific topics. Posts are added regularly, whereas pages are more static and aren't generally expected to change that much.

In short, I would advise you to think of pages as pieces of static content, and posts as a series of articles that are published in a timely manner. In other words, pages are meant to hold content that is equally up to date, no matter when someone reads it. For instance, the things that people publish via WordPress pages are most commonly details pertaining to their company or business, team, and other related and evergreen details. Posts are often very time-sensitive and present advice/news that's important today/now. For most blogs, posts are the pillars of their content and make up more than 90 percent of the entire content catalog.

When you first install WordPress, one page is created for you automatically (along with the first post and the first comment). You can see that page by going to `http://YOURSITE.com/sample-page/`.

Adding a page

To add a new page, go to your `wp-admin` and navigate to **Pages** | **Add New**, or use the drop-down menu in the top menu by clicking on **New** and then **Page**. This will take you to the block-based editor. As you'll notice, this is the same editor that we used when working on blog posts. The block editor is very universal and WordPress uses it for both posts and pages.

The minimum you need to do to create a new page is type in a title and some content. Then, click on the blue **Publish** button, just as you would for a post. Your new page will become available under its unique URL.

You'll recognize most of the sections in the settings sidebar of the block-based editor. They work the same for pages as they do for posts. Let's talk about the one section that's new—the one called **Page Attributes**, consisting of elements such as **Parent Page** and **Order**:

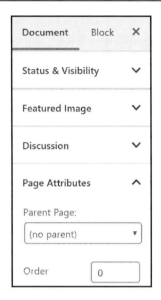

Parent

WordPress allows you to structure your pages hierarchically. This way, you can organize everything into *main pages* and *subpages*, which is useful if you're going to have a bigger number of pages on your site. For example, if I were to write a blog along with three other authors, we would each have one page about us on the site, but those would be subpages of the main **About** page. If I was adding one of these pages, I'd first create a new **About** page (the main one), then create another page just for me, called *About Karol*, and finally choose that main **About** page as the parent for the new page.

Order

By default, all pages you create will be presented in alphabetical order by page title. If you want them in some other order, you can specify this by entering numbers in the **Order** box for each of your pages. Pages with lower numbers (for example, 0) will be listed before pages with higher numbers (for example, 5). You can easily test this by editing some of your pages and assigning various numbers to them.

That being said, to be honest, this isn't a very clear method of rearranging pages, especially if you want them displayed in a menu. You can do this much more easily by working with menus directly (as described in Chapter 8, *Customizing Your Website Appearance/Design*). In the end, I would advise you not to trouble yourself with setting the **Order** attribute at all.

Managing pages

To see a list of all the pages on your website in `wp-admin`, navigate to **Pages** from the main menu. You'll see something similar to what's shown in the following screenshot:

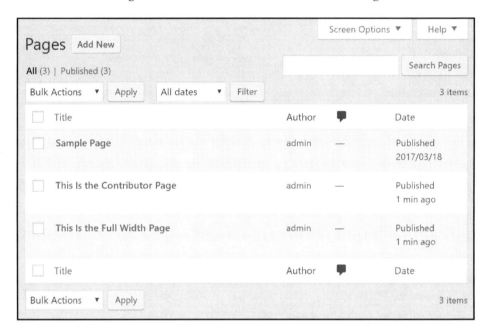

By now, this list format should begin to look familiar to you. You've got your list of pages, and in each row, there are a number of useful links allowing you to **Edit**, **Quick Edit**, **Trash**, or **View** the page. You can click on an author's name to filter the list by that author. You can use the two links at the top, **All** and **Published**, to filter the pages by status (if you have pages saved as **Drafts** or **Pending Review**, then they will also appear here). There's also filtering by date, through the drop-down menu just above the list of pages. Additionally, you can check certain boxes and mass edit pages using the **Bulk Actions** menu at the top and bottom of the list. Finally, you can search through your pages with the search box at the top.

Setting up a home page

There's one page that's very special among all the other pages that you can create on your website. That is the *home page*, also called the *front page*. In simple terms, the home page is what the visitors see when they go to your main website address—usually something like `YOURSITE.com`.

By default, WordPress displays a list of your most recent blog posts on the home page—in reverse chronological order. While having your latest blog posts there is okay for some types of websites, it's not optimal for everyone. Usually, you're going to be better off exploring the possibility of setting up a completely customized home page and picking by hand what you want to have displayed on it.

Going forward, we're going to assume that you're using the default WordPress theme—**Twenty Nineteen**. If you're on a different theme, parts of the process described in this section of the chapter might work differently.

Creating a placeholder home page

The first thing we need to do may seem a bit counter-intuitive, but it'll all make sense in a minute. Let's start by creating two blank pages. You can do this in the normal manner; just go to **Pages | Add New**:

- Title the first one **HOME**, the save, and publish it. Don't add any other content there for now, just the title.
- Title the second one **BLOG**; also save and publish it.

Enabling the custom home page

We need to instruct WordPress to start using those two pages when determining the contents of your home page.

Go to **Settings | Reading**. Once there, switch the first setting on the page from <**Your latest posts** to **A static page**. From the drop-downs, assign your new page **Home** as the **Homepage** and the page **BLOG** as the **Posts page**, as follows:

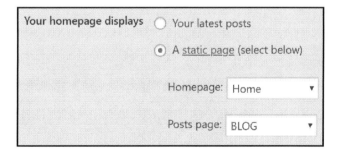

Click on **Save Changes**.

With that, one of your new pages—**Home**—has become the home page for your entire website. However, currently, there's nothing much going on there since the page is blank.

The other page—**BLOG**—has been tasked with listing your latest blog posts in reverse chronological order. In other words, the **BLOG** page now does what was previously done by the out-of-the-box default home page. You can see the blog page if you go to `YOURSITE.com/blog`.

Customizing your home page

A blank home page is surely not what you want, so let's customize it a bit:

1. Go to **Pages** and click on the **Home** page to start editing it. Start by giving the page a title—something that you want your visitors to see first as they land on your website. I'm not going to be creative here and simply type in `Welcome to my website!`.

2. Next, add whatever copy you think should find its place on the home page. If it's a business site you're building, you should probably mention what your business does and how it can serve its customers. Again, I'm not going to be creative and simply add a couple of random sentences. Here's what I have so far:

> # Welcome to my website!
>
> Welcome to my website! Here, we're all about cooking!
>
> - Healthy!
> - Tasty!
> - Fast!

3. In the next step, let's present some of the most recent posts on the blog, just so that people can get an idea about the kind of content they can expect from you. To begin, you can type a simple line, inviting people to check out your latest posts.

4. After that, let's add a new block that we haven't worked with yet. The block is called **Latest Posts**, and you can find it in the **Widgets** section. Refer to the following screenshot:

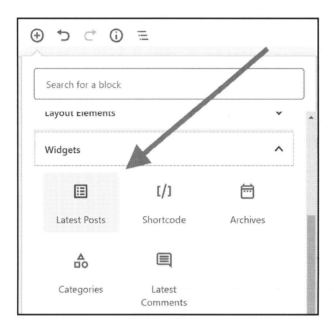

5. As soon as you add this block, it's going to be populated with your most recent blog posts. I'm going to customize that block slightly. First, I'll change the view from *list* to *grid* by clicking on the following button:

6. Next, I'll adjust a couple of other settings via the settings sidebar, like so:

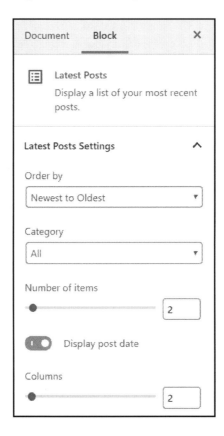

The things I've changed are as follows:

- Columns: Set to 2
- Number of items: Set to 2
- Display post date: Set to yes

As you can see, these settings are quite straightforward, so you can adjust them however you see fit for your specific website.

When I click on the **Preview** button at this moment, I'll see two of my latest posts set side by side right there on the page:

Welcome to my website! Here, we're all about cooking!

- Healthy!
- Tasty!
- Fast!

Check out some of my latest blog posts:

My First Blog Post
December 3, 2018

My Top 3 Favorite Dishes
November 27, 2018

Lastly, let's set a featured image for the home page. This image will be displayed in the header section of the entire website, so it's best to pick something representative that you're going to be proud to see there.

Assigning the featured image works just the same as it does for blog posts.

7. From the settings sidebar, switch to the **Document** tab and scroll down to the section labeled **Featured Image**. Pick the image that you want to have set, and save the settings. When done, you'll see your image assigned:

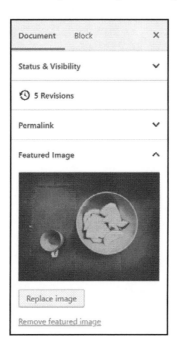

At this stage, we're done working on our custom home page. Of course, there's a lot more that can be included on the home page, and it all depends on what you want your home page to represent. That's the whole magic of WordPress—you don't have to settle for what's already there but instead make the website truly yours.

8. To see your current home page in all its glory, just navigate to your main website address. Here's what's on my home page:

Media library

The media library is where WordPress stores all of your uploaded files, such as images, PDFs, music, and videos. To see your media library, navigate to **Media** in the main menu (there's probably not a lot of media there at the moment):

What you're seeing is a nice grid layout that makes looking through media very user-friendly. My media library has four photos in it at the moment. Once I click on any of them, I will see the **Attachment Details** screen that we talked about in Chapter 3, *Creating Blog Content*. On this screen, there are a lot of options to modify the file that's been selected.

We can edit details, such as **Title**, **Caption**, **Alt Text**, and **Description**, and also delete the file permanently or view it on the frontend of the site:

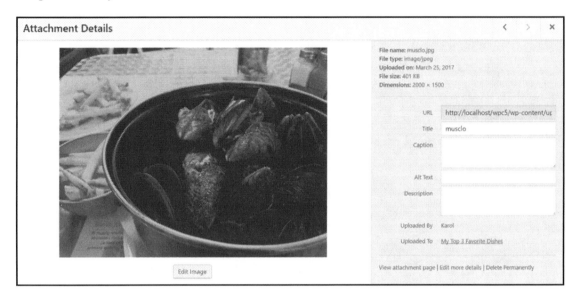

You can also add a new file to the media library. Navigate to **Media** | **Add New** to access a page, similar to the upload media page that you got while uploading a file for a post. When you click on the **Select Files** button and pick the file to be uploaded, or drag and drop it directly from your desktop, WordPress will upload the file and then display it along with the other media files in the library. Your new item will be unattached to any post or page at this point.

To include it somewhere (in a post or page), go to **Posts** or **Pages** and proceed to edit one of the posts/pages. Click on the **+** button in the top-left corner and pick the **Image** block. Now, instead of uploading a new file, just select it from the media library. We covered the entire process more extensively in the previous chapter:

Creating an image gallery

WordPress not only allows you to add individual images to your posts and pages, but also allows you to create great-looking galleries comprised of multiple images. Here are the steps for creating a new image gallery and have it displayed inside a post or page.

Choosing a post or page

You can add a gallery (or multiple galleries) to any new or existing page or post. I, for example, went with one of my existing posts, which you can see in the following screenshot:

My Top 3 Favorite Dishes

Here you can see them all.

The first step to add a gallery to this post is to click the + button in the top-left corner of the page and pick the **Gallery** block:

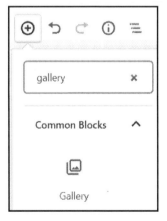

Adding images to Gallery

This new **Gallery** block looks very similar to the standard **Image** block, and it gives you a couple of main options:

Additionally, aside from the possibility of uploading images or picking them from the media library, you can drag and drop multiple images straight from your desktop. WordPress will immediately start turning them into a gallery. For this example, if you want to pick the images from the media library, just click on the **Media Library** button. You'll see a panel that should be familiar at this point. In there, just click on the images that you want to have included in the gallery. As an example, I've selected three images (see the checkboxes in the upper-right corners):

At this stage, you can adjust the titles and descriptions of the images if you want to, and then click on the **Create a new gallery** button. In the next step, you have the opportunity to rearrange your images by dragging them around the display area. You can also adjust the captions (the captions will be saved so that they can be reused later on if you're creating a gallery using the same images). When you're done, just click on the **Insert gallery** button:

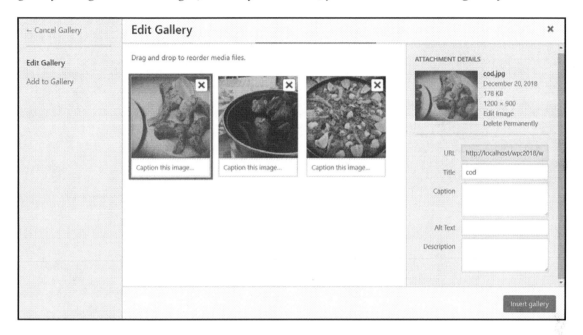

You'll see a nice preview of the gallery right on the canvas of your post. By clicking on the **Gallery** block, you'll also see some additional options. For instance, you can change the number of columns in the gallery, set if you want the images to be linked to anywhere, and crop them to fit the space available in the block. You can also upload additional images and add them to the gallery. You can see these options in the following screenshot:

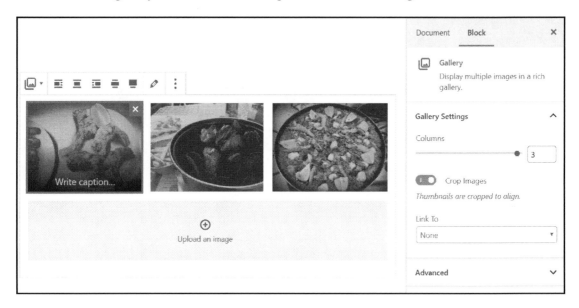

For example, if you decide to change the number of columns to 2, WordPress will do whatever it can to still make your gallery look great. Here's what happens to my gallery when I do this:

As you can see, WordPress makes each picture fit perfectly on the page although, the degree of this perfection depends on the theme you're using.

Importing/exporting content

The final thing we're going to discuss in this chapter is the feature of importing and exporting your content. By default, WordPress allows you to *take* content from other places and publish it on your site. Though, keep in mind that this doesn't happen automatically. WordPress will only help you import the content so that then you can decide what to do with it next.

There are a number of platforms supported, including **Blogger**, **LiveJournal**, **Tumblr** blogs, and more. You can see the complete list by navigating to **Tools | Import** (it's also the starting point when importing content):

Import

If you have posts or comments in another system, WordPress can import those into this site. To get started, choose a system to import from below:

Blogger Install Now	Details	Import posts, comments, and users from a Blogger blog.
Blogroll Install Now	Details	Import links in OPML format.
Categories and Tags Converter Install Now	Details	Convert existing categories to tags or tags to categories, selectively.
LiveJournal Install Now	Details	Import posts from LiveJournal using their API.
Movable Type and TypePad Install Now	Details	Import posts and comments from a Movable Type or TypePad blog.
RSS Install Now	Details	Import posts from an RSS feed.
Tumblr Install Now	Details	Import posts & media from Tumblr using their API.
WordPress Install Now	Details	Import posts, pages, comments, custom fields, categories, and tags from a WordPress export file.

If the importer you need is not listed, search the plugin directory to see if an importer is available.

Importing content

If you want to import content from any source, you first need to click on either of the **Install Now** links that are under the available platforms (visible in the preceding screenshot). WordPress uses additional plugins to handle the importing, and it first needs to install them to carry out the procedure.

Importing content from each of the available platforms is a bit different, but the general process looks similar, so we're going to use another WordPress site as an example here—that is, we're going to import content from another WordPress website. For that to work, all we need to do is click on the **Install Now** link that's within the **WordPress** section (it's the last one in the preceding screenshot), and then, when the installation completes, click on the new **Run Importer** link that will have just appeared. Refer to the following screenshot:

WordPress   Import posts, pages, comments, custom fields, categories, and tags from a WordPress
Run Importer | Details   export file.

This will take you straight to the importer panel:

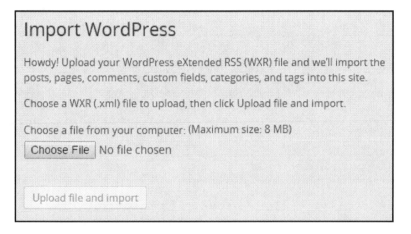

It is a very simple interface where all you have to do is take a WordPress export file and upload it to your site. The platform will take care of extracting the archive and importing the content into it. As a result, your site is going to be filled with new posts, pages, custom fields, navigation menus, and even comments.

The main purpose of this feature is to help everyone who's migrating their sites from platforms such as **Blogger** or **LiveJournal**. Imagine if someone had a Blogger blog with over a hundred posts in it. Going through each one individually and inputting it in to WordPress by hand would be too time-consuming. With this feature, it can be done in under a minute.

Exporting content

Exporting content is even simpler than importing. To begin, navigate to **Tools** | **Export**:

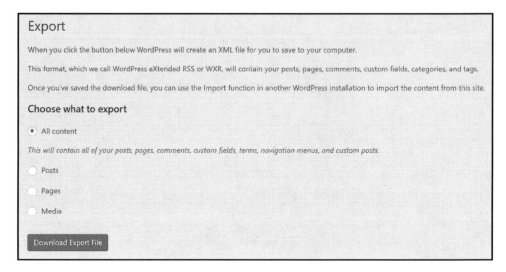

There's not much you can do here except select what you want to export and then click on the big button to download your WordPress export file:

- Selecting **All content** will export your posts, pages, comments, custom fields, terms, navigation menus, and custom posts
- Selecting just **Posts, Pages** or **Media** is pretty self-explanatory

When you click on the **Download Export File** button, you will end up with a file that's just like the one we used when importing. This means that you can take that file and create a mirror copy of your site somewhere else on another domain name.

Summary

In this chapter, we explored the content that WordPress can handle that's not directly about blogging. You learned about static pages, the home page, the media library, image galleries, and importing/exporting content.

You are now fully equipped to use the WordPress **Admin** panel to control all of your website's content. Next, you'll learn how to expand your site's functionality by installing new plugins, which we'll be discussing in the following chapter.

Section 2: Customizing WordPress

2

This section is your next step up after you've installed WordPress and gotten familiar with its basic features. In this section, we'll explore the many different ways in which you can extend WordPress' default features.

This section will cover the follow chapters:

5
Plugins - What They Are and Why You Need Them

The role of plugins has grown a lot in recent years. Nowadays, it's hard to imagine any WordPress site that could operate without at least a handful of (essential) plugins installed.

In this chapter, you will get to know what plugins are, why to use them, how to use them, where to get them, and how to be up to date with any new useful plugins that get released to the community. We will also talk about some of the most basic and popular plugins in the WordPress world, and why having them might be a good idea. Okay, let's get on with it!

Let's take a look at the topics that will be covered in this chapter:

- Breaking down plugins
- Installing a plugin
- The must-have pack of plugins

Breaking down plugins – what are they?

Simply speaking, plugins are small scripts (files with executable PHP code) that allow you to include new functionality in your WordPress site—functionality that is *not* available or enabled by default. One of the best advantages of WordPress is that it's quite an optimized platform. It makes your site load fast and doesn't contain much redundant code. However, WordPress itself only offers the absolute essential range of features—the features that are useful to everyone. At the same time, the platform provides a straightforward way of expanding the abilities of your site by introducing, you guessed it, plugins. The idea is simple—if you want your site to be able to handle a specific new task, there's undoubtedly a plugin for that. Much like in the Apple world and the popular expression, *there's an app for that*.

Why use plugins?

The best thing about plugins is that you don't need any specific programming knowledge to use them. Essentially, they are just like standard applications for iOS or Android— you can install them and enjoy the things they have to offer without knowing what's going on inside. This being said, not all plugins are safe to use in regards to data security or code quality. We will discuss this topic later in this chapter.

Furthermore, the right combination of plugins can make your site more optimized, more user-friendly, more attractive, more social media friendly, properly backed up, protected against spam, and, ultimately, unique. Plugins really are one of the best things about WordPress.

Before content management systems like WordPress were popularized, there was no easy way for site owners to introduce new functionalities to their sites. Doing so always required hiring a professional programmer and investing in the whole development process. Nowadays, this is no longer the case, and virtually anyone can have an impressive site without losing their shirt.

Where to get plugins?

The community behind WordPress plugins is a huge one. There's not a central plugin-building company or anything. Developers all over the world create plugins and then distribute them across the internet. And, very often, they receive no direct compensation whatsoever. The best and the safest place to visit for WordPress plugins is the official directory at `https://wordpress.org/plugins/`:

There are more than 55,000 different plugins available in the directory at the time of writing this book, and that number is constantly expanding, with around 100+ new plugins being added every week. This is really impressive because many of those plugins are very advanced pieces of web software and not just simple, one-script add-ons.

There's a search field available in the center of the page in the directory (visible in the preceding screenshot), which allows you to search plugins by topic and by tag. You can also view a list of the most popular plugins as well as featured plugins. In short, the official plugin directory is where you should always go first when looking for a plugin. It's also a good habit to always check how popular the plugins you're interested in are. Downloading plugins that already have a proven track record of happy users will improve your chances of getting a quality product that you'll enjoy using. This is really important since your site security should never be underestimated. By getting your plugins from the official WordPress directory, you can at least be certain that the plugins are not malicious in any way. We'll talk more about website security in the next chapter.

You can also carry out Google searches when looking for plugins on a per-task basis. I recommend searching for the problem you're trying to solve and see what plugins other users recommend and why. Often, multiple plugins perform similar functions, and you will find feedback from other WordPress users valuable in choosing between them. However, as you do this, be sure to keep an eye out for malicious or poorly coded plugins that could break your website or allow someone to hack into it. Be careful when installing new plugins with no reviews, comments, or feedback from users, in addition to those plugins that have bad feedback about them on the internet.

To get even more in-depth into your plugin investigation, you can also check out the change logs and support forums for each plugin you're considering for your site (every plugin page inside the official `plugin` directory has a tab labeled **Support**). This should give you an idea of how well or how poorly a given plugin is coded, supported, and so on.

Apart from free plugins, there's also a big set of premium plugins (paid ones). However, you won't find them in the official directory. Most of those plugins have their own websites for handling sales, customer support, and usage tutorials. If you're interested, one of the more popular premium plugin directories can be found at `https://codecanyon.net/category/wordpress`.

Finding new plugins

Generally speaking, if a given plugin proves that it's a quality solution and gains some popularity, it will be showcased on the home page of the official directory in the **Featured Plugins** section. But if you want to be up to date with things as they happen, you can pay attention to what's going on at `https://wordpress.org/plugins/browse/new/`.

Additionally, a great way to discover new plugins is to become a regular on the popular blogs about WordPress. Although these blogs are not official creations (they are run by independent owners), they do provide an impressive range of tips and advice, not only on plugins, but also on other aspects related to WordPress. The list includes the following:

- `https://wptavern.com/`
- `https://codeinwp.com/blog/`
- `https://themeisle.com/blog/`
- `http://www.wpbeginner.com/`

Installing a plugin – how to go about this

The steps for installing a plugin are simple:

1. Find your plugin
2. Download it to your WordPress site, either manually or through the automatic installer
3. Install and activate it
4. Configure it (if necessary)

There are two ways to get the plugin into your WordPress installation:

- Install it manually
- Install it directly from within `wp-admin`

The first option—installing plugins manually—generally requires a bit more effort than the second one, but sometimes it's the only way to work with certain plugins (mostly premium ones). The second option—installing from within the `wp-admin`—is generally quicker and easier, but it's not possible in all cases. You need to be on a server that's configured correctly, in a way that lets WordPress add files (we talked about installing WordPress and server configuration in `Chapter 2`, *Getting Started with WordPress*). Plus, the plugin you want to install has to be available in the WordPress plugin repository, that is, the official plugin directory.

In the following section, we'll go over the auto-installation first (since it's easier to do), and then handle the manual method.

Auto-installation

If the plugin you want to install is available in the official plugin directory at `https://wordpress.org/plugins/`, then you can search for and install the plugin from within `wp-admin`. Just navigate to **Plugins | Add New**. You will find a search field in the top-right corner. Type in your desired plugin's name there (as shown in the following screenshot):

Once you see your plugin, click on the **More Details** link to see some more information about the features it has to offer:

I recommend you always look at this information carefully. Be sure to watch for version compatibility. There's a parameter labeled **Compatible up to** listed with the plugin's details. In some cases, you can risk installing a plugin that's a little outdated, but you should proceed with caution. It's also a good idea to have a glance at the number of downloads a plugin has had. The more downloads, the more people had the chance to take a look at the plugin and evaluate its quality.

After installation, you need to test the plugin carefully and verify that it's behaving correctly. Most of the time, if the **Compatible up to** parameter indicates an older version of WordPress, it doesn't necessarily mean that the plugin will fail to work with a newer version. It just means that it hasn't been thoroughly tested, hence the importance of performing your own tests. However, I strongly advise against installing any plugins that haven't been updated in more than two years. Luckily, whenever you encounter such a plugin, WordPress itself will either warn you through a message on the official plugin page, as shown in the following screenshot, or, inside the plugin details section in `wp-admin`, there will be a parameter labeled **Last Updated**:

 This plugin **hasn't been updated in over 2 years**. It may no longer be maintained or supported and may have compatibility issues when used with more recent versions of WordPress.

If everything is fine, you can proceed by clicking on the **Install Now** button. After a couple of seconds, you will be able to activate the plugin. You'll see the **Activate** button that will appear. Consult with the following screenshot:

At this point, the plugin has been installed and activated. In other words, it should be fully operational.

Manual plugin installation

The following procedure allows you to install any WordPress plugin you can get your hands on, irrespective of whether it comes from the official directory at WordPress.org (`https://wordpress.org/`) or elsewhere.

To install a plugin manually, you must start by downloading the plugin archive either from the official directory at `https://wordpress.org/plugins/` or from another website or source (usually when dealing with premium plugins).

In this case, the Jetpack plugin is available in the official directory at `https://wordpress.org/plugins/jetpack/`:

Just click on the blue **Download** button and save the resulting ZIP file on your computer in a place where you can find it easily. Once you have the plugin downloaded, and if your server is set up correctly, you should be able to upload the ZIP file directly via the **Plugins | Add New** page. Go to that page, click on the **Upload Plugin** button at the top, and choose the ZIP file of the plugin, as shown in the following screenshot:

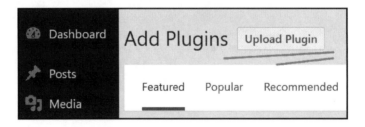

If this automatic uploader doesn't work for you, you can do it the old-fashioned way. First unzip, that is, extract the ZIP file you downloaded so that it's a directory, probably named `jetpack` (at least in this case). Then, using your FTP client, upload this directory inside the `wp-content/plugins/` directory of your WordPress installation. You'll also see the two plugins in that directory that WordPress came with—`akismet` and `hello.php`.

If you need any assistance with FTP software, review `Chapter 2`, *Getting Started with WordPress*, where we talked about the topic of installing WordPress.

After the upload finishes, you will be able to activate the plugin. This is required to effectively turn the plugin on. This can be done by clicking on the **Activate Plugin** button, as shown in the following screenshot. At this point, you're done, and the Jetpack plugin is working:

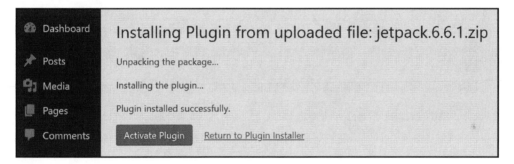

What to do after plugin installation

With your plugin installed and ready to go, there's just one more thing that you might want to do. While some plugins are perfectly functional right after activation, others require some additional tuning. The following are the four most likely scenarios:

- You may not have to do anything. Some plugins simply change the way WordPress does certain things, and activating them is all you have to do.
- You may have to configure the plugin before it begins to work. Some plugins need you to make choices and set new settings.
- You may also get a set of shortcodes or other elements that you can use to include additional content that the plugin provides inside your posts or pages.
- There may not be a configuration page, but you may have to add some code to one of your theme's template files.

If you're unsure of what to do after you've uploaded and activated your plugin, be sure to read the README file that most likely came with the plugin or look at the FAQ on the plugin's website.

 Many plugin authors accept donations. I strongly recommend giving donations to the authors of the plugins that you find useful. It helps to encourage everyone in the community to continue writing great plugins that everyone can use. Even if you can only donate a small amount, it will still count. Think how much time you saved thanks to the developer of your favorite plugin. If it's significant, maybe you should indeed consider donating.

The must-have pack of plugins

Even though there are more than 55,000 plugins available in the official directory, you surely don't need all of them on your WordPress site at the same time. There is a small set that we might call the *must-have pack*. My list of must-have plugins can be different from the next guy's, so treat the following information more as guidance rather than as a written-in-stone necessity. That being said, if I am honest here, and despite the fact that some of my blogs feature more than 25 plugins all working at the same time, the essential must-have list consists of only seven plugins. All these plugins handle a specific task geared toward making a WordPress site better and more functional.

Backing up

Backing up is probably the most critical task for any website owner, and I'm saying this in all seriousness. For instance, can you imagine a situation in which you lose your whole site overnight with no ability to restore it? This might sound a bit hard to believe right now, but it does happen. If it's a personal blog you've been running, then it's not that tragic. But for a business website, it's an entirely different story.

So, one of the main problems with backing up is that it's only effective if it's done regularly. In other words, you need to create backups often and keep them somewhere safe. While that's all fine, who has the time to do this manually? No one, honestly. That's why we'll be using a plugin that does its magic in the background without any supervision required on our part—introducing **UpdraftPlus**—a WordPress backup plugin, available at `https://wordpress.org/plugins/updraftplus/`:

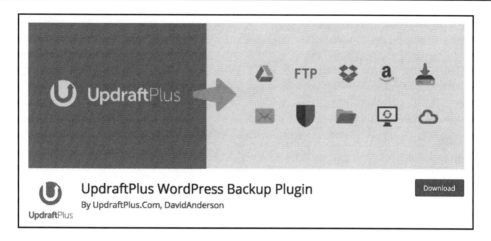

This plugin allows you to handle website backups in an easy to grasp and hassle-free way. It connects with your remote storage account, such as Dropbox (but there are more possibilities here), and then backs up your site regularly on autopilot. It requires only minimal initial setup.

 If you don't have an account yet, you can sign up to Dropbox for free at `https://www.dropbox.com/`. As part of the free package, you get 2 GB disk space, which will be more than enough to keep your site backed up.

Here are the steps necessary to integrate UpdraftPlus with Dropbox. After installing and activating the plugin, navigate to **Settings** | **UpdraftPlus Backups** in your `wp-admin`, and then switch to the **Settings** tab. There, click on the **Dropbox** logo:

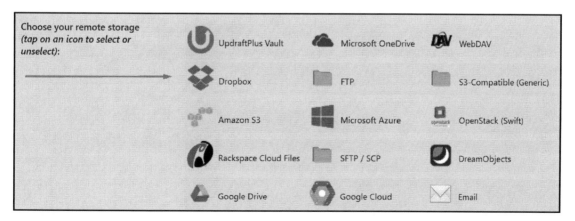

Right after clicking on the logo, scroll down and click on the main **Save Changes** button. This will reload the page, and you'll see a notification that additional authorization with Dropbox is required, as follows:

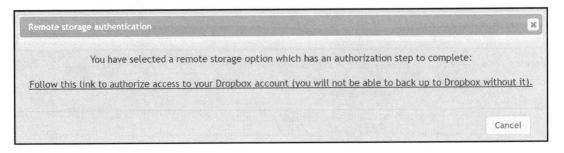

Just click on the link in the notification, and you'll be taken to the Dropbox authorization page. To proceed, you'll need to log in to your Dropbox account and then confirm the authorization. After a couple of seconds, you will be redirected back to your site and your settings will be in place. At this stage, you have integrated the plugin with Dropbox. All that needs doing now is telling the plugin to back up your website automatically.

Go back to the **Settings** tab of the plugin. The two fields to pay attention to now are the following ones:

- **Files backup schedule**
- **Database backup schedule**

This depends on your personal preference, but for a website that doesn't publish multiple entries every day, setting the former to **Weekly** and the latter to **Daily** is going to be just fine, as follows:

With this plugin, you can also trigger backups manually (on top of the backup scheduling feature). Doing so is a good idea when you first install the plugin, just to check whether everything's working fine and to have your initial backup done. You can start the backup in **Settings | UpdraftPlus Backups**. You will be presented with the following screen:

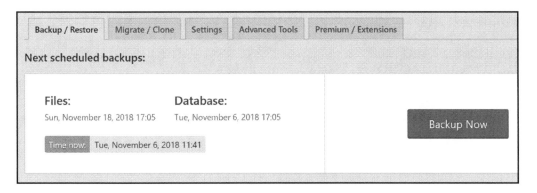

All you need to do is just click on the big **Backup Now** button.

Enabling Google Analytics

Google Analytics is a very popular site stats and analytics solution. It's free, easy to use for a beginner, and very powerful for anyone willing to get into it a little more deeply. In short, Google Analytics lets you in on a set of stats and data regarding the web traffic your site is getting, including things such as the exact number of visitors (daily, monthly, and so on), traffic sources, your most popular content, and a virtual myriad of other statistics. Google Analytics is available at `https://www.google.com/analytics/`.

To enable Google Analytics on your site, you have to sign up for a Google account first, enable **Analytics**, and then add your site in the control panel (all available on the official Google Analytics page, along with extensive tutorial documentation). Next, take the tracking code that Google gives you and include it on your site. This last step is where the **Google Analytics for WordPress by MonsterInsights** plugin comes into play and makes the whole thing a lot simpler. You can get it at `https://wordpress.org/plugins/google-analytics-for-wordpress/`:

Once you download and activate it, proceed to **Insights | Settings**. Although the plugin has a lot of settings, the only thing you must do to make it work is to authenticate the plugin so that you can enable a connection with your Google Analytics account. Just click on the **Authenticate with your Google account** button:

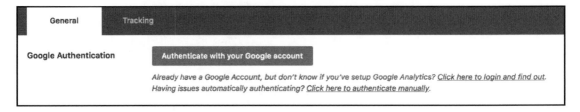

This will redirect you to a page on Google where you have to click on another button, **Grant access**, and then you'll be taken back to your wp-admin. Now, you can select what's called your *UA-profile*, which is what you want to use for monitoring the site. If you're having problems with this semi-automatic way of authentication, you can simply input your Google Analytics code (called the UA code) manually. This code is visible in your profile at Google Analytics (it usually begins with UA- and is followed by nine numbers).

Once you're done with the authentication procedure, your site is fully connected to Google Analytics and the traffic stats are being collected. After a while, you can navigate to your profile in Google Analytics and see how your site's been doing in terms of visitor popularity. Also, to get a more immediate indication of whether the tracking code has been set correctly or not, you can navigate to the **Real-Time** traffic section inside Google Analytics.

Caching

To be honest, caching is a pretty complicated concept. If you speak *engineering*, then here's the definition: *in computer science, a cache is a component that transparently stores data so that future requests for that data can be served faster*. What it means in plain English is that if you have caching enabled on your site, it will load faster and be much more accessible for your audience/visitors. Luckily, even though the concept itself is not that straightforward, the plugin that enables you to *cache* is. Currently, the top of the line plugin is called **W3 Total Cache**, and is available at https://wordpress.org/plugins/w3-total-cache/:

And it's not just me recommending it. Actually, a number of major hosting companies and experts say that it provides *the* way to get your site optimized fast. More than that, the plugin is also in use on some major blogs around the web.

The installation procedure is the same as with any WordPress plugin. But right after you activate it, you'll see that the usage is quite different. For one, it's accessible through a completely new section in the left sidebar. It's labeled **Performance**, and it's placed right below **Settings**. Less than a second after you click on it, you will realize that this plugin is a huge one. It could probably have a completely separate book written about it. So here, I will only provide a quick start guide, so to speak.

Go to **Performance** | **General Settings**, and browse through the page. There are a number of checkboxes labeled **Enable**. Just to get started with the plugin, I advise you to enable (check the following checkbox) the following blocks:

- **Page Cache**
- **Database Cache**
- **Object Cache**
- **Browser Cache**

Then, click on any of the **Save all settings** buttons. From now on, caching will be fully enabled on your site and your visitors should start experiencing performance improvements right away. Obviously, we've only touched on the possibilities and customizations that this plugin brings to the table, so I encourage you to give it a closer look in your spare time.

Search engine optimization

Search engine optimization (SEO) is one of the most popular topics online (at least among website owners). The simple truth is that working on your site's SEO, if done right, will raise its position in search engines (such as Google) and will bring you more visitors on a daily basis. The concept is pretty simple in theory, but the work involved to achieve this can become a full-time job. If you're not interested in devoting a big chunk of your time to SEO, then, at the very least, get the **Yoast SEO** plugin, available at `https://wordpress.org/plugins/wordpress-seo/`, and have the basics handled. The plugin is very popular in the blogosphere, and it's in use on some of the most popular blogs out there:

Similar to the previous plugin, W3 Total Cache, this one has a custom section within `wp-admin` too. It's visible right below **Settings**, and it's called **SEO**. The best way to get the core how-to on this plugin is to go through the configuration wizard. You'll see the link leading to it right after visiting the plugin's section, **SEO**, in the `wp-admin`:

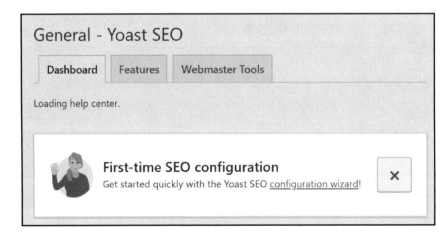

The wizard is really well made and it'll take you step by step through the whole configuration phase of the plugin, along with its most basic settings and features. I really encourage you to spend a while optimizing your site with this plugin because this work will surely pay off in the long run, or maybe even much sooner:

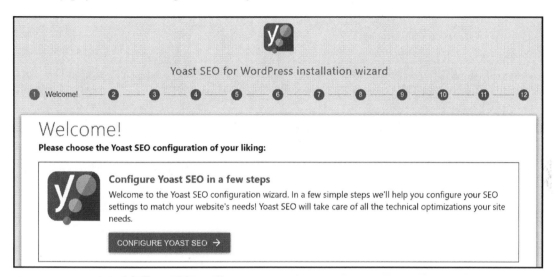

 There's a separate resource that was published by the author of the WordPress SEO plugin—Joost de Valk. It's where you should go to get further in-depth information on how to set up the plugin and what else you can do to make your site SEO-friendly. You can find it at https://yoast.com/wordpress-seo/.

Social media integration

Social media has taken the online space by storm and, these days, we can hardly imagine a website existing without at least some level of social media integration. The benefits of such integration are clearly visible. With a good social media plugin for WordPress, you will be able to share your posts with friends and family on all of the most popular social platforms out there. More than that, your readers will be able to do it too, effectively growing your audience and making your site more popular. Ultimately, publishing content that goes viral on social media can skyrocket your traffic and make your site visible to thousands of new people every week, or even every day.

So, the way we're going to make it easier for your readers (and you) to share your content is by displaying some social media buttons on your site, and more accurately, on each post and page that your site consists of.

The social media plugin called **Simple Social Media Share Buttons** is a great free solution that gives you the requisite functionality. It is available at `https://wordpress.org/plugins/simple-social-buttons/`:

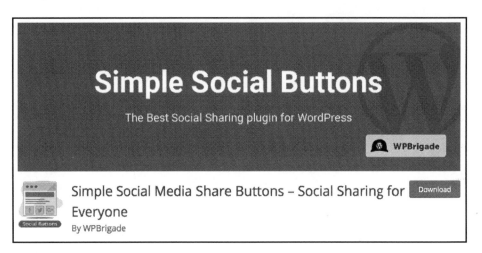

After installing and activating it, you can go to the plugin's settings section in **Social Buttons | Settings**. There, you can review the default settings that the plugin comes with out of the box. The good news is that if you don't want to deal with any of those, you can just leave things as they are—all of the settings are optional. If you do want to play around, however, you can change a load of things about how social media buttons are presented on your site:

As you can see, the interface is really easy to grasp, lets you pick from a range of different social networks, and also gives you some basic customization options (such as changing the size of the buttons, their position on the page, and whether or not you want the share counter to be displayed). When you're done experimenting with the settings, click on **Save Changes**.

For example, the settings I have selected in my setup include only Facebook, Twitter, and LinkedIn buttons, plus a slick minimal theme to make those buttons stand out. Here's what they look like under a blog post:

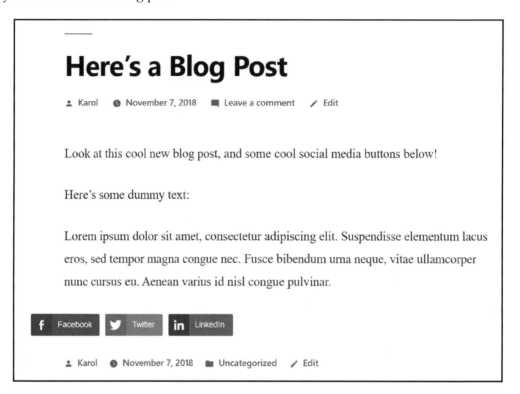

Jetpack

This mysterious name is exactly what one of the most popular plugins of today is called. Jetpack, by the guys behind WordPress.com, offers a truly exceptional range of features and functionalities. The plugin consists of a number of modules that can be enabled or disabled one by one. This gives you full control over the features you want and don't want to use. Jetpack is available at `https://wordpress.org/plugins/jetpack/`:

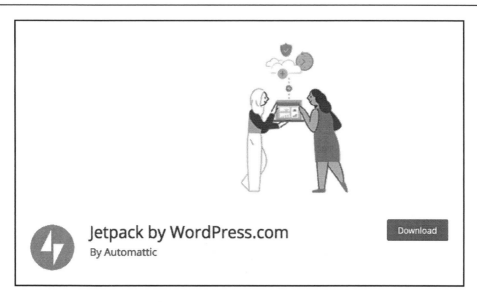

Jetpack by WordPress.com
By Automattic

Download

After downloading and activating it, you'll see a new section in `wp-admin`, but this time, it's right below **Dashboard**, as shown in the following screenshot:

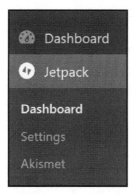

Inside, you can see all of the available modules and functionalities. First, you should navigate to **Jetpack** | **Settings** to enable or disable the modules you need/don't need. There are over 30 modules there, so you have a lot to choose from. Luckily, they've been grouped into a handful of categories:

- **Writing**: Everything that makes writing content easier, together with settings for site speed-up
- **Sharing**: Some additional social media integration

- **Discussion**: Tools that help your readers discuss and interact with your content
- **Traffic**: Tools and settings that help you monitor the traffic that your website is getting
- **Security**: Backups, added security, and spam protection

I won't go over each of the modules here in detail because it would probably require a chapter of its own. Instead, I encourage you to click on the name of each module you'd like to look into and get all the info yourself. In general, each of the modules is quite user-friendly, so you shouldn't experience any trouble during installation or using them later on.

Comment spam

Comment spam is one of the most annoying things on the internet if you're an online publisher. Basically, a spam comment is a comment that has been submitted for the sole purpose of getting a link back to a specific website. The main reason why people submit spam comments is SEO. Generally speaking, in terms of SEO, the number of links pointing to a site is a known ranking factor, and website owners around the world do whatever they can to get as many links as possible. Unfortunately for us, sometimes it means using various spam methods as well.

The way WordPress comments are set up by default makes it possible for anyone to get a link from your site just by submitting a comment and entering a website address in one of the comment fields. If they do so, and the comment gets approved, whatever was typed into the **Name** field of the comment becomes the text of the link, and the **Website** field becomes the link's destination.

The worst thing about comment spam is that once your site gets even remotely popular, you can start getting hundreds of spam comments a day; hence, dealing with them by hand becomes almost impossible.

Unfortunately, fighting comment spam is not something built into WordPress by default. This means that you have to get some plugin(s) to enable this functionality. For now, let's focus on the most popular spam protection plugin out there—Akismet. The good thing about this is that it comes along with the standard WordPress installation incorporated directly, so you should be able to find it in the **Plugins** section in your wp-admin. The only thing you need to do is activate it.

Working with Akismet

Right after you activate the plugin, you'll see a prompt in the top section of your `wp-admin`. Click on the big button that's in it:

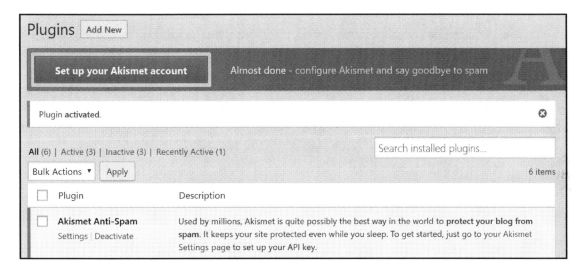

The Akismet plugin requires that you have a special API key. Getting this API key isn't something particularly difficult, but we still need to go through a couple of steps. First, click on the **Get your API key** button:

You will be redirected to akismet.com (`https://akismet.com/`), where you will be able to complete the process. The on-screen instructions are very clear and take you through everything step by step. To get started, you first need a WordPress.com profile account. If you don't have one yet, you will be prompted to create it. Nothing fancy—just standard information is needed during signup. We covered this in an earlier chapter.

Once you do have the account and begin setting up Akismet, the thing you should pay special attention to is the specific subscription plan that you're going to select. At the time of writing, there are three available: Basic (free), Plus ($5), and Enterprise ($50). To get standard spam protection, you can confidently go with Basic, as shown in the following screenshot:

Now, this is tricky. The plan you've selected is based on voluntary donations. If you're not willing to spend any money, just take the slider that's in the center and slide it to the left, all the way to $0.00/yr:

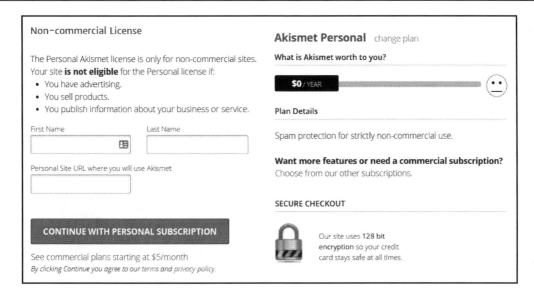

After clicking on the final activation link, you will be redirected back to your WordPress website, and the API key is going to be already in the right field in Akismet settings.

If you're feeling confident, you can check the box labeled **Silently discard the worst and most pervasive spam so I never see it**. Akismet is relatively good at identifying which comment is actually spam, and checking this box will make those comments disappear. However, if you're concerned about Akismet misidentifying comments, leave this unchecked. All you have to do is click on the **Save Changes** button, and your blog is now protected from comment spam! This is demonstrated in the following screenshot:

Comments	☐ Show the number of approved comments beside each comment author
Strictness	○ Silently discard the worst and most pervasive spam so I never see it.
	◉ Always put spam in the Spam folder for review. **Note:** Spam in the spam folder older than 15 days is deleted automatically.
Privacy	◉ Display a privacy notice under your comment forms.
	○ Do not display privacy notice. To help your site with transparency under privacy laws like the GDPR, Akismet can display a notice to your users under your comment forms. This feature is disabled by default, however, you can turn it on above.

Disconnect this account | Save Changes

Summary

This chapter was all about expanding the features available on your site and making your content more attractive without the need to touch any source code. Basically, that's the whole idea behind plugins.

Some developers might not need plugins because they can code things on their own. However, for the rest of the world, plugins are what makes WordPress easy to use and attractive for everyone.

At this point, we know how to control the content of our WordPress site, but that's only the beginning. In the next chapter, we will learn how to take care of basic website security and prevent hackers from taking over our sites.

6
Securing your WordPress Website

The topic of website security can be an intimidating one. On the one hand, we all want our websites to be secure, but, on the other, we fear that we might not have the skills to battle hackers trying to break into our sites. But hold off on that thought for a second; why would anyone even attack your site in the first place?! You're not a financial institution or a popular online publication, so why would anyone care to spend their time trying to harm your site?

Well, the reality can be harsh in this case. Most hacker attacks are not about stealing your revenue or taking over your site as a whole. Usually, they are about including a small piece of code on your site that links out to other external sites (most of the time, either fraudulent sites or *naughty* content). What does the hacker get out of it? This varies, but usually, those kinds of attacks are done to use your site as part of a network that is meant to achieve a specific goal. Effectively, your site becomes a zombie—it does whatever the hacker tells it to do, and it's part of a bigger network of similar *zombie sites*.

So how can we prevent this *zombification* of your site from happening? That's what this chapter is about. Let's start with the basics.

Let's take a look at the topics that will be covered in this chapter:

- The principles of WordPress security
- The best practices for WordPress security
- Installing an SSL
- Security plugins and which ones to get
- Setting up secure user accounts
- User roles and abilities
- Managing users
- User management plugins

The principles of WordPress security

Before we get into any specific tips and techniques for WordPress security, let's set some groundwork in place. Your number one objective is to set the most fundamental elements in place so that you can avoid 99% of the attacks. Remember that the hackers are not targeting your site individually. Instead, they target a whole cluster of sites and aim to take advantage of known vulnerabilities. Therefore, if you erase that given vulnerability from your site, then you're effectively preventing the attack from happening.

Again, our number one goal: prevention through implementing best practices. Or, to say it another way, let's do the 20% of the work that'll give us 80% of the result. To achieve that, let's start with some overall best practices for website security.

The best practices for WordPress security

The good thing about the most essential best practices for your WordPress website security is that they are all very simple to implement. Let's start with the basics.

Using strong passwords

This sounds really simple, but the value of a strong password cannot be overstated. Many hacker attacks try to capitalize on the user having a simple password that's either a dictionary word or is one of the most commonly used passwords. In other words, if you can see your WordPress password on the following list, then you're doing it wrong:

• 123456 • Password • 12345678 • qwerty • 12345 • 123456789 • letmein • 1234567 • football • iloveyou	• admin • welcome • monkey • login • abc123 • starwars • 123123 • dragon • password • master • hello

For a more complete list of the most commonly used passwords, visit this page: `https://en.wikipedia.org/wiki/List_of_the_most_common_passwords`.

So, how do you set a strong password? There are two schools:

- Either use a selection of random characters with lowercase and uppercase letters, numbers, and special symbols (like hyphens); for example: `noUYhf56%%6fJJJ-Njh`
- Come up with an actual sentence, and then join it together into a password using hyphens; for example: `I-like-pizza-but-cake-is-good-too`

To change your password, go to **Users** | **Your Profile**. Once there, click on the **Generate Password** button (refer to the following screenshot). WordPress will suggest a password, but you can also input your own. Click on **Update Profile** when done:

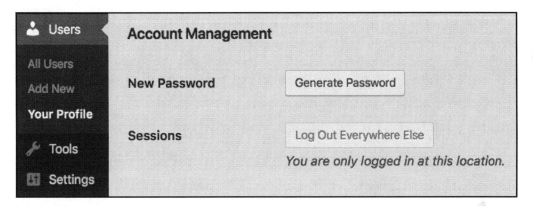

Keeping your WordPress updated

With every new release of the WordPress software, you get a range of improvements and upgrades. Some of those are entirely new features, some are improvements to old features, and some are improvements in the realm of security. For that reason, keeping your WordPress up to date is the best way to stay out of trouble and make sure that your WordPress website remains in tune with the current developments in website security.

Whenever a new version of WordPress is available, you'll see an update prompt in `wp-admin`. Please make sure to pay attention to those prompts. It really can't be emphasized enough how important they are.

Keeping your theme and plugins updated

Staying with the idea of updates, just like the WordPress core gets updated, themes and plugins get updated as well. You should install them as soon as they're available for the very same reason you want to be installing WordPress updates.

To see what updates are available for your site in general, go to **Dashboard** | **Updates**. You'll see a summary there, along with links enabling you to get the updates installed, as can be seen in the following screenshot:

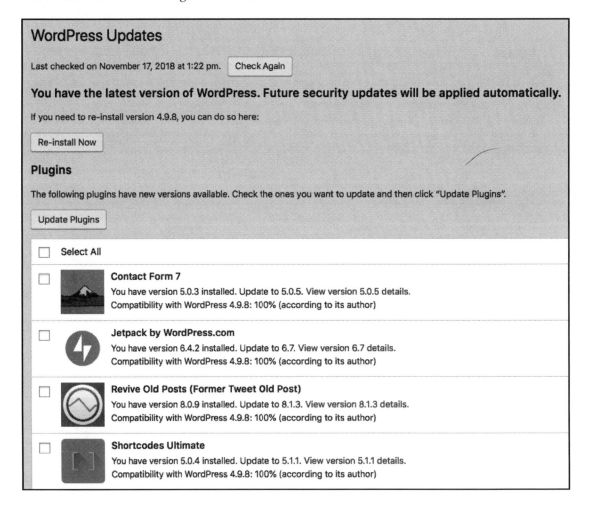

Avoid installing unneeded plugins

There are thousands of WordPress plugins available on the web. As exciting as some of them might appear, you should think twice before installing some of the less popular plugins, or plugins that haven't been tested by users.

Generally speaking, first of all, you shouldn't install anything that's not essential for your website to do its job efficiently. If a plugin is just a cool thing to have, but not essential, you should probably skip it.

Over and above that, also pay attention to the ratings, compatibility info, and the popularity numbers of the plugin that you're considering. For example, here are some relevant fields from the Jetpack plugin's official page at `https://wordpress.org/plugins/jetpack/`:

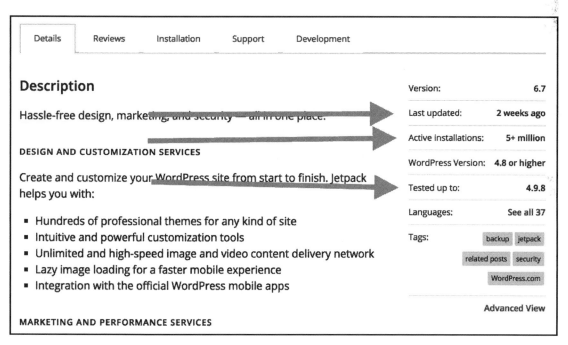

When installing a new plugin, try not getting anything with low ratings, a small number of installs, or a plugin that hasn't been tested with the current versions of WordPress.

That's it in terms of the topic of WordPress security best practices. Now, let's get down to some additional work.

Installing an SSL

Secure sockets layer (SSL) is a web technology that was created to encrypt the connection between a web server (a website) and the client's browser (the person reading the website).

With an encrypted connection, it's basically impossible to intercept the data that's being sent back and forth, thus making it secure to perform sometimes even the most sensitive of tasks, such as handling bank transfers, for instance.

In simple terms, once you enable SSL on your website, you'll make it incredibly more difficult for hackers to breach and/or distort the connection between your site and its visitors.

Luckily, these days, installing an SSL is a straightforward thing to do. Most of the popular web hosts offer a free SSL certificate as part of your main hosting plan. The only thing you need to do is check a couple of boxes in your user panel to enable it.

Unfortunately, the specific steps differ from host to host. Here's how to get this done with some of the popular providers:

- **Bluehost**: `https://my.bluehost.com/hosting/help/free-ssl`
- **SiteGround**: `https://www.siteground.com/tutorials/getting-started/configure-ssl-with-one-click/`
- **GoDaddy**: `https://www.godaddy.com/garage/enable-https-server/`
- **HostGator**: `https://support.hostgator.com/categories/ssl-certificates/ssl-setup-use/`

If you're hosting your site with someone else, you'll likely find a similar guide in their documentation as well.

However, even after going through the steps in the user panel of your host, you still have the SSL only *partly* enabled on your WordPress site. This brings us to the topic of security plugins.

Security plugins and which ones to get

There are tons of different security plugins on the web, all promising to handle one thing or the other for your WordPress website. However, not all of them are essential to have, or rather, few are. So, let's take a minute to discuss the ones that can be truly useful to have on your site. We didn't list them in the previous chapter specifically so that we can cover them in greater depth here.

SSL plugin

With SSL enabled on your host's end, it's time to prepare your WordPress website to receive it:

1. This can be done with a plugin called **Really Simple SSL**, which is available at `https://wordpress.org/plugins/really-simple-ssl/`:

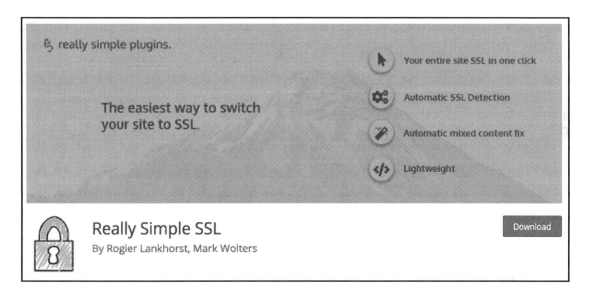

2. After activating the plugin, you'll see a message like this:

Almost ready to migrate to SSL!

Some things can't be done automatically. Before you migrate, please check for:

- Http references in your .css and .js files: change any http:// into //
- Images, stylesheets or scripts from a domain without an ssl certificate: remove them or move to your own server.

You can also let the automatic scan of the pro version handle this for you, and get premium support and increased security with HSTS included,

Go ahead, activate SSL!

3. Click on the **Go ahead, activate SSL!** button. After doing so, you'll immediately get signed out of your WordPress dashboard, but don't worry, this is just part of the process. When you log back in, you'll see that your dashboard is now available under `https` instead of the standard `http`.

4. To make sure everything works as it should, visit your website normally and look for the characteristic padlock next to your website's address:

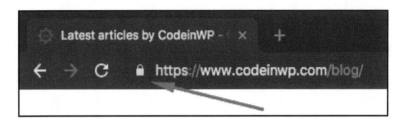

General security plugin

Apart from SSL, you should also get a general security plugin that's going to take care of some other common holes in website security. The plugin we're going to use is called **Wordfence Security**, which is available at `https://wordpress.org/plugins/wordfence/`:

Getting started with this plugin requires only basic setting up. Immediately upon installing and activating it, you will see an invitation to take the tour and enter your admin email to get notifications about your site's security, as shown in the following screenshot:

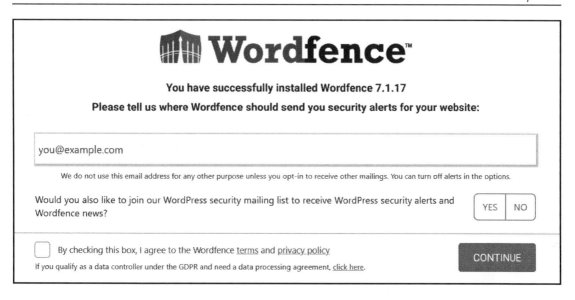

This tour, although short, will present all of the most important features to you and tell you how to work with the plugin effectively. For the most part, the plugin doesn't require any supervision, and thanks to the notification emails, you can just sit back, relax, and wait for the plugin to reach out to you, so to speak:

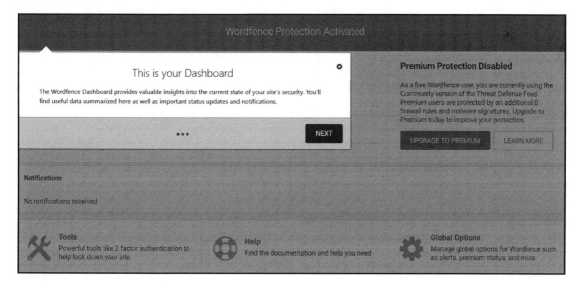

The best way to get started with the plugin is to go to **Wordfence | Scan** from `wp-admin`, and then click on the big **START NEW SCAN** button, as shown in the following screenshot:

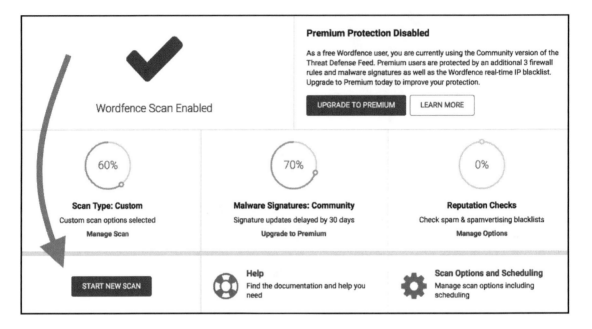

Right after doing so, you will see the scan running. When the scan is done and everything is okay, you will see a row of check marks confirming that the scan was successful:

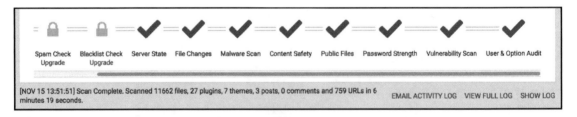

In the event of any problems, Wordfence will display them to you further down the page and will also give you tips on how to solve them. In any case, you can always view the full log of the scan by clicking on the link labeled **VIEW FULL LOG** or **SHOW LOG** (visible in the preceding screenshot).

Apart from the basic scanning functionality, this plugin also gives you the ability to block individual IP addresses from accessing your site, improve your site's performance with caching, and even make your site inaccessible to whole countries (in case some geographical area causes you serious problems).

The most important aspect in this regard, however, is that from now on, Wordfence protection runs automatically, and you don't have to do anything yourself actively to keep your site safe. Whenever your attention is required, Wordfence will send you a notification via email and let you know what you should do. This really is a set-it-and-forget-it kind of solution for the most part.

Other plugins to consider

With SSL and Wordfence out of the way, let's now have a quick look at other popular security plugins. Installing them is optional, depending on what you think is a good direction to follow with your website, security-wise:

- **Google Authenticator** (`https://wordpress.org/plugins/miniorange-2-factor-authentication/`): Use it to enable two-factor authentication
- **Force Strong Passwords** (`https://wordpress.org/plugins/force-strong-passwords/`): Gives you a password strength indicator and doesn't allow weak passwords to be used
- **WP Security Audit Log** (`https://wordpress.org/plugins/wp-security-audit-log/`): Keeps a log of all activity going on in the admin section of your website
- **Login LockDown** (`https://wordpress.org/plugins/login-lockdown/`): Protects your login page by recording the IP addresses and timestamps of every failed login attempt, and then locks out specific IP addresses based on failed login attempts
- **Sucuri Security** (`https://wordpress.org/plugins/sucuri-scanner/`): An alternative to Wordfence, and another great security scanning plugin

 Learning more: If you want to learn more about website security and WordPress security in particular, you should subscribe to the Sucuri blog (at `https://blog.sucuri.net/`). Sucuri is a highly respected company and the leader when it comes to all matters of website and WordPress security. Whenever a new vulnerability is discovered in the WordPress space, it's Sucuri that often breaks the news.

Setting up secure user accounts

So far in this book, we've focused on working with a personal website—one that belongs to, and is used by, just one person. However, many blogs are used differently—there may be a single blog or website with a variety of writers, editors, and administrators. This makes the site more like a community project or even an online magazine. Also, it's by no means uncommon for bigger online publishers to use WordPress as the base of their websites, in which case the site has a number of authors, editors, reviewers, and overall contributors with varying responsibilities, not to mention the technical staff or designers. All those people should have their own user accounts when interacting with the site.

Furthermore, even if it's just you managing your personal WordPress website, you should still make your own account as secure as possible. In this section, you'll learn all the ins and outs of how to make user accounts secure and how to go about creating them in the first place.

There are three main rules that you should keep in mind whenever creating new user accounts:

- Each new user account should have sufficient privileges that allow the user to carry out their work, but not more
- Don't use obvious usernames, such as `admin` or `user`; instead, make things a tiny bit more complex, such as by using `firstname.lastname`
- Use strong passwords—you already know that

Let's cover that first aspect in a bit more detail—account privileges. Based on who you're creating the user account for, that person will probably not need full admin-level access to your website. In most cases, people will just want to be able to write and publish new posts or pages, and they don't need admin credentials for that. The following is a breakdown of all the user account types available in WordPress, together with what they're intended for.

User roles and abilities

WordPress allows you to work with an unlimited number of user accounts on your website. Each user can be assigned one of five different roles. Let's look at these roles one at a time, starting with the most powerful one.

Administrator

When you installed WordPress, it automatically created a user with administrative powers for you. This role is called *administrator*, and every WordPress site must have at least one admin account (you will not be allowed to delete them all). As you have already seen in the earlier chapters, administrators can do everything.

 The administrator's primary purpose is to manage everything about the website.

In general, you don't want to have a lot of administrators on a single blog or website. It is best to keep just one administrator account on a blog with 10 to 20 authors and editors, or perhaps up to three administrators for a blog with dozens of users.

Some examples of the actions that only a user with the administrator role can perform are as follows:

- Switch blog theme
- Add, edit, activate, or deactivate plugins
- Add, edit, or delete users
- Manage general blog options and settings

When creating more administrator accounts (or managing the main one), make sure to use only complex passwords that are hard to break using any sort of brute-force methods. As we mentioned previously, a lot of hacking attempts revolve around password guessing, so the more complex your password is, the tougher it will be to break.

Editor

After the administrator, the *editor* has the most powerful role. This role is meant for those users who need to manage everything about the content of a website, but who don't need to be able to change the basic structure, design, or functionality of the website itself (that's for administrators).

 The editor's primary purpose is to manage the content of the website.

To get an idea of what the screen looks like when a user logs in as an editor, let's take a look at the editor's menu (on the right) in comparison to the administrator's menu (on the left):

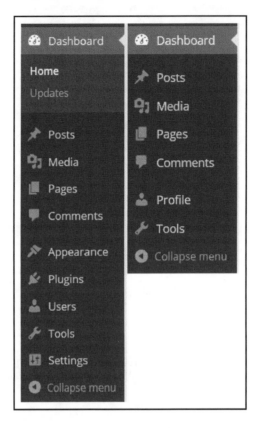

As you can see, the top section is unchanged (apart from the **Updates** link). However, nearly the entire bottom menu, with **Appearance**, **Plugins**, **Users** (which is replaced with **Profile**), and **Settings**, has disappeared. We can see that the editor is left with only the ability to edit their own profile and to access the **Tools** section, which includes any plugin pages that allow editor-level users.

The examples of actions that a user with the editor role can perform are as follows:

- Manage all posts
- Create and edit pages
- Moderate comments
- Manage categories, tags, and links
- Edit other users' content

There's one advantageous aspect of the editor's role. If you take a closer look, you'll see that it has all the credentials that you would need to publish any piece of content on a given WordPress site. This makes it perfect for everyday use, even for single-author blogs/sites. Therefore, what I actually encourage you to do is set a separate editor account for yourself, and then use it for posting and editing content, instead of working with the default administrator account. This setup is a lot safer, particularly if someone tries to hijack your password, or in the event of any other mishap to your account, the site itself won't get harmed (because editors can't install new plugins or delete any existing ones).

For multi-author blogs/sites, the editor role is meant to be assigned to users who are in charge of the content published on the site. As the name itself indicates, the *editor* role is perfect for editors.

Author

Authors have much less access than editors. Authors can add and edit their own posts, and manage the posts made by their subordinates. However, they can neither edit posts made by other authors nor manage comments on posts that don't belong to them.

 The author's primary purpose is to manage their own content.

To get an idea of the experience of a user with the *author* role, let's take a look at the author's menu (on the right) in comparison to the editor's menu (on the left):

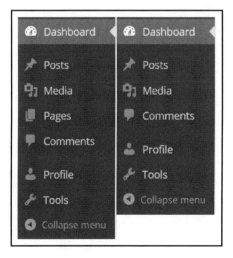

As you can see in the preceding screenshot, the **Pages** section has disappeared. Additionally, if the author looks at the complete list of posts, they will only have the ability to **view**, but not **edit**, **quick edit**, or **delete** posts that they did not author (highlighted):

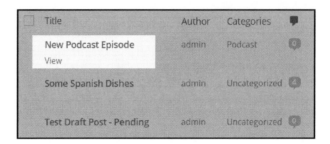

As you would imagine, the author role is perfect for, well, authors—users who are actively involved in creating content for your site. Authors can, for example, do the following:

- Submit and publish their posts
- Manage their posts after the publication
- Moderate the comments under their posts

Contributor

Contributors are only able to write posts and submit them for review. These posts will be in **Pending Review** status until an editor, or administrator, agrees to publish them. Contributors cannot upload images or other files, view the media library, add categories, edit comments, or any of the other tasks available to more privileged users.

 The contributor's primary purpose is to submit content for consideration.

One important thing worth mentioning is that although contributors can create and submit their work for review, once the article is published, they no longer have the ability to edit it in any way. However, they do get access to the comments section (for moderation).

When it comes to the real-world applications of this role, it's most commonly used when working with guest bloggers or any other regular contributors who are not part of your in-house team. Guest blogging is really popular nowadays, and handling it through contributor accounts is much less labor-intensive than receiving articles via email and then having to copy and paste them to WordPress.

Subscriber

Subscribers cannot do anything at all, as weird as that might sound. They can only log in and edit their profile (adjust their first name, last name, password, bio information, and so on), and that's it. Depending on the permissions set in **Settings | Discussion**, blog visitors may have to sign up as subscribers in order to be able to post comments. Also, there are some plugins that handle sending info updates to subscribers, such as newsletters or email notifications of new posts.

A subscriber has no editorial power over the website.

Most of the time, this role is used as a placeholder. Take, for example, a specific author who had been contributing to your site regularly in the past, but who hasn't submitted anything in months. Instead of deleting their account completely, you can simply change the role to that of a *subscriber*.

Managing users

To manage users, log in (as the administrator, of course) and navigate to **Users**. You'll see a list of your existing users, as seen in the following screenshot:

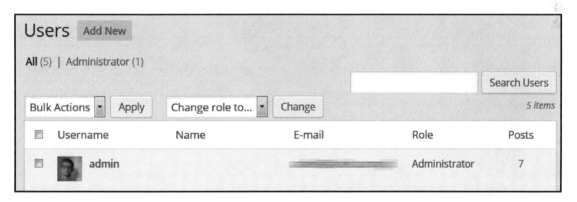

When we installed WordPress, it just created our first user (which is how we've been logging in all this time). So let's create a new user, and assign that user the next most powerful role—*editor*.

1. To do this, navigate to **Users** | **Add New**. You'll see the **Add New User** form, as shown in the following screenshot:

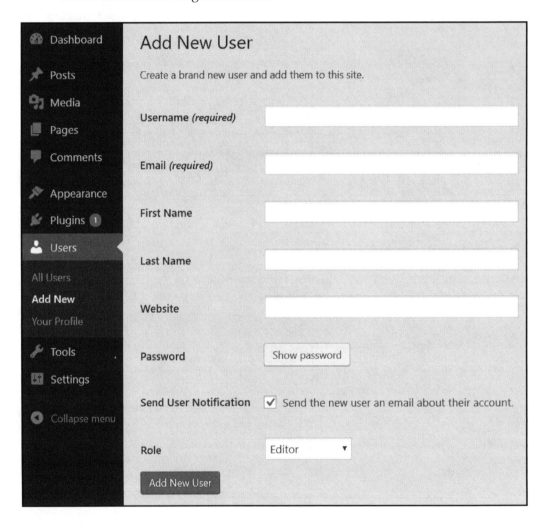

In this form, only the **Username** and **Email** fields are required. The **Password** is handled automatically. WordPress will generate a safe password on its own and then send it to the new user once done. You can also change the **Role** from the default (**Subscriber**) to one of the other roles. In this case, I've selected **Editor**.

2. Then, click on the **Add New User** button. Apart from the required fields, it's also good practice to fill in **First Name** and **Last Name**. This can make the task of further managing the user accounts much clearer.

3. In this example, I'll repeat this process to add an **author**, a **contributor** and a **subscriber**. When I'm done, the **Users** page (where the users can be managed) appears as in the following screenshot:

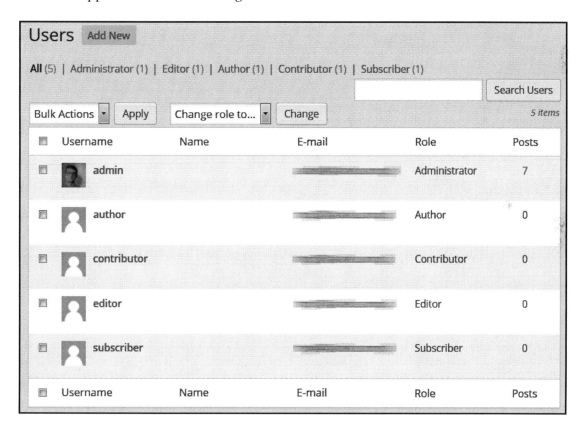

To see the actions that you can perform on each of these new user accounts, just hover your mouse cursor over any of the rows. In this case, you can **edit** or **delete** users. You can use the checkboxes and the **Bulk Actions** menu, or use the filter links to view only users with particular roles. You can change the role of one or more users on this page by checking the box (or boxes) and using the **Change role to...** drop-down menu.

Enabling users to self-register

Adding users by yourself is not the only way to add users to your WordPress website. You can also give your users the ability to register on their own.

1. First, navigate to **Settings** | **General** and make sure you've checked **Anyone can register** next to **Membership**.

2. I strongly recommend picking **Subscriber** as the **New User Default Role**, though **Contributor** would also be fine if the purpose of your blog requires it. However, allowing new users to be assigned a role with more power automatically is just asking for trouble.
3. Next, add a link somewhere on your blog that points people to the login and registration pages. The easiest way to do this is to use the widget named **Meta**, which comes with your WordPress installation. It will add a box to your sidebar with a few useful links, including **Log in** and **Register**.
4. Users who click on **Register** will be taken to the following basic registration page that asks only for their **Username** and **Email**, as seen in the following screenshot:

After submitting this form, the user will be emailed a password, and the main site administrator will be sent an email notification of the new registration taking place. The user can now log in and edit their profile, or do more if an administrator changes their role.

You can learn more about the built-in WordPress roles and capabilities at https://codex.wordpress.org/Roles_and_Capabilities.

User management plugins

At the time of writing, there are hundreds of plugins tagged with *users* in the WordPress plugin directory (`https://wordpress.org/plugins/tags/users`). We can divide those plugins into many groups, as the functionality offered is extensive. For example, there are plugins for the following:

- Dealing with various author accounts, co-authoring posts, and multi-author sites
- Constructing membership sites around WordPress where members can get access to premium packages of content based on their subscription model
- Building a classic e-commerce store where everyone can make a purchase from the available directory of *things*
- Creating an online forum based on WordPress
- Building an email newsletter sent to a given site's users directly from WordPress, instead of using external services
- Launching a social network on WordPress
- Managing user profiles for registered users

As you can see, the possibilities are striking. If we want to, we can do virtually anything with a WordPress site and its users. Only our imagination imposes a limit. That being said, you should always think about website security when considering any such plugins.

Summary

In this chapter, you learned about the principles of WordPress security and how to make sure that your website won't fall victim to hackers or malicious scripts/software. You also learned how to manage a group of users working on a single website or blog.

With that out of the way, it's about time we learn a thing or two about how to control the design of your website. In the next chapter, we discuss themes, and why they're the most exciting part of WordPress.

7
Choosing and Installing Themes

One of the greatest advantages of using a **content management system (CMS)** for your website is that you are able to change the look and feel of your website without being knowledgeable about HTML and CSS. Almost every CMS allows users to customize the look of their website without having to worry about their content being changed. These managed looks are referred to as themes. On other platforms (for example, Blogger, Joomla, and Drupal), themes are sometimes called **templates** or **layouts**.

Thousands of WordPress themes are available for download free of cost, and thousands more are available at a pretty low cost. Some of the free themes are developed by members of the WordPress community and listed on WordPress' main website at `https://wordpress.org/themes/`, while others can be found across the web on independent sites.

Before you are ready to set about changing the theme of your website, you will want to know the following:

- Some basic factors about the theme you're considering
- How to find quality themes
- How to choose the theme that best suits your content and audience
- How to install a theme

In this chapter, we will discuss all of these topics. This chapter is a ground-up guide to using themes. And, in the following chapters, we will discuss the advanced topic of developing your own themes.

Finding themes

There are dozens of websites that offer WordPress themes for you to download and to install on your own website. Many theme developers offer their themes for free, whereas some charge a small fee. Of course, if you cannot find a free theme that fits your needs, you can always hire a theme developer to create a customized theme for you, or you can be your own theme developer (see `Chapter 9`, *Developing Your Own Theme*).

WordPress Theme Directory

The first place you should always go to when looking for a theme is the official WordPress **Theme Directory** at `https://wordpress.org/themes/`. This is where everyone in the WordPress community uploads their free themes and tags them with keywords that describe the basic look, layout, and functions of their themes, as shown in the following screenshot:

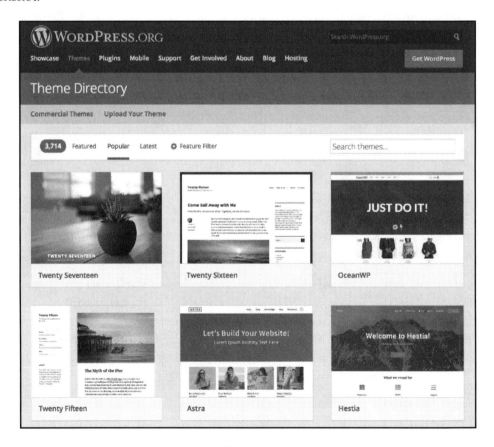

To get a better idea of what a theme looks like, apart from what's offered by the thumbnail, just click on the title of the theme (in my case, **Hestia**, at `https://wordpress.org/themes/hestia/`). You'll be taken to the theme's details page, as shown in the following screenshot:

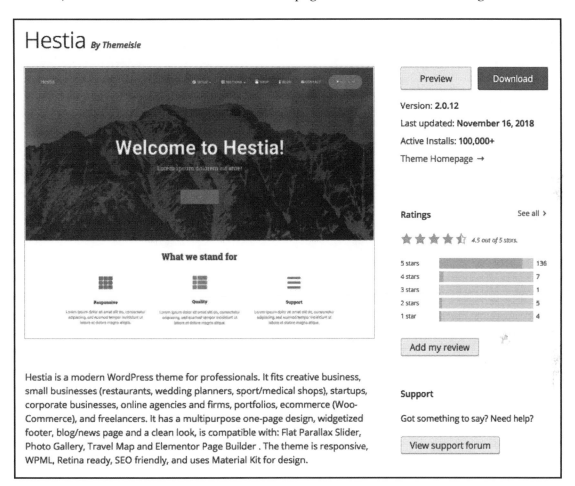

The preceding page shows you the theme's description, all of the tags that apply to it, the average rating given to it by other users, and some comments on the theme. If you click on the **Preview** button, you'll get to see the theme actually in action, as shown in the following screenshot:

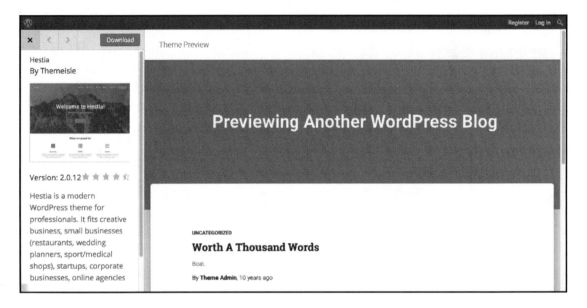

As you browse through the theme directory, make sure to take note of any theme you find that you like; we'll discuss how to add it to your WordPress site later on in this chapter.

It's also worth pointing out that each theme in the official directory comes with its own **Support** section and user reviews section. You can view them by clicking on one of the links available in the right sidebar, as highlighted in the following screenshot:

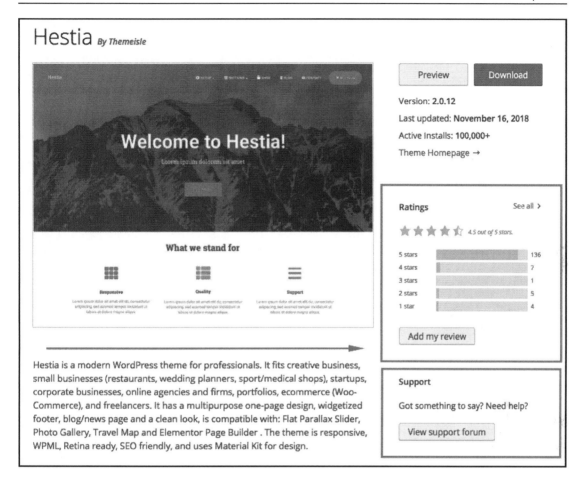

Main types of themes

As we mentioned before, there are two main types of themes—**free themes** and **premium (paid) themes**. Also, if you don't consider price being a factor here, we can also divide themes into four other groups—**standard themes**, **child themes**, **starter themes**, and **theme frameworks**:

- **Child themes**: We will discuss this in detail in the following chapters, so, for now, let's say that a child theme is a theme that inherits the functionality of another theme, the parent.

- **Standard themes**: These are themes that are meant to work in their original form while allowing some basic customizations and tuning up (just like the default theme, **Twenty Nineteen**).
- **Starter themes**: These are a relatively new concept in the WordPress world. In short, when using them, you are encouraged to modify the theme files directly, and effectively make them the foundation of the theme you're currently building. As the name suggests, they provide a great starting point for your own theme to be built upon. They are a great solution for developers, but not so much for regular users, who just want to download a great theme and be able to use it right out the box.
- **Theme frameworks**: These are somewhat similar to starter themes (they are meant to be used as the base for your custom theme development), but they usually deliver a larger range of various built-in features, plus they can be used straight out of the box as a standalone theme (at least to some extent).

In some way, the main difference between starter themes and theme frameworks is that when you get a starter theme, you must put work into it beforehand to make the theme functional. With frameworks, you get a functional theme right away, but then you are expected to spend time tweaking its various elements to make it fit your site hand-in-glove. The thing with both theme frameworks and starter themes is that they are usually highly code-heavy products, which means that you can't really take full advantage of them if you don't possess any programming skills or don't have anyone on your payroll who does. This may not sound that clear right now, and that's okay. We will explain this concept some more in the following chapters.

In the end, standard themes are what most bloggers and site owners work with during their WordPress journeys, especially if they don't need any advanced customizations or don't run purpose-specific websites (such as animated sites and interactive sites).

Finding more themes

If you can't find a theme that you would like in the official directory, you have other options. There are third-party sites with free themes, and also sites that sell themes for a price. Most commercial themes are offered at two or three price points:

- The first price is simply the cost of buying the theme for your own use, and can be anywhere from $20 to $100. Such a license allows you to use the theme on a single site.

- The second price is the price you pay if you want to be able to use the theme on multiple sites (domains), or when you need the project graphics (for example, Photoshop documents) and other development files. In this case, it's usually from $60 to $200.
- The last price point, although not that popular nowadays, is the *exclusive license.* You can get it if you want to be the only user of the theme. This can be anywhere from $500 to $1,500, or even more.

Let's focus on free versus paid themes for a minute. While every theme in the official directory is free, the rest of the internet is split in half on this. Some sites provide free themes exclusively, while others offer paid ones exclusively. There are also a number of distributors who sit in-between. I, personally, don't advise getting any free themes from anywhere other than either the official directory or one of the respected theme stores (which offer some free themes by way of a promotion).

The reason is simple. Only quality themes are allowed into the official directory, and I'm not just talking about the looks or the design. What matters, apart from the design, is also the code structure and code quality. There's no single theme that features any mysterious blocks of code (such as encrypted code or suspicious external links) that will ever find its way into the official directory. That's what ultimately makes the official directory one of the best sources of free WordPress themes on the web.

When it comes to various free themes being released in theme stores, the story is quite similar. The *first league* of WordPress themes, so to speak, consists of respected, serious companies. So, even when they release a free theme, they can't afford it being low quality or lacking in any other way. Therefore, in most cases, they are safe to use as well.

The last thing we can witness online are hundreds, if not thousands, of free themes being released on random websites, promoted through paid advertising, *top themes* lists, advertorial articles, and so on. Let me say this again: I don't advise you to get any of those, even if the designs are attractive. The fact is that you'll never know what sits on the inside and what security breaches can be taken advantage of to hack into such a theme. They are also almost never supported by their creators and there's no theme documentation or updates. In short, it is not worth it.

Finally, if you have some money you'd like to invest in your site and its quality, consider getting a full-blown premium theme, or even a premium theme framework. As I mentioned earlier, the price range is around $20 to $100, depending on the manufacturer and the features the theme comes with.

You are welcome to check out any theme provider you wish. But just to make things quicker, the following is my go-to-first list of quality theme stores:

- **ThemeIsle**: `https://themeisle.com/`
- **Elegant Themes**: `https://www.elegantthemes.com/`
- **ThemeForest**: `https://themeforest.net/category/wordpress`

Also, here's a separate list of the top WordPress theme stores on the web, based on sales and product quality: `https://www.codeinwp.com/blog/wordpress-theme-shop-directory-2016/`.

In general, most good commercial theme websites let you see a preview of the theme in action before you buy it. Some also let you customize the theme before downloading it. As with any other online shopping experience, do some research before buying to make sure you'll be getting a quality theme with decent support. There are plenty of badly coded themes out there and even themes with malicious code. Before buying a theme, verify the source of the theme and see whether you can find feedback or reviews from anyone else who has purchased it.

To find even more websites that offer themes, just do a Google search for `WordPress themes` or `premium WordPress themes`, and you'll get over 100 million hits. Also, keep in mind that choosing a theme is not final. You can always review your decision later on and change the theme in a couple of clicks.

The factors to consider when choosing a theme

Let's take a quick look at some factors to consider when choosing and installing themes, just so that you'll be better informed.

The structure of a theme

A WordPress theme is actually a collection of files in a directory. There are no special or unusual formats, just a few requirements for those files in the theme directory. The only requirements for a directory to be a valid WordPress theme are as follows:

- It should have a `style.css` file and an `index.php` file
- The `style.css` file must have the basic theme information in its initial lines

There are a number of additional files that you'll find in most themes. They are as follows:

- A `screenshot.png` file that is the little thumbnail that shows what the theme looks like.
- An `images` directory where all images associated with the theme reside.
- A variety of files that are used for different purposes (for example, `functions.php`, `header.php`, `footer.php`, `page.php`, `single.php`, and `archive.php`). Read the following article to learn about the most commonly used files: `https://codex.wordpress.org/Theme_Development#Template_Files`.

 To learn more about the structure of various theme files and their hierarchy, feel free to read the following articles at `https://developer.wordpress.org/themes/basics/organizing-theme-files/` and `https://developer.wordpress.org/themes/basics/template-hierarchy/`.

You don't have to worry about these details now, but knowing them will help you identify what is going on inside the themes that you download. This will also be useful in the following chapters, where we will discuss making our own theme from scratch.

Also, don't worry if you download a theme and its directory structure looks very different from what's described here. Some theme developers decide to go with their own structure to provide some extra features and a more customizable environment. This is mostly the case with various theme frameworks and big premium themes that come with their premade child themes.

Factors to consider when choosing a theme

As you look through the themes that available out there, you'll see that there is quite a variety in terms of look, feel, and layout options. To be honest, picking the perfect theme involves effort and some thought. A couple of years ago, there were just a handful of quality websites and stores where you could get your hands on some themes. Now, there are hundreds to thousands of them. All of this results in a situation where there are multiple factors to consider when selecting a theme. It's best if you start with the following.

The purpose of the theme

As I've already mentioned multiple times in this chapter and the previous chapters, nowadays, WordPress is perfectly capable of running any kind of website, and this situation is reflected in the number of available themes. Therefore, the first question to answer is: *what do you need the theme for?*

Depending on the kind of site you're planning to launch, you should focus on different types of themes. The following are some of the popular possibilities:

- **Traditional blogs**: These are the ones where the content is presented in a reverse chronological order, with only several pages of static content.
- **Photo blogs**: These are very much like traditional blogs when it comes to content organization, but in this case, the content consists mainly of photos. This is a popular type of blog among photographers and other creative individuals.
- **Video blogs**: These are much like photo blogs, except now we're dealing with videos.
- **Small business websites and corporate websites**: Most small business sites don't feature a lot of *posts* like traditional blogs. They usually focus on static pages for providing the most important information about the business (such as contact data and offers). This type is most commonly used by local businesses such as restaurants, cafes, hotels, and other similar businesses. Corporate sites are very similar in nature, but are much bigger and feature much more content.
- **One-page micro-websites**: Some people know very well that they need only a minimal online presence, effectively treating their new website as a modern business card. In this case, a solution like a one-page site is perfect for them. In short, one-page sites are just what they sound like; they consist of only a single page. However, due to clever design and structure of that page, the visitor can still get a rich experience browsing it.
- **Online magazines**: The main difference between traditional blogs and online magazines is that the latter feature a lot more content, with usually as many as ten or more posts being published every day. This requires good content layout and clear presentation.
- **E-commerce stores**: Traditionally known as online stores or shops, an e-commerce store is every website that offers a shopping cart functionality and allows its visitors to buy products, much like they'd do in a traditional store or supermarket.
- **Software/app websites**: These are websites that are devoted to promoting/selling a specific product. Nowadays, it's usually some kind of app or other piece of mobile software.

The trick when choosing a theme for your site is to understand its purpose and make your decision based not only on the appearance of the theme, but also on the thing you need the theme for, such as its capabilities, as well as options for further customization. The easiest way to do this is to pay attention to the categories of themes on the site where you're looking for them. For instance, if you go to one of the popular theme stores, such as the ones at https://themeisle.com/wordpress-themes/ or https://themeforest.net/category/wordpress, you'll see that they feature mechanisms for filtering themes by purpose. Here's how ThemeForest does this:

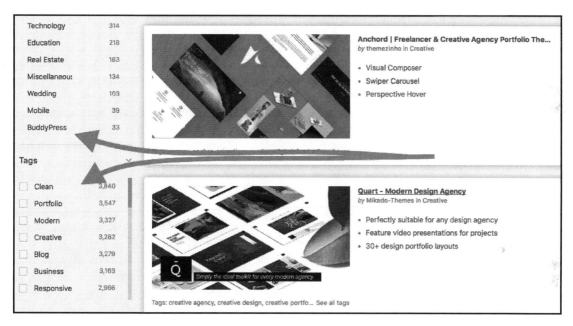

You can also do some research on the internet and notice what the standard is when it comes to the themes being used in your niche and for your type of site. For example, if you're thinking of launching a photo blog, find out what sort of themes other photo blogs use—do they feature a lot of sidebars? How big are the photos they publish? Are there a lot of static pages? And so on. The idea is this: don't reinvent the wheel. If there's a significant number of sites that are similar to the one you're planning to launch, then you should always try learning from them and then making an educated decision when choosing your theme.

Theme licensing

If you're getting a theme from the official directory, then this part doesn't concern you.

However, when getting a theme from a professional theme store, you usually have two or more options regarding the license. As I mentioned earlier, the price range is usually between $20 to $100. Now, there are many licensing models, but the following two examples are the most popular web-wide:

- **Standard, one-site license**: This allows you to launch a site using the theme. It's the recommended choice if you're just searching for a theme for yourself and are not going to use it on other people's sites as well. This is the cheapest kind of license.
- **Developer license**: This is targeted toward developers and people who want to launch more than one site with a theme. Additionally, the package usually includes PSD project files and other mid-development files (note that some one-site licenses include those as well). Developer licenses can be as much as twice as expensive as standard, one-site licenses.

Up-to-date themes only

This is probably the most important parameter here. Your theme has to be up to date or it will fail to take advantage of the newest features in WordPress. The only bad news is that you can't know for sure whether a theme is a modern one or not. You can only rely on the details provided by the theme seller. But as bad as it sounds, it's actually not that big of a problem, because serious theme stores can't afford to lie in their marketing materials. So, whenever you see a message that the theme is *compatible with WordPress version X.X*, it's most likely true. Additionally, with WordPress 5 being released, and all the significant changes it brought to the table (compared to the previous versions), it's important to use only themes that have been verified to work with WordPress 5.

Also, a good rule of thumb is to check when the last update took place. Depending on the theme store you're getting the theme from, this information can be displayed in various places, so I can't give you any specific advice on where to look for it. Nevertheless, if you're getting your theme from the official directory at `https://wordpress.org/themes/`, then you can find this detail in the right sidebar on every individual theme's page (labeled **Last Updated**).

Themes that are customizable

When considering a theme, make sure to find answers to the following questions:

- Are the sidebars flexible? Can I choose how many sidebars I want to display?
- Is it widget-ready?
- Does it support custom menus?
- Does it work with the new WordPress block editor that got introduced in WordPress 5.0?
- Is the theme complex or simple? Which do I prefer?
- Does it support the Customizer panel? Or does it offer a *Theme Settings* page where I can customize the layout, category display, home page, and other options?

At this point in WordPress' development, I recommend rejecting any theme that does not support widgets, custom menus, does not deliver good customization features, or doesn't seem to work well with the new WordPress block editor. The idea behind all of this is that, these days, a situation where you can use a theme right out of the box rarely happens, so having at least a couple of customization possibilities goes a very long way.

Themes with a responsive structure

This is one of the new parameters among modern themes. Back in the day, if you wanted to make your site mobile-friendly, you needed to get some plugins and additional mobile themes and then enable them to work at the same time. Now, with HTML5 and CSS3, you can use just one theme and be certain that it's going to look great on every possible device (from desktop computers to laptops, and mobile devices). The keyword to all this is *responsive design/structure.*

Whenever a theme developer indicates that their theme is responsive, it means that it's compatible with all the devices people use to access the internet these days. In a nutshell, whenever a theme is responsive, this fact will surely be mentioned on the official sales/download page.

Support, reviews, and documentation

This is especially important if you're getting a paid premium theme. Quite simply, since you're paying money, you naturally want to be sure that the product you're getting is a quality one that provides good customer service and well-designed functionality, hence the importance of documentation, reviews, and customer support. It's a simple as that.

I do admit that selecting a theme can take a while, especially if you have to remember all of what we've just covered, but this is work that will surely pay off. Let's not forget that you're probably going to use that theme for at least a year or two (a common scenario), so you surely don't want to spend money on a low-quality product.

Installing and changing themes

Now that you've chosen the theme you want to use, you'll need to install it onto your WordPress website. You'll have the following two choices, as you did when adding new plugins:

- If the theme you want is in the WordPress **Theme Directory**, you can add the theme straight from within `wp-admin`
- Otherwise, you'll have to download the theme's ZIP archive and then upload it to your site by hand

Adding a theme from within wp-admin

As we mentioned in the preceding section, you can add a theme directly from within your `wp-admin` if you've chosen a theme from the WordPress **Theme Directory**:

1. First, navigate to **Appearance**, and then click on the **Add New** button (visible at the top), as shown in the following screenshot:

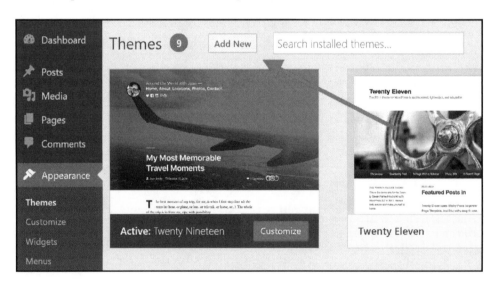

The screen that's going to appear will be very similar to the **Add New Plugins** screen. At the top, you'll see some familiar elements, such as various sub-navigation links (**Featured**, **Popular**, **Latest**, **Favorites**, **Feature Filter**), along with a search box to the right. You can click on any theme displayed on the grid to see its details, along with a nice preview.

2. Using **Feature Filter** (as shown in the following screenshot), you can filter out some of the themes based on the functionality they have or don't have. The **Feature Filter** is a great way to find a theme that offers a specific range of functionalities that you require for the site you're currently building. For instance, you can choose to display themes featuring a responsive layout only. This will make sure that your website is going to look great on all devices, and that's including all desktop computers, as well as mobiles and tablets:

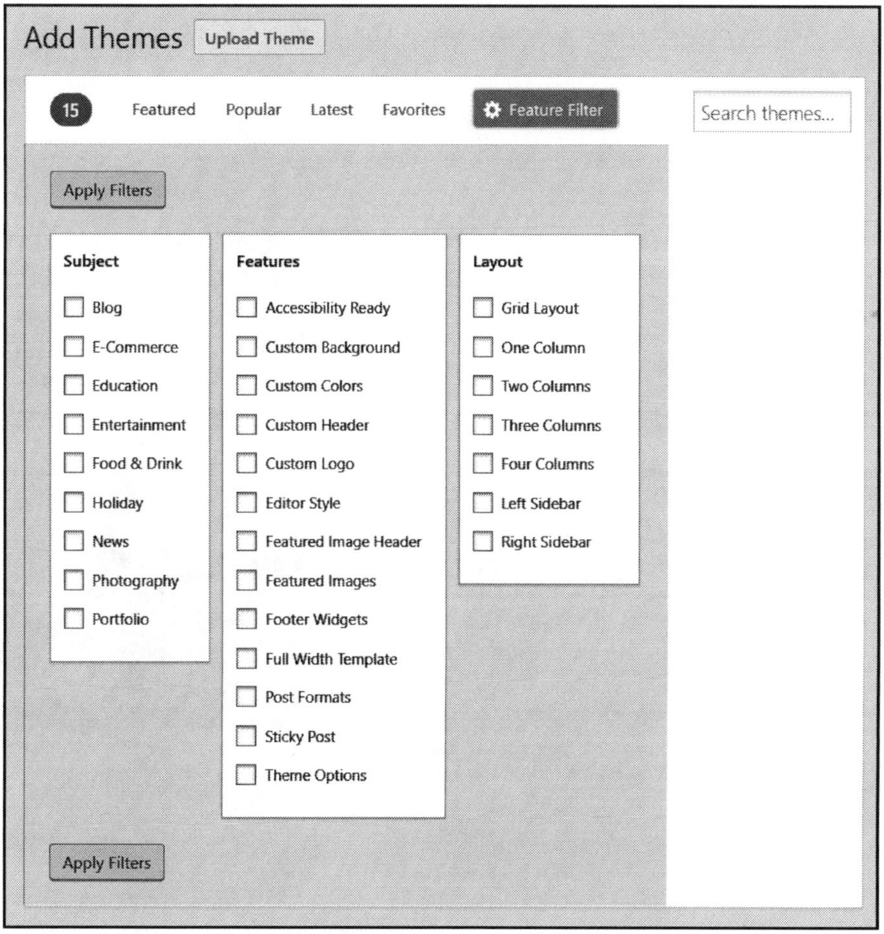

3. Now, I've already found a theme I like, so I won't bother with filtering and just put the name of the theme in the search box, as shown in the following screenshot:

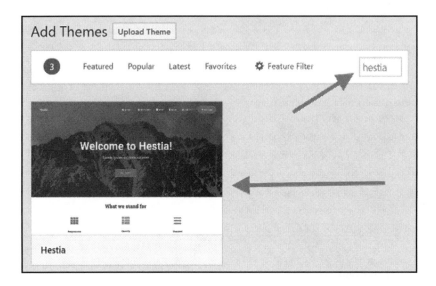

4. When I hover over the theme block, I will see additional links for details, preview, and installation. Clicking on **Preview** is a great way to see what the theme is most likely going to look like in action. When I click on **Install**, the theme will be downloaded and added to my collection of themes automatically (and will be visible in the **Appearance** section in wp-admin), as shown in the following screenshot:

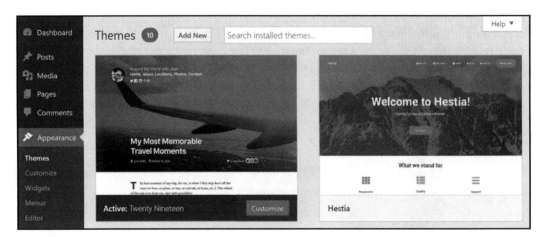

5. By clicking on the theme, I will see a larger block containing all the details, along with two more links to activate and see the live preview of the theme, as shown in the following screenshot:

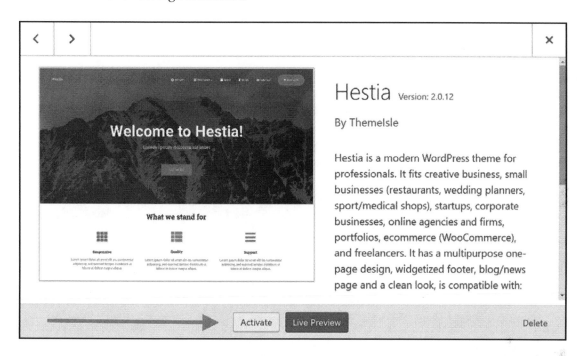

At this point, clicking on the **Activate** button will result in *turning the theme on* and setting it as the new design on the website - instead of **Twenty Nineteen** (which is the default, out-of-the-box theme when you first install WordPress).

Downloading, extracting, and uploading

If you can't install a theme from within `wp-admin` for whatever reason, you'll have to use the following procedure instead.

Additionally, due to the growing popularity of external theme sources, such as various theme stores and independent developers, downloading and installing a theme manually becomes the default way of handling things, and gradually replaces the traditional approach of getting a theme from the official directory.

Therefore, to provide a good example when explaining the manual installation, I'm going to get a theme (a free one) and guide you through the process of having it installed:

1. To get started, what you need is to download your desired theme and save its ZIP archive somewhere on your desktop. Don't extract the archive. The theme I'd like to try out is called *Underscores*, and it's a free starter theme that's available at `https://underscores.me/`.

2. Depending on the source of your theme, in order to actually get it, you might be required to either create a user account, make a purchase, or sign up for a newsletter, and so on. Of course, sometimes, there's just a direct download link. Underscores uses a pretty straightforward model. All you need to do is input the name that you want to use for your theme in the field at `https://underscores.me/` (it can be whatever name you wish). Then, after clicking on **GENERATE**, you'll get a ZIP download:

3. At this point, you can upload that ZIP file through `wp-admin` by navigating to **Appearance | Themes** and clicking on the **Add New** button. There, click on the **Upload Theme** button, which will take you to the place where you can finally perform the manual installation, as shown in the following screenshot:

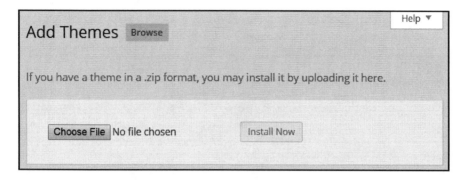

4. The only thing you need to do there is choose the ZIP file from your desktop and then click on the **Install Now** button. After a short while, you will be redirected to the success page, where you will be able to activate your new theme.

   If this doesn't work, continue with the following steps to extract and upload the theme files manually.

5. If you're on Mac, the ZIP file may have automatically been unzipped for you, in which case you'll see a directory on your desktop instead of the ZIP file, or in addition to the ZIP file. If not, then just do the extraction/unzipping manually so that you have the theme directory on your desktop.

6. The following screenshot shows the file contents of the Underscores theme that I downloaded. Apart from the mandatory `style.css` file and the `index.php` file, it also has a number of other files that handle different tasks and take care of various aspects of the display and the functionality of the theme:

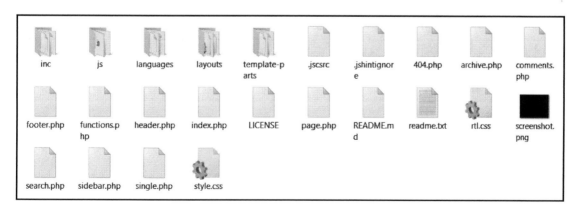

7. You need to upload the theme directory to your WordPress website. As you did in `Chapter 2`, *Getting Started with WordPress*, you need to start an FTP connection with your server. Once there, navigate to your WordPress website's installation directory.

8. Next, go to the `wp-content` directory and then to the `themes` directory. You'll see one theme directory in here already named `twentynineteen` (and possibly others as well). These are the themes that came pre-installed with WordPress. The only thing you have to do here is upload the directory that you've just unzipped a minute ago so that it sits alongside the default `twentynineteen` directory. And that's it!

At this point, when you go back to **Appearance** in your `wp-admin`, you will see the new theme waiting there. All that's left to do now is activate it and use it as the main design of your site.

Summary

This chapter described how to manage the basic look of your WordPress website. You learned where to find themes, why they are useful, what the basic differences between various themes are, how to select the perfect theme for your site, and how to install themes manually as well as through `wp-admin`.

In the next chapter, you will learn how to customize existing WordPress themes, therefore making your website appear exactly how you want it to appear.

8
Customizing your Website Appearance/Design

At this stage, you already know how versatile WordPress is when it comes to the range of designs you can have on your site—all because of themes. However, just getting a theme and using it as is isn't necessarily the most optimized approach. Therefore, in this chapter, we're going to take it up a notch—you'll learn how to customize your theme and make your website look exactly as you want it to.

We'll start by discussing how to manage navigation menus and work with the basic layout customization features to further enhance the capabilities of your entire website. Then, we'll talk about widgets and how to use them to make your sidebars even more functional and reader-friendly. We'll cover the topic of WordPress Customizer, and what it can do for your overall website presentation. Lastly, we'll talk about Google AMP and how to make sure that your site is more than optimized to be viewed on mobile devices.

Let's take a look at the topics we'll dive into in this chapter:

- Menus
- Widgets
- WordPress Customizer
- Optimizing for mobile and working with AMP

Menus

Menus serve a very important role for any website's ease of navigation and helping readers find things. A classic website menu is one displayed near the top of the page, listing individual sub-pages that are part of the website. Those very often are pages such as *About*, and *Contact*. Under the hood, menus are just simple lists of links that point to different areas within your website.

It just so happens that WordPress handles menus in a very user-friendly way. You can easily create menus featuring links to pages, posts, category archives, and even arbitrary links to any URL. And when you're done configuring the menu itself, you can add it to be displayed in your design/theme.

Adding a menu

Let's take a look at the menus management screen.

1. To get there, just navigate to **Appearance** | **Menus**:

2. To create your first menu, enter a title (for example, *Main*) where it says **Menu Name**, and then click on **Create Menu**.

3. After doing so, you can select individual *pages* from the panel on the left and click on the **Add to Menu** button to confirm:

4. If you want to add specific blog posts to the menu, you can do that too. Just click on the **Posts** heading in the panel and then pick the exact post you want to link to. To confirm, click on **Add to Menu**:

5. You can add some custom links to the menu as well. This can be done after clicking on the **Custom Links** heading on the left and then filling out the required link information. To confirm, click on **Add to Menu**:

6. Next, you can add some category links. Click on the **Categories** heading on the left and then proceed to click on the checkboxes next to the categories you want to include. Click on **Add to Menu** to confirm:

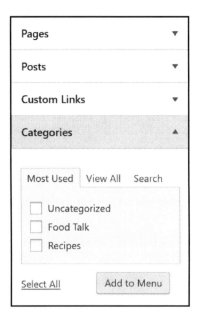

7. Finally, be sure to click on **Save Menu** in the upper-right corner. The following is what my new menu looks like now:

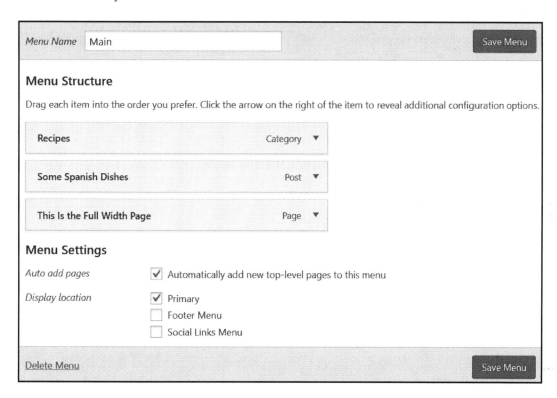

8. You can also drag items to the right to make them sub items of the item immediately above. For example, I'll drag one of my posts as a sub item under the **Recipes** category. Now, my menu looks like the following screenshot:

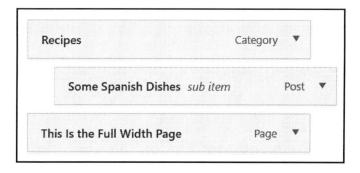

You can make more menus by clicking on the **Create a new menu** link at the top and repeating the process.

Now, you might ask: *I created my new menu, but how do I make it show up on my site?*

Displaying a menu

If you have a menu-enabled theme (which you probably do), then, once you have one menu, a new box will appear on the **Menus** page showing you the menu locations. **Twenty Nineteen** has three menu locations, and they're named **Primary**, **Footer Menu**, and **Social Links Menu**:

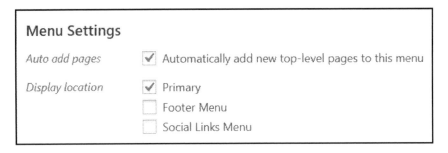

All you have to do to assign your newly created menu to the predefined menu area in **Twenty Nineteen**, is to check one of the boxes, as shown in the preceding screenshot. Right now, my primary navigation on the website looks like the following screenshot:

When I click on the down arrow next to **Recipes**, I will also see my other post that was saved as a sub item, as shown in the next screenshot. **Twenty Nineteen** displays sub items in a rollover menu:

Widgets

Widgets are one of the native mechanisms in WordPress. Their main purpose is to provide us with an easy-to-use way of customizing the sidebars, footers, and headers of our sites, with the addition of extra content. Even though the most common placement of widgets is indeed the sidebar, the only actual rule is that a widget must be displayed inside a *widget area,* and a widget area can be anywhere a theme developer wants it to be. Common widgets contain the following:

- A monthly archive of blog posts
- A clickable list of pages
- A clickable list of recent posts
- A metadata box (containing logon/logutout links, RSS feed links, and other WordPress links)
- Recent comments posted on the blog
- A clickable list of categories
- A tag cloud
- A block of text and HTML
- A search box

These days, nearly all themes are widget-enabled, with one or more widget areas available for use. If I were to simplify this a bit, I'd say that widget areas behave like locations for menus.

To control the widgets on your new website, do the following:

1. Navigate to **Appearance** | **Widgets**. **Twenty Nineteen** comes with just one widget area. It's called **Footer**, as shown in the following screenshot:

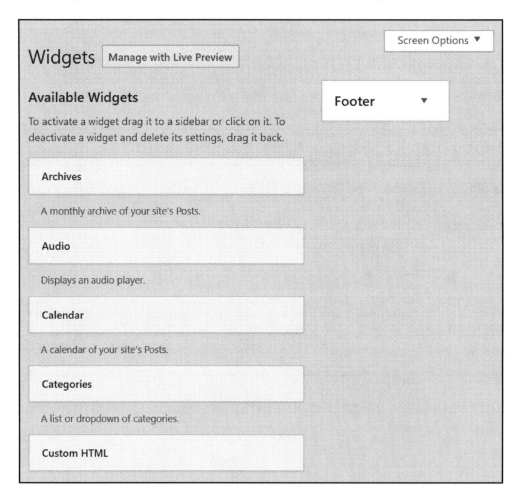

2. As the name indicates, this widget area appears in the footer of the site. The way you work with widgets is very simple. The only thing you have to do is take any of the widgets visible on the left-hand side and drag and drop them into the right-hand area under any of the available widget areas. For example, let's take the **Navigation Menu** block and drag it all the way to **Footer**. The result is as shown in the following screenshot:

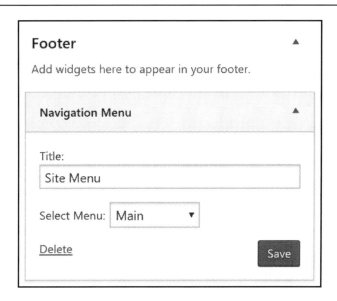

3. Now, we can give this block a title and also use the dropdown to select the custom menu we want to include in this widget. Currently, there's only one menu, which we created a while ago, **Main**. Once we click on the **Save** button (visible in the preceding screenshot), our menu is going to be added in place.

4. At this point, we have the main menu displayed twice on the site. There's one in the top area, and the second one is inside the footer. As you can see, if you want to place a menu somewhere on the site, you have two ways of doing so. You can either assign it inside the **Appearance** | **Menus** section, or use it as a navigation menu widget and place it in any widget area that your theme supports.

5. Enabling any other type of widget is very similar to the process described just now. All you need to do is drag the widget you like and drop it onto the area where you want to have it displayed. Then, once the widget is in place, you can adjust its settings and content.

6. When it comes to working in the **Appearance** | **Widgets** section, you can click on the little down arrow to the right of any widget to expand the details and see the options. You can drag a new widget in from the collection of available widgets on the left, you can drag existing widgets up and down to change their order, and you can delete a widget by expanding it and then clicking on **Delete**.

7. Experiment with putting widgets into different widget areas and then refresh your blog to see what they look like. Always be sure to click on **Save** if you make any changes to a widget.

8. Also, at the bottom of the screen, there's one more section labeled **Inactive Widgets**, as shown in the following screenshot. Many widgets have their settings and parameters. Therefore, even if you don't want to display a particular widget on your site at the moment, but don't necessarily want to lose its settings (in case you'd like to use the widget again in the future), this section is where you put it. Just like the label says, it's where you can drag your widgets to remove them from display but keep their settings. This is also where you will find any widgets that were previously active, but that got deactivated automatically after switching to a theme that didn't use the same widget area naming convention:

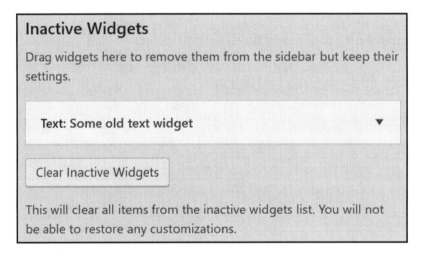

WordPress Customizer

Yet another feature in WordPress that's highly dependent on your theme is the **Customizer** module. If you still have the welcome box enabled in your Dashboard's screen settings, you can access this module by clicking on the big **Customize Your Site** button, as shown in the following screenshot:

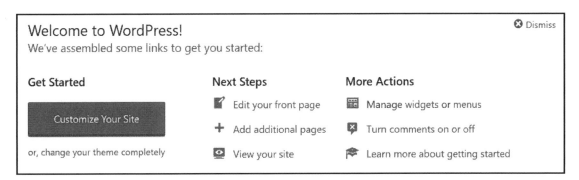

Another way of accessing this module is by visiting `http://yoursite.com/wp-admin /customize.php`. This is what you'll see (provided you're working with the default theme):

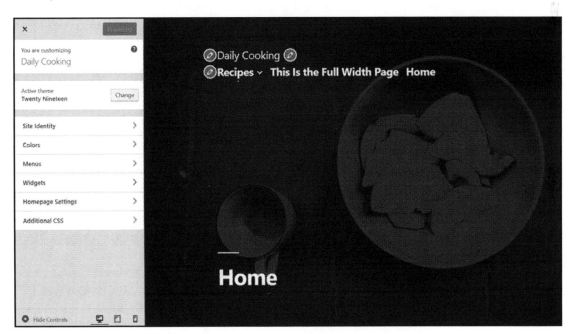

By going through the individual tabs on the left, you can adjust various aspects of your site—some that we've already talked about in this chapter, as well as some that are completely new. We're going to look through them here. The customizations that are available in most themes are as follows:

- **Site Identity**
- **Colors**
- **Header Media**
- **Menus**
- **Widgets**
- **Homepage Settings / Static Front Page**
- **Additional CSS**

The best thing about this module is that it provides a live preview, which makes editing the basic aspects of your design much quicker. When you're done, you can click on either the **X** button or the **Save & Publish** button that are visible in the top-left corner.

Before we get into the individual sections of the Customizer, let's have a glance at those curious-looking pencil icons in various parts of the interface. You can see an example in the following screenshot:

In a nutshell, those are shortcut icons. Meaning, they get displayed next to specific interface elements that can be edited within the Customizer. So, instead of having to search for a given customization in the left sidebar, you can simply click on the shortcut icon corresponding to it, and you will be immediately taken to the correct options panel. For example, if you click on the site's title, you will be taken to the exact section where you can edit it, as shown in the following screenshot:

We'll explore the options one by one as we go through the Customizer.

Site identity

Site Identity is the first block that's available in the Customizer's sidebar:

When you click on it, you will be able to adjust things such as the site's **Logo, Site Title**, **Tagline**, and **Site Icon**. What needs to be said here, however, is that the effect all those options have on your site depends greatly on your current theme. For example, one theme will display the logo in a completely different place than the other, and the same can be said for the site title, and so on. It's therefore always a good idea to experiment with the settings there, and find out on your own what effect they have. Under the hood, the options we're dealing with here are just standard input fields and image/media selection panels. This is everything that we have already covered in the previous chapters of this book

The one element that usually works the same for most WordPress themes is the **Site Icon** setting. A site icon is this small icon that's visible in the corner of your web browser window. For instance, if you go to this book publisher's website, at `https://www.packtpub.com/`, you will see the site icon presented in the following screenshot:

Overall, site icons are a nice way of giving your website some visual representation in the visitor's web browser, so that they can identify it more easily when having a handful of browser tabs open at the same time. You can pick your site icon easily by selecting it through the Customizer. The currently recommended image dimensions for the icon are at least 512 pixels wide and tall.

Colors

The second section in the Customizer sidebar is labeled **Colors**. In it, you can pick one of the current theme's predefined color schemes for the site. The **Twenty Nineteen** theme has two options there, as seen in the following screenshot. Furthermore, there's also an additional setting to define whether the primary color will have an effect on your pages' or posts' featured images (play around with it to see the effect yourself):

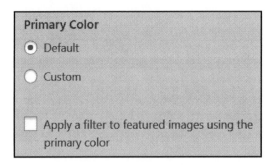

Changing from **Default** to **Custom** switches the site design from white background colors to whatever you want them to be. If you click on **Custom**, you get to use a color picker to adjust some of the colors used in the design in a more freehand way.

Header Media

Header Media is another popular section in the Customizer sidebar. That being said, this is not a section that's available in the current default theme, **Twenty Nineteen**. However, I'm describing it here since you're likely to find it in many other themes. To demonstrate this, I'll switch to the previous default theme of WordPress, **Twenty Seventeen**. This is what the **Header Media** section looks like when using that theme. Refer to the following screenshot:

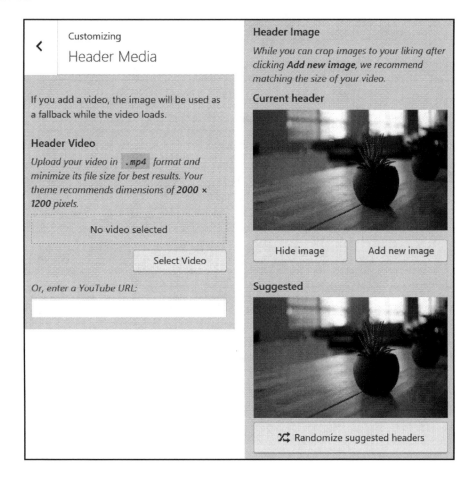

Most themes will allow you to select any image to be placed inside the header, and sometimes even a video, as **Twenty Seventeen** does. **Twenty Seventeen** also has some specific requirements for the header image (actually, most themes have, and **Twenty Seventeen** is only an example of that). The suggested size is 2,000 pixels wide by 1,200 pixels tall, but you don't have to worry all that much about this because WordPress also provides some handy image editing tools. All you have to do here is use the **Choose image** or **Add new image** buttons and select one of the pictures from your **Media Library**, or upload a new one. WordPress will immediately redirect you to the aforementioned image editing tools, where you can adjust and crop your image, as shown in the following screenshot:

After clicking on the **Crop Image** button and then **Save & Publish**, we're done with setting up the header image. Here's what the site might look like afterward:

Background

Some WordPress themes also allow you to adjust not only the header but the entire background of the site as well, meaning that you can place any image in the background of the whole site, and have it remain there at all times. This works similarly to a desktop wallpaper, but for your WordPress website. Although the current default theme, **Twenty Nineteen**, doesn't offer this functionality, this is still a very common feature to find in other themes, so let's discuss it here using another former default theme, **Twenty Fifteen**.

If you use that theme, and you go to the Customizer, you will see a new section in the sidebar called **Background Image**, as shown in the following screenshot:

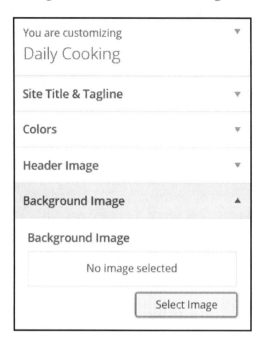

The first thing we have to do is select an image we want to place in the background of our whole site. Let me say that again: our whole site. Right after selecting an image (just click on the **Select Image** button that's visible in the preceding screenshot), the preview block will be refreshed, and you will be able to see what your background looks like at the moment. Immediately, there are some new options visible at the bottom of the options block:

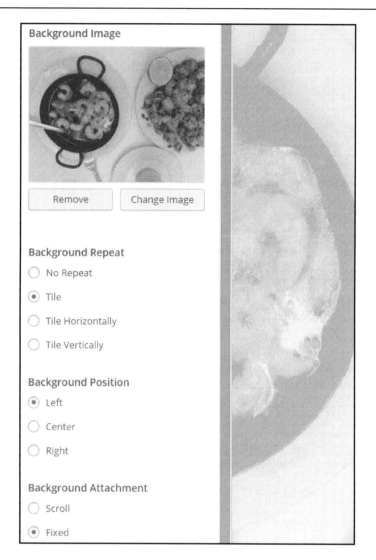

The various options are as follows:

- **Background Repeat**: This can be **No Repeat**, **Tile**, **Tile Horizontally**, or **Tile Vertically**:
  - **No Repeat**: This means that your background image will be displayed only once, and after the visitor scrolls down, they will simply *run out* of the background image.

- **Tile**: This is the most popular setting and actually the default one as well. This means that WordPress will repeat your image in both dimensions (width and height). No matter what part of your site the visitor is browsing, the background image will always be visible.
- **Tile Horizontally**: This tiles your image horizontally.
- **Tile Vertically**: This tiles your image vertically.
- **Background Position**: This can be **Left**, **Center**, or **Right**. This decides whether the background image should be aligned to the left, center, or right.
- **Background Attachment**: This can be either **Scroll** or **Fixed**:
    - **Scroll**: Your image scrolls along with the content.
    - **Fixed**: Your image remains in a fixed position. In other words, it stands still in the background at all times.

I encourage you to play around with these settings for a while when adjusting your site.

Widgets

Even though we did discuss widgets earlier in this chapter, the Customizer offers you an alternative way of working with them. You can do it in the section called **Widgets**.

Once you click on it, you will see all the *widget areas* currently available in your theme. Then, when you click on any of those, you will see all the *individual widgets* that are assigned to that given area. All those widgets can be easily edited much like we did earlier in this chapter; the methodology is the same.

Homepage settings or Static Front Page

This next section in the Customizer is commonly called either **Homepage Settings** or **Static Front Page**, based on the specific theme you're using. Once you navigate there, you will be able to change the main settings of the page that is displayed when a visitor comes to your home page—the main address of your website. You can set a couple of things here:

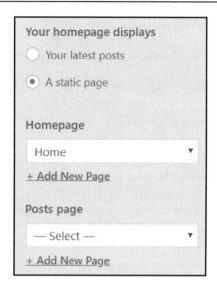

Once you go there, you will be able to choose between the default setting of **Your latest posts** (in this mode, the home page is just a classic listing of your latest blog posts; this is the default setting that you're probably used to) and a new setting labeled, **A static page**. That second one gives you the possibility to set whatever page you wish as the home page of your website. You can either select an existing page from the dropdown list under **Homepage** or create a new page by clicking on the **+ Add New Page** link.

As you might recall from Chapter 4, *Pages, Media, and Importing/Exporting Content*, what we did there was create a new page and set it as the custom home page for the site. We called the page **Home**—quite fittingly. It's important to remember that any page that you assign as your home page still remains an otherwise normal page, meaning that you can edit it like any other page via the **Pages** section of wp-admin.

Apart from the **Homepage**, there's also another block here, labeled **Posts page**. If you change your home page to a static one, it's always a good idea to assign a new **Posts page** as well. Since the classic listing of your latest posts will no longer be displayed on the home page, the new **Posts page** is meant to handle this task from now on. As with the home page, you can select an existing page to serve as the new posts page, or create a new one.

In this case, however, it's actually more convenient to create a completely new page rather than picking an existing one. You can call yours **BLOG** or another similar name that conveys the page's purpose. What's interesting about this page is that you don't need to edit it manually or place any content on it. WordPress will populate this page with content on its own, so the only thing you need to do is just create it, and that's it.

If you do create a new **posts page**, don't forget to link it from your main menu. Otherwise, your audience will have no way of finding it when they visit your website. We talked about menus earlier in this chapter.

Additional CSS

Additional CSS is the final block of Customizer. This one can be handy if you want to include some custom changes in your current theme, changes that can't be achieved in any other way. Once you click on **Additional CSS**, you will see a text input block where you will be able to incorporate any CSS code you wish. Be careful here, though. Working with raw CSS code can quickly cause problems if you're not sure what you're doing. Overall, this section is meant for advanced theme customizations:

Add your own CSS code here to customize the appearance and layout of your site. Learn more about CSS ➡

When using a keyboard to navigate:

- In the editing area, the Tab key enters a tab character.

- To move away from this area, press the Esc key followed by the Tab key.

- Screen reader users: when in forms mode, you may need to press the escape key twice.

The edit field automatically highlights code syntax. You can disable this in your user profile ➡ to work in plain text mode.

Close

1

Scheduling your design changes

One more interesting thing that you can do in WordPress Customizer is schedule your changes to be made public on a given date, rather than being rolled out right away.

By default, when you click on the main **Publish** button, whatever changes you made to your site will go public immediately. In order to schedule the changes instead, click on the *gear icon* right next to the main **Publish** button of WordPress Customizer. Then, from the section that will appear, select **Schedule** and then pick the exact date and time you want your changes to be made public. Refer to the following screenshot:

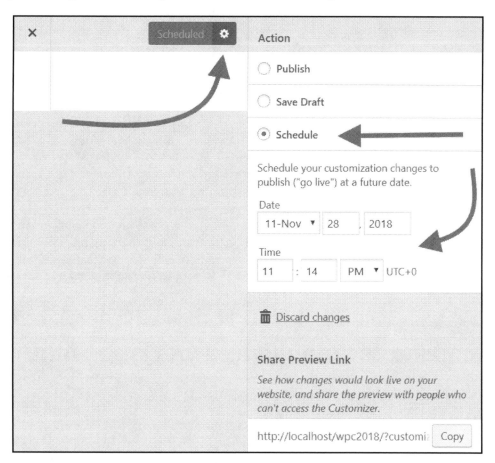

Apart from that, one thing you might have noticed in the preceding screenshot is that there is also a *preview link* available. You can use it to share your changes with other people or to review them later on yourself.

This whole functionality can be advantageous in actual real-world scenarios when working on a live website. You simply don't always want your changes to go live the second you're done working on them. Preparing for a scheduled launch is often a more appealing perspective. Also, thanks to this feature, you can avoid rolling out changes at your website's peak traffic hours.

Customizer previews

Last but not least, there are four interesting icons sitting in the bottom-left corner of the Customizer window, as demonstrated in the following screenshot:

From the left, they are the **Hide Controls** button (this hides the whole Customizer sidebar to give you a bigger canvas when adjusting your website), the *desktop view* icon, the *tablet view* icon, and the *mobile view* icon. Those final three icons are particularly important. These days, more people tend to browse the web on their mobile devices than on classic desktop computers. Because of that, it's crucially important for you to make sure that your website displays properly on those devices. These three icons—the desktop view icon, the tablet view icon, and the mobile view icon, allow you to do just that. When you click on any of them, the whole Customizer window will change in size to emulate the display mode on tablets and mobile devices. Switching back and forth between the modes, you can make sure that your site looks great on all devices. We will expand on the topic of mobile optimization in the very next part of this chapter.

Optimizing for mobile and working with AMP

Accelerated mobile pages (AMP) is an open source project introduced by Google in an effort to make the viewing of content on mobile more streamlined and user-friendly, no matter what device the user might be using.

A couple of years ago, the idea of mobile web was only getting started, and a lot of websites were incredibly poorly optimized for mobile viewing. Back in the day, mobile wasn't so important, since the technology didn't allow for effective media consumption on a mobile phone. However, with the introduction of smartphones, this all changed. Nowadays, more people access the web on mobile than on desktops and laptops combined.

Clearly, websites needed to adapt and deliver an optimized interface for mobile viewing alongside their default, desktop-only view.

This is where AMP comes into play. In many cases, making an existing website mobile-friendly isn't the easiest of tasks. If your theme/design didn't come as mobile-optimized out of the box, retrofitting mobile on top of it can prove difficult. AMP provides an easier solution. Instead of forcing you to rebuild parts of your site manually, you can install an add-on AMP module, and have it done automatically. What you get as a result is an AMP version of your website. This new version will be displayed only to your mobile visitors. Here's what makes AMP a good idea:

- It's optimized for high performance—AMP pages load almost instantly, which is a preferable scenario for a mobile user than waiting a couple of seconds before starting to see anything appear on the page—a situation that's common for pages that are not optimized for mobile viewing
- Google prefers AMP pages when displaying results for mobile searches
- The design of AMP is simplified, putting content first and thus letting your visitor quickly get to the part that's of interest to them

Let's add to that the fact that AMP is getting popular rather quickly. As data tells us (`https://theblog.adobe.com/google-amp-one-year-later`), in February 2017, AMP pages accounted for a whopping 7% of all web traffic for top publishers in the United States.

How to enable AMP in WordPress

Unsurprisingly, there's a plugin that handles the integration for you. It's simply called **AMP for WordPress**, and you can get it from `https://wordpress.org/plugins/amp/`:

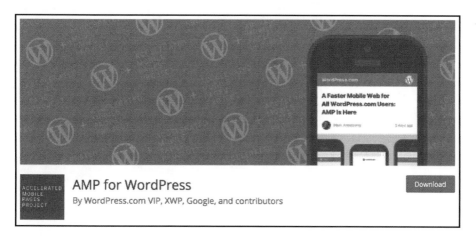

This plugin literally couldn't be easier to use. The only thing you need to do is install and activate it. After that, it picks up on its own and works on autopilot. There are only a few optional settings you can adjust. The first one can be found in **AMP | General**. By default, AMP for WordPress is enabled only for blog posts. You can change that by turning it on for your pages as well:

At this stage, your website is fully integrated with AMP. Whenever someone tries to access one of your posts or pages on mobile, they will be redirected to the AMP version of it. You can find those if you append /amp/ to the end of your standard post URLs, for example:

- **Standard version of a post**: yoursite.com/some-post/
- **AMP version of a post**: yoursite.com/some-post/amp/

The second thing you can customize is the color scheme of the AMP theme. To do that, go to **Appearance | AMP**. You will be able to change the colors and the general vibe of the color scheme:

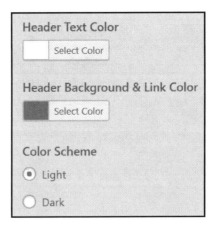

Here's what an example post might look like when converted to AMP and viewed on mobile:

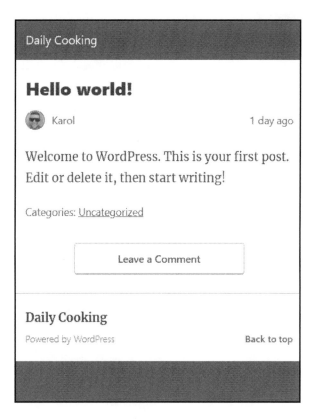

Learning more:

- If you want to learn more about the AMP project, the official website is a good start: `https://www.ampproject.org/`
- Here's an *AMP quick start guide* for developers: `https://www.ampproject.org/docs/getting_started/quickstart`
- Here's an online validator for AMP pages: `https://validator.ampproject.org/`

Summary

In this chapter, you learned the basics of theme customization. You now know about menus, widgets, header and background settings, how to work with the WordPress Customizer, how to make your site ready for AMP, and more. At this stage, you know how to pick a great WordPress theme for your website and then how to customize it to suit your requirements precisely.

In the next chapter, you will learn, step by step, how to build your own theme from scratch.

Developing your Own Theme

9

At this point, you know how to find themes on the web and install them for use on your WordPress website. But, there's a lot more that WordPress has to offer, particularly in the theme development department. In this chapter, you'll learn how to turn your own design into a fully functional WordPress theme, which you'll then be able to use on your website. You'll also learn how to share your WordPress theme with other users on the web.

All you will need before we get started is the following:

- Your own website design
- The ability to slice and dice your design to turn it into an HTML structure

We'll start out with tips on slicing and dicing, so that your HTML and CSS files are as WordPress-friendly as possible, and then cover the steps for turning that HTML build into a fully functional theme.

 Note that I assume you are already comfortable writing and working with HTML and CSS.

The topics we will be covering in this chapter include the following:

- Setting up your design
- Converting your build into a theme
- Creating template files within your theme
- Making your theme widget-friendly
- Enabling a menu in your theme
- Making your theme editable in the WordPress Customizer
- Creating a child theme
- Sharing your theme

This chapter covers only the very basics of theme creation. This topic actually deserves a whole book, and it has one! I highly recommend *WordPress Theme Development: Beginner's Guide, Rachel McCollin and Tessa Blakeley Silver, Packt Publishing*. This book covers everything you could possibly want to know about creating your own theme in detail, including details such as choosing a color scheme, considering typography, writing the best CSS, and laying out your HTML using rapid design comping. If this chapter leaves you wanting more, go there!

Setting up your design

Just about any design in the world can be turned into a WordPress theme. However, there are some general guidelines you should follow—regarding both the design and the HTML/CSS build of your theme.

Designing your theme to be WordPress-friendly

While you can design your blog any way you want, a good starting point would be with one of the standard blog layout, as shown in the following screenshot:

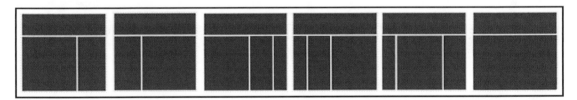

Note that, while these standard layouts have a differing number of columns, most of them have the following essential parts:

- A header
- A main column
- A side column(s)
- A footer

WordPress expects your theme to follow this pattern, for the most part. While you can be creative and not include one or more of these blocks in your design, you will get the most educational value out of this experience if you don't skip anything. WordPress will provide you with functions that make your work easier. Also, a build that stays within the same general design patterns of WordPress themes will easily accommodate the existing plugins and widgets.

That said, a common situation in the WordPress world is to build custom home pages or landing pages (that is, purpose-specific pages, which are mostly commercial) that feature completely different designs. Therefore, you might stumble upon websites that don't look like they're built with WordPress at first glance. Also, many modern theme frameworks give you the possibility to create such custom home pages, as well as other custom page templates. This is all part of the trend to make WordPress capable of running any kind of website.

In this chapter, you're going to learn how to build a basic WordPress theme that offers a classic blog layout. The following screenshot demonstrates what the final product will look like:

The HTML structure of the design is built on top of the _S starter theme (you can read more about underscores at `https://underscores.me/`), and the visual elements are all done through CSS, with only minimal modifications to the original HTML structure.

Three paths to theme development

Essentially, there are three paths that you can follow when developing your new theme:

- You can either work from the ground up, by building the HTML structure and the functional structure of the theme by hand
- You can work on top of an existing theme framework, where you only have to adapt your design to work on the structure provided by the framework itself
- You can go for a solution that sits somewhere in between

All of these paths have their pros and cons.

Building a theme from the ground up

The main advantage of building a theme from the ground up is the massive educational value you get. When you develop a theme from scratch, you learn the basics of theme construction and function. This kind of knowledge will go a long way for your future projects in WordPress.

On the other hand, it's also the longest of the three paths. In a professional production environment (among people designing and developing themes as a profession), creating themes from scratch is a highly time-consuming approach, making it quite ineffective. And it's not that much about adapting the design (which must always be done with theme frameworks as well); it's more about building the core functionality of the theme.

Building a theme with a framework

The main advantages of this approach are its time-efficiency and the quality of the final result. For instance, if you're building a theme from scratch, you have to make sure to keep your theme up-to-date long after the development process has finished. The thing is, WordPress gets updated very frequently (around once every 50-90 days), and the purpose of many features changes over time—they might even get completely erased or replaced by new ones. In such a scenario, only modern themes that are kept up-to-date can take full advantage of these features. Updating your theme will obviously take a massive amount of work. This is where theme frameworks come into play. In essence, theme frameworks are themes with a very minimalist design and no visually-complicated aspects.

The purpose of frameworks is to make them the base of any future theme by acting as the parent theme. The fact that the framework itself has no design allows every creator to introduce almost any design imaginable, while taking full advantage of the features and constructions provided by the framework. Now, the strength of quality frameworks is that they get updated almost as frequently as WordPress plugins. In short, if you're using a framework, you don't have to worry about your theme going out of date. Whenever there's an update available, you can simply perform it and forget about the whole thing.

This brings me to the main disadvantage of using theme frameworks. Most of the time, theme frameworks are big, complex pieces of web software (**Hypertext Preprocessor**, or **PHP** scripts). So, if you want to be able to use them effectively, you'll have to spend a significant amount of time learning the framework itself. On top of this, if you decide to switch to a different framework later down the road, you'll have to learn all over again (frameworks are usually very different from each other). As you can see, reaping the benefits of using frameworks has its price.

Here are some of the popular theme frameworks (both paid and free ones), as follows:

- **Gantry** (free): `http://gantry.org/`
- **Cherry Framework** (free): `http://www.cherryframework.com/`
- **Hybrid Core** (free): `https://themehybrid.com/hybrid-core`
- **Unyson Framework** (free): `http://unyson.io/`
- **Genesis** (paid): `https://my.studiopress.com/themes/genesis/`
- Some frameworks are listed on the official WordPress website: `https://codex.wordpress.org/Theme_Frameworks`

Building a theme with a starter theme

Finally, there's also a third solution, one that's somewhere between building a theme from the ground up and using a framework—using a starter theme.

A starter theme, like the one we'll be using in this chapter, is a great solution to make sure that the theme you're building has the right scaffolding, it's up to date with modern practices, and is optimized to be used for a WordPress site. Apart from that, a starter theme leaves you with all of the freedom in the world to adjust your creation however you wish (you have almost the same freedom as you do with from-the-ground-up theme building).

In other words, a starter theme provides you with the best of both worlds; that is, starting from scratch and using a framework. You can learn the basic structure of WordPress themes this way, and at the same time, you don't need to worry about making any silly mistakes because the core of the task is handled by the starter theme itself.

The main idea in the following sections is to learn the craft and get to know all of the basic structures and mechanisms sitting inside WordPress. Your journey with theme development starts once you have a graphic design prepared in Photoshop, or some other similar tool. You can also take the code bundle for this chapter and work with the design from there. Either way, the next step is to turn it into some HTML code.

Converting your design into code

For the purpose of this chapter, I assume that you already know how to take a graphic website design and turn it into an HTML plus CSS structure. With that, we'll cover some pointers on how to do your slicing and dicing as we go through this chapter.

Let's get down to business and take a look at the HTML structure that was generated (by the _S starter theme) for the purpose of the theme we're building here. Just to remind you, the starter theme can be generated at `https://underscores.me/`.

Examining the HTML structure

The following is the very basic layout of the main HTML file for my food blog design; I'm showing it here just to give you a general idea of what we're going to be working with:

```
<!DOCTYPE html>
<html lang="en-US">
<head>
<meta charset="UTF-8">
<meta name="viewport" content="width=device-width, initial-
scale=1">
<link rel="profile" href="http://gmpg.org/xfn/11">
<link rel="stylesheet" id="open-sans-css"
  href="//fonts.googleapis.com/css?family=Open+Sans%3A300italic
  %2C400italic%2C600italic%2C300%2C400%2C600&subset=latin%2
  Clatin-ext&ver=4.0.1" type="text/css" media="all" />
<! - embedding Google Fonts - >
<link rel="stylesheet" id="daily-cooking-custom-style-css"
  href="style.css" type="text/css" media="all" />
<! - embedding the style sheet for the design - >
<title>Daily Cooking</title>
</head>
```

```
<body>
<div id="page">
  <header id="masthead" class="site-header" role="banner">
    <div class="site-branding">
      <h1 class="site-title">Daily Cooking</h1>
    </div>
    <nav id="site-navigation" class="main-navigation"
    role="navigation">
      <! -  placeholder for site navigation  - >
    </nav>
  </header>

  <div id="content" class="site-content">
    <div id="primary" class="content-area">
    <main id="main"  class="site-main" role="main">
    <article>
      <header class="entry-header">
        <h1 class="entry-title">Hello world!</h1>
      </header>

      <div class="entry-content">
        <p>Welcome!</p>
        <! -  main content block  - >
      </div>

      <footer class="entry-footer">
        <! -  footer of the content block  - >
      </footer>
    </article>
    </main></div>

    <div id="secondary" role="complementary">
      <! -  sidebar  - >
    </div>
  </div>

  <footer class="site-footer" role="contentinfo">
    <! -  main footer of the page  - >
  </footer>
</div>
</body>
</html>
```

This HTML structure can be found in the official code bundle for this chapter—called `phase 1`.

You can see that I've separated out the major parts, as follows:

- The header is in an HTML5 `<header>` tag.
- As part of it, there's the main site navigation, also in an HTML5 `<nav>` tag.
- Next, we have the main content block, `<div id="content" class="site-content">;;` each individual post will be displayed inside separate HTML5 `<article>` tags.
- After this, we have a section that handles the sidebar, `<div id="secondary" role="complementary">`. The sidebar is set with the `role="complementary"` attribute. Essentially, the role attribute describes the role that the element plays in the context of the document. In this case, the sidebar is complementary to the main content (and if you pay close attention, you'll notice that the main part, that is, the content, is indeed set to `role="main"`). In general, such attributes are meant to explain the purpose of elements in the HTML structure.
- Finally, there's the footer, using the `<footer>` tag. Keep in mind that this is HTML5, and it may not work on older web browsers.

Now that I've got my basic layout, I'm going to add a few more HTML elements to flesh it out a bit, including more information in `<head>`, as well as in the main content box, plus some additional CSS. Then, I'll fill up the sidebar, header, content, and footer.

Examining the CSS

Generally, a very good practice in web development is to start your CSS design by resetting all of the default styles used by various web browsers. The main issue, and the reason why this is an important step, is that most popular web browsers (or, should I say, every single one of them) have their own default set of CSS styles. And, if you want your theme to look exactly the same in every browser, you have to start your work by resetting those styles, whatever they might actually be. The good thing about this is that you don't have to do it by hand. You can just use one of the reset scripts available on the internet. Keep in mind that every piece of code that's listed in this chapter is also available in the official code bundle that came with your book. So, what we'll do first is just have the following CSS at the beginning of our new `style.css` file:

```
/* setting up the basic elements - starter setup */
html, body, div, span, applet, object, iframe,
```

```css
h1, h2, h3, h4, h5, h6, p, blockquote, pre,
a, abbr, acronym, address, big, cite, code,
del, dfn, em, font, ins, kbd, q, s, samp,
small, strike, strong, sub, sup, tt, var,
dl, dt, dd, ol, ul, li,
fieldset, form, label, legend,
table, caption, tbody, tfoot, thead, tr, th, td {
  border: 0;
  font-family: inherit;
  font-size: 100%;
  font-style: inherit;
  font-weight: inherit;
  margin: 0;
  outline: 0;
  padding: 0;
  vertical-align: baseline;
}

html {
  font-size: 62.5%;
  overflow-y: scroll;
  -webkit-text-size-adjust: 100%;
  -ms-text-size-adjust: 100%;
  box-sizing: border-box;
}
*, *:before, *:after {
  box-sizing: inherit;
}

body {
  background: #fff;
}

/* resetting the basic content blocks */
article, aside, details, figcaption, figure, footer, header, main,
  nav, section {
  display: block;
}

/* resetting the lists */
ol, ul {
  list-style: none;
}

table {
  border-collapse: separate;
  border-spacing: 0;
}
```

```
caption, th, td {
  font-weight: normal;
  text-align: left;
}

blockquote:before, blockquote:after, q:before, q:after {
  content: "";
}
blockquote, q {
  quotes: " "";
}

a:focus {
  outline: thin dotted;
}
a:hover, a:active {
  outline: 0;
}
a img {
  border: 0;
}
```

Let's now take a look at the actual CSS—the things that build our design and not just reset it. First, we'll review the CSS that displays everything you see in the design. Note that I have styles for all of the key elements, such as the header, sidebar, main content area, and footer.

Also, note that this is just the scaffolding, so to speak; it only indicates the individual areas of the final CSS style sheet. Talking about CSS isn't the main thing we're focusing on in this book. Therefore, I'm including the complete version of the aforementioned code bundle, and right now, I'm only presenting the individual areas of the CSS. This is just to make the whole thing easier to grasp once you look at the complete style sheet. To be honest, the final CSS isn't actually that complex from a CSS design point of view, but it is quite lengthy. Here's the simplified version:

1. Let's start with the typography settings and various standard content elements. I'm not showcasing the individual styles here, as they are kind of basic and don't play a huge role in our WordPress site structure:

   ```
   /* -  -  -  - -
   Typography
    -  -  -  -  - -*/
   body, button, input, select, textarea {}
   h1, h2, h3, h4, h5, h6 {}
   h1 a, h2 a, h3 a, h4 a, h5 a, h6 a {}
   p {}
   ```

```
b, strong {}
dfn, cite, em, i {}
blockquote {}
address {}
pre {}
code, kbd, tt, var {}
abbr, acronym {}
mark, ins {}
sup, sub {}
small {}
big {}
/* -  -  -  -
Elements
  -  -  -  - -*/
hr {}
ul, ol {}
dt {}
dd {}
img {}
figure {}
table {}
button, input, select, textarea {}
```

2. What follows next is a set of rules that will take care of the alignment, the general design structure, the headers, and other typical HTML elements:

```
.site-header {
  width: 15%;
  float: left;
  height: auto;
  background: #279090;
  margin-right: 2.5%;
  border-radius: 6px;
}
#page {
  width: 1160px;
  margin: 0 auto;
  margin-top: 50px;
  position: relative;
  overflow: auto;
}
#primary {
  width: 56%;
  float: left;
}

/* Navigation */
.main-navigation {
```

```
    clear: both;
    display: block
    float: left;
    width: 100%;
}

/* Alignments */
.alignleft {
    display: inline;
    float: left;
    margin-right: 1.5em;
}
.alignright {
    display: inline;
    float: right;
    margin-left: 1.5em;
}
.aligncenter {
    clear: both;
    display: block;
    margin: 0 auto;
}
```

3. The center part of the site structure is where the posts and pages will be displayed. The code for it is as follows:

```
.site-content .page, .site-content .post {
    margin-bottom: 40px;
    background-color: white;
    border-radius: 6px;
}
.entry-header h1.entry-title {
    text-align: center;
}

.site-content .entry-content {
    padding: 10px 20px;
}
```

4. The code for the main sidebar is demonstrated as follows:

```
#secondary {
    width: 24.5%;
    float: left;
    height: auto;
    margin-left: 2%;
    opacity: 0.6;
    background-color: white;
```

```
  border-radius: 3px;
  padding: 0 10px;
}
```

5. And finally, the code for the footer is as follows:

```
.site-footer {
  float: right;
  padding: 20px;
}
```

Inside this style sheet, you will find many specific classes that aren't just my own creations, but instead come from WordPress itself. Here's what I mean: when WordPress creates all of the items, which includes page lists, category lists, archive lists, images, and galleries, it gives many of these items a particular class name. If you know these class names, you can prepare your style sheet to take advantage of them. This is one more reason why we're using a starter theme here. With it, we don't have to worry about any of this.

For example, when you add an image to a post or page, WordPress gives you the option to have it to the right or left, or at the center of the text. Depending on what you choose, WordPress will assign either of these classes to the image: `alignleft`, `alignright`, or `aligncenter`. These specific classes are handled in the *Alignments* section of our CSS style sheet. Another thing is that, when you add an image with a caption, WordPress gives it the `wp-caption` class. This particular thing is handled in the *Captions* section of the style sheet. WordPress uses many other classes that you can take advantage of when building your style sheet. I've listed a few of them in `Chapter 13`, *Creating a Non-Blog Website Part Two – E-Commerce Websites and Custom Content Elements*.

Now that you've got your HTML and CSS lined up, you're ready for the next step—turning your HTML build into a WordPress theme.

Converting your build into a theme

You'll be turning your HTML build into a theme, which is composed of a number of template files and other scripts. We are going to first dig into the inner workings of a theme, so as to get familiar with how it's put together. Then, we'll actually turn our HTML build into a theme directory that WordPress can use. Finally, we'll include WordPress functions that populate the theme with content. As I mentioned in an earlier chapter, doing development for your WordPress website in a local environment can make the whole process much smoother. Consider getting a server up and running on your home computer using WAMP, MAMP, or some other way to install Apache and MySQL.

Creating the theme directory

The first step to turning your HTML build into a theme, is to create your theme directory and give it everything it needs to be recognized as a theme by WordPress. Let's look at an overview of the steps and then take them one by one, as follows:

1. Name your directory and creating backup copies of your build files
2. Preparing the essential files
3. Adding a screenshot of your theme, named `screenshot.png`
4. Uploading your theme directory
5. Activating your theme

Let's take these steps one by one now.

Naming your directory and creating backup copies of your build files

You'll want to give your build directory a sensible name. I'm naming my theme **Daily Cooking Custom**. I'll name the directory `daily-cooking-custom`. Now, I suggest creating backup copies of your HTML and CSS files. As you'll eventually be breaking up your build into template files, you could easily lose track of where your code came from. By keeping a copy of your original build, you'll be able to go back to it for reference.

Preparing the essential files

WordPress has only the following two requirements to recognize your directory as a theme:

- A file called `index.php`
- A file called `style.css`

Just rename your main design's HTML file `index.php`—this takes care of the first requirement. To satisfy the second requirement, your style sheet needs to have an introductory comment that describes the basic information for the whole theme: title, author, and so on. Also, it has to be at the very top of the style sheet. I've added this comment to my `style.css` file, as follows:

```
/*
Theme Name: Daily Cooking Custom
Theme URI: http://nio.tips/
Author: Karol K
Author URI: http://karol.cc/
Description: Daily Cooking Custom is a custom theme created for the buyers
of "WordPress Complete"
Version: 1.0
License: GNU General Public License v2 or later
License URI: http://www.gnu.org/licenses/gpl-2.0.html
Text Domain: daily-cooking-custom
Tags: brown, orange, tan, white, yellow, two-columns, right-sidebar,
flexible-width, custom-header, custom-menu, translation-ready
*/
```

The preceding structure has been created on the basis of the template available at `https://codex.wordpress.org/Theme_Development#Theme_Stylesheet`. Whenever you're creating a new theme, it's always good to check the currently recommended template beforehand. When you add this comment section to your style sheet, just replace all of the details with those that are relevant to your theme.

Adding a screenshot

Remember when you first learned how to activate a new theme that there were thumbnail versions of the themes in your **Appearance** tab? You'll want a thumbnail of your own design. It should be a PNG file with the name `screenshot.png`. Just do the following:

1. Flatten a copy of your design in Photoshop or in a similar tool
2. Change the image width to 1200 px and the height to 900 px
3. Save it for the web as a PNG-8 file

The preceding requirements (1200 px by 900 px) are the current ones at the time of writing. To get the latest guidelines at any point in time, revisit the official Codex at `https://codex.wordpress.org/Theme_Development#Screenshot`.

Create a screenshot

Name your file `screenshot.png` and save it in your build directory. This is all it takes to have the screenshot enabled and allow WordPress to recognize it when it loads your theme.

Uploading your directory

Using FTP software, upload your template directory to `wp-content/themes/` in your WordPress build. It will share the themes directory with `twentynineteen`, and any other theme you've added as you installed WordPress. In the following screenshot, you can see my `daily-cooking-custom` theme living in the `themes` directory:

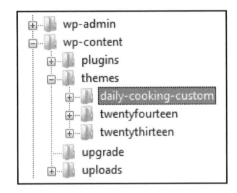

Activating your theme

You've got the absolute basic necessities in there now, so you can activate your theme (although, it won't look like much yet). Log in to your `wp-admin`, and navigate to **Appearance**. There, you'll see your theme waiting for you. As you can see, I've created a nice screenshot for my theme, with the name of the theme on it for easier identification:

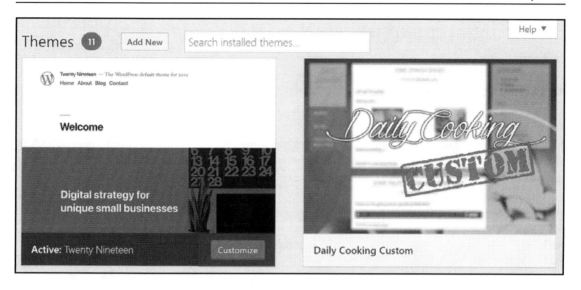

At this point, you can activate your new theme and continue working on it to include WordPress-generated content and make it into a full-fledged WordPress theme in general. Don't be alarmed if the theme doesn't look perfectly right after activation, though. There's still some work to do. This is another good reason to have a development server. You wouldn't want to have this incomplete theme active on a live site while you finish the final pieces in the background.

Note that not every theme installation goes as expected. Sometimes, you have to deal with errors. In most cases, WordPress will let you know what went wrong with a notification. Every once in a while, however, activation can result in a critical error and your whole site could go blank. If that happens, simply rename the new theme's directory, or delete it completely. This will force WordPress to switch to the default theme, and things should go back to normal. From there, you can start looking for the issue that caused the crash in the first place.

Speaking of final pieces, your theme is now ready to have all of the WordPress content added, so let's do just that!

How to create basic WordPress content

Right now, your `index.php` file is your only theme file. We'll be breaking it up into template files a bit later. First, we need to include WordPress functions that will spit out your content into your theme.

The functions.php file

In short, the `functions.php` file is meant to set up your theme and provide some helper functions and settings to make using the theme easier. Apart from this, the functions file also has many other applications that we're not going to discuss here, as they are beyond the scope of this book. In essence, `functions.php` is a file that allows you to perform a very wide scope of modifications. Even though there is a set of standard things that should always be taken care of when dealing with a functions file, they don't restrict you from doing virtually anything you wish. For instance, you could create a classic PHP function, such as `my_function_name()`, and then call it from within one of your template files (such as `index.php`) through `<?php my_function_name(); ?>`, but this is just one of the possible scenarios.

Although this isn't a requirement, it's always good to start your functions file with the following lines of code (just as a good reference point):

```php
<?php
/**
 * Daily Cooking Custom functions and definitions.
 *
 * @package Daily Cooking Custom
 */
```

The preceding lines of code provide essential information about the theme.

The next part is the setup of the default features that the theme is going to enable, as follows:

```php
if(!function_exists('daily_cooking_custom_setup')) :
function daily_cooking_custom_setup() {

  //Make theme available for translation.
  //Translations can be filed in the /languages/ folder.
  load_theme_textdomain('daily-cooking-custom',
  get_template_directory().'/languages');

  //Adds RSS feed links to <head> for posts and comments.
  add_theme_support('automatic-feed-links');

  //Let WordPress manage the document title.
  add_theme_support('title-tag');

  //This theme uses wp_nav_menu() in one location.
  register_nav_menus(array(
    'primary' => __('Primary Menu', 'daily-cooking-custom'),
  ));
```

```
//Switch default core markup for search form, comment form,
//and comments to output valid HTML5.
add_theme_support('html5', array(
  'search-form', 'comment-form', 'comment-list', 'gallery', 'caption',
));

//Set up the WordPress core custom background feature.
add_theme_support('custom-background', apply_filters(
  'daily_cooking_custom_custom_background_args', array(
  'default-color' => 'ffffff',
  'default-image' => '',
)));

}
endif; //daily_cooking_custom_setup
add_action('after_setup_theme', 'daily_cooking_custom_setup');
```

The preceding function, `daily_cooking_custom_setup()`, will be executed at just the right time, triggered by the `after_setup_theme` action called at the end to set up the basic features of our theme properly. Most of the code is pretty self-explanatory, due to the comments, but there's just one thing I'd like to mention individually, which is the following (registering the menu):

```
register_nav_menus(array(
  'primary' => __('Primary Menu', 'daily-cooking-custom'),
));
```

This is a small piece of code that will let us assign any custom menu to appear as the primary menu later on. It is also what we'll use to set our new theme. In addition, the preceding function allows you to register even more menu areas if you wish—and all you'll have to do is add `'secondary' => 'Secondary Menu'`.

Next, let's enable our style sheet CSS file to load with our theme, or more accurately, to be *enqueued,* and then load precisely the right moment. Here's how to do so:

```
function daily_cooking_custom_scripts() {
  wp_enqueue_style('daily-cooking-custom-style', get_stylesheet_uri());
}
add_action('wp_enqueue_scripts', 'daily_cooking_custom_scripts');
```

As you can see, there's only one style sheet here. It is enabled by the very first line in the function.

The preceding code closes our first template-like `functions.php` file. Later, we will add new lines to it to make it even more functional. Now, the interesting part is that there is no closing PHP tag in the functions file (no `?>`). This is not a typo; it is intentional. Since most of the file is pure PHP, we don't need this tag. The complete file is as follows:

```php
<?php
/**
 * Daily Cooking Custom functions and definitions
 *
 * @package Daily Cooking Custom
 */

if(!function_exists('daily_cooking_custom_setup')) :
function daily_cooking_custom_setup() {

  //Make theme available for translation.
  //Translations can be filed in the /languages/ folder.
  load_theme_textdomain('daily-cooking-custom',
  get_template_directory().'/languages');

  //Adds RSS feed links to <head> for posts and comments.
  add_theme_support('automatic-feed-links');

  //Let WordPress manage the document title.
  add_theme_support('title-tag');

  //This theme uses wp_nav_menu() in one location.
  register_nav_menus(array(
    'primary' => __('Primary Menu', 'daily-cooking-custom'),
  ));

  //Switch default core markup for search form, comment form,
  //and comments to output valid HTML5.
  add_theme_support('html5', array(
    'search-form', 'comment-form', 'comment-list', 'gallery', 'caption',
  ));

  //Set up the WordPress core custom background feature.
  add_theme_support('custom-background', apply_filters(
    'daily_cooking_custom_custom_background_args', array(
    'default-color' => 'ffffff',
    'default-image' => '',
  )));

}
endif; //daily_cooking_custom_setup
add_action('after_setup_theme', 'daily_cooking_custom_setup');
```

```
function daily_cooking_custom_scripts() {
  wp_enqueue_style('daily-cooking-custom-style', get_stylesheet_uri());
}
add_action('wp_enqueue_scripts', 'daily_cooking_custom_scripts');
```

The <head> tag

Okay, let's move on to our index.php file and the things we can do inside of it. In the following section of the chapter, we're going to be altering specific lines of code from the original HTML structure. Let's see how to do that:

1. Set up the <head></head> section of your HTML file. Let's start with charset and the device-width parameter. Here are the two lines to begin with right after the opening <head> tag:

   ```
   <meta charset="<?php bloginfo('charset'); ?>">
   <meta name="viewport" content="width=device-width, initial-scale=1">
   ```

   The first one holds the character set that your blog uses. The other defines the width of the viewport used. Here, it's set to the width of the device being used (this allows everyone to view the site correctly, including desktop computer users, iPad users, and Android phone users).

2. You need to add another important chunk of code—first, to put header tags into your theme for the pingback URL; second, other miscellaneous WordPress stuff. Add the following lines in your <head> section:

   ```
   <link rel="profile" href="http://gmpg.org/xfn/11">
   <link rel="pingback" href="<?php bloginfo('pingback_url'); ?>">
   ```

3. Add the following line right before the closing </head> tag (it takes care of displaying your site's title and enabling a number of WordPress-specific functionalities):

   ```
   <?php wp_head(); ?>
   ```

4. Now, add the body_class() function to the body tag, so it looks like the following:

   ```
   <body <?php body_class() ?>>
   ```

5. Your header now look like the following:

```
<!DOCTYPE html>
<html <?php language_attributes(); ?>>
<head>
<meta charset="<?php bloginfo('charset'); ?>">
<meta name="viewport" content="width=device-width, initial-scale=1">
<link rel="profile" href="http://gmpg.org/xfn/11">
<link rel="pingback" href="<?php bloginfo('pingback_url'); ?>">
<?php wp_head(); ?>
</head>
<body <?php body_class(); ?>>
```

The header and footer

It's time to start adding some content. Here, we'll take care of things such as displaying a link to the blog's home page, displaying the blog's title, displaying the tagline, and displaying the main navigation. All of these operations are pretty simple, so let's just take a look at the lines of code that take care of them. Then, we'll put these lines of code in just the right place within our HTML structure.

First, we have the code that displays the site's main URL, as follows:

```
<?php echo esc_url(home_url('/')); ?>
```

Next, the code that displays the site's title is as follows:

```
<?php bloginfo('name'); ?>
```

The following is the code for displaying the tagline:

```
<?php bloginfo('description'); ?>
```

The preceding two lines pull information from where you set the blog name and description in wp-admin, and you can simply change them from the **Settings** | **General** page.

Lastly, displaying the main navigation is done with the following code:

```
<?php wp_nav_menu(array('theme_location' => 'primary')); ?>
```

The wp_nav_menu() function is a built-in way of displaying the navigation menu. It takes care of the proper HTML structure of the menu and all of its elements. In other words, you don't have to worry about anything else other than using this one line of code.

Now, the part of your HTML that describes the header looks similar to the following listing. Additionally, as you can see, we're linking the logo to the home page, which is a standard practice:

```html
<div id="page" class="hfeed site">
  <a class="skip-link screen-reader-text" href="#content">
  <?php _e( 'Skip to content', 'daily-cooking-custom' ); ?></a>

  <header id="masthead" class="site-header" role="banner">

    <div class="site-branding">
      <h1 class="site-title"><a href="<?php echo
        esc_url(home_url('/')); ?>"
        rel="home"><?php bloginfo('name');?></a></h1>
      <h2 class="site-description"><?php bloginfo('description');?>
      </h2>
    </div><!- .site-branding - >

    <nav id="site-navigation" class="main-navigation"
      role="navigation">
      <button class="menu-toggle" aria-controls="menu"
        aria-expanded="false">
      <?php _e( 'Primary Menu', 'daily-cooking-custom' ); ?></button>
      <?php wp_nav_menu(array('theme_location' => 'primary')); ?>
    </nav><!- #site-navigation - >

  </header><!- #masthead - >

<div id="content" class="site-content">
```

Are you wondering why you should bother with some of this when you could have just typed your blog title, URL, and a description of the theme? One reason is that if you ever want to change your blog's title, you can simply do it in one quick step in `wp-admin` and it will change all over your site. The other reason is that if you want to sharing your theme with others, you'll need to give them the ability to easily change the name through their own `wp-admin` panels. Keep in mind that anything (anything at all) that will change from site to site based on the site's purpose and content should not be hardcoded into the theme, but should be dynamically generated.

Now, when I refresh the site, there's the actual blog title in the header, as shown in the following screenshot:

The two links visible in the header are live links from one of my custom menus. Just to tie things up, I'm going to add some code to my footer to display the "proudly powered by WordPress" message, and to include the `wp_footer()` function/hook that's often used by many plugins in one way or another, so every theme should feature it. The code for my footer section now looks like the following:

```
</div><! -  #content  - >

<footer id="colophon" class="site-footer" role="contentinfo">
  <div class="site-info">
    <a href="<?php echo esc_url( __( 'http://wordpress.org/',
     'daily-cooking-custom' ) ); ?>">
    <?php printf( __( 'Proudly powered by %s', 'daily-cooking-custom' ),
     'WordPress' );?></a>
    <span class="sep"> | </span>
    <?php printf( __( 'Theme: %1$s by %2$s.', 'daily-cooking-custom' ),
     'Daily Cooking Custom', '<a href="http://karol.cc/" rel="designer">
     Karol K.</a>, and
     <a href="http://underscores.me/" rel="designer">_S</a>' ); ?>
  </div><! -  .site-info  - >
</footer><! -  #colophon  - >

</div><! -  #page  - >

<?php wp_footer(); ?>

</body>
</html>
```

One thing you might have noticed inside the previous listing is the mysterious `__()` function. It's a native WordPress function that retrieves the translated string corresponding to the parameters given in the function. It's a feature meant for the internationalization of your site. More details about the function can be found at `https://codex.wordpress.org/Function_Reference/_2`.

The sidebar

Now, we can move along to adding WordPress-generated content in the sidebar. Essentially, this part of our work is pretty simple. All we have to do is include some WordPress functions that will handle displaying various bits of dynamic content. In this case, it is the categories, tags, and archives.

Starting at the top, include the following piece of code in the sidebar area:

```
<div id="secondary" class="widget-area" role="complementary">
  <?php if(is_active_sidebar('sidebar-1')) dynamic_sidebar('sidebar-1' );
?>
</div><! -  #secondary  - >
```

This code takes care of displaying whatever widgets have been assigned to that particular widget area. Placing widgets in the sidebar of your HTML structure is the easiest, and probably the most usable way, of widget-enabling your theme. Also, WordPress will take care of actually displaying everything properly, so you don't have to worry about any weird-looking elements on your site. For instance, every menu is displayed as a <ul> list, and every menu element is inside <li>. This is as in tune with the standards as it can be.

Main column – the loop

This is the most important section of our WordPress code. It's called the loop, and it's an essential part of your new theme. The loop's job is to display your posts in reverse chronological order, choosing only those posts that are appropriate. You need to put all of your other post tags inside the loop. The basic loop text, which has to surround your post information, is displayed using the following code:

```
<?php if (have_posts()) : ?>
<?php while (have_posts()) : the_post(); ?>
  <?php get_template_part('content', get_post_format()); ?>
<?php endwhile; else: ?>
  <?php get_template_part('content', 'none'); ?>
<?php endif; ?>
```

The get_template_part() function call that's right in the middle, fetches another file that contains the rest of the loop; but for now, let's just focus on the main section here.

There are two basic parts of the loop, as follows:

- Individual post information
- What to do if there are no appropriate posts

The first part is handled by a standard PHP while loop that goes through every post and, for each element, calls the appropriate content-[TYPE].php file. The second part is similar, as it calls the content-none.php file if there are no posts that can be displayed. The use of these various content-[TYPE].php files is currently the standard for handling the different types of content that WordPress displays. It's a lot more effective and clear than working with the individual if or switch clauses.

So, in order to get started with this, let's create a basic `content.php` file that will serve the role of a placeholder for the default type of content. In this file, let's place the following code, which handles the loop:

```
<article id="post-<?php the_ID(); ?>" <?php post_class(); ?>>

<header class="entry-header">
  <?php the_title(sprintf('<h1 class="entry-title">
  <a href="%s" rel="bookmark">', esc_url(get_permalink())), '</a></h1>');
  ?>

  <?php if('post' == get_post_type()) : ?>
  <div class="entry-meta">
    <?php daily_cooking_custom_posted_on(); ?>
  </div>
  <?php endif; ?>
</header>

<div class="entry-content">
  <?php
  the_content(sprintf(__('Continue reading %s <span class="meta-nav">&rarr;
  </span>', 'daily-cooking-custom'), the_title('<span class="screen-reader-
  text">"', '"</span>', false)));

  wp_link_pages(array('before' => '<div class="page-links">' . __('Pages:',
  'daily-cooking-custom'), 'after'  => '</div>'));
  ?>
</div>

<footer class="entry-footer">
  <?php daily_cooking_custom_entry_footer(); ?>
</footer>

</article><! -  #post-##  - >
```

If you take a closer look, you'll notice that it's very similar to the static HTML version I shared earlier in this chapter. The only difference is that, instead of the dummy text, there are calls to specific WordPress functions and custom-made functions that we'll discuss shortly.

Let's take it from the top; the file starts with these two lines:

```
<article id="post-<?php the_ID(); ?>" <?php post_class(); ?>>
  <header class="entry-header">
```

This is just some standard HTML and basic WordPress function calls to display proper element IDs and CSS classes. For instance, the `the_ID()` function displays the ID of the post. Next, we have the following line:

```
<?php the_title(sprintf('<h1 class="entry-title"><a href="%s"
rel="bookmark">', esc_url(get_permalink())), '</a></h1>'); ?>
```

This displays the link and the title of the current content element (which is usually a post), instead of using the dummy text. The `the_title()` function takes three parameters (which are all optional). Right here, we're using just two. The first one defines the text to place before the title (in this case, we're making a `sprintf()` function call), and the second one defines the text to place after the title. The following is a piece of code that displays various types of meta information about the current content element:

```
<?php if('post' == get_post_type()) : ?>
<div class="entry-meta">
  <?php daily_cooking_custom_posted_on(); ?>
</div>
<?php endif; ?>
```

If what we're dealing with is a standard post, a custom function is called to display the details. This way of handling things—through an additional function—makes everything much clearer in comparison to placing the code right there. Here's what the function looks like (we can place it in our main `functions.php` file, or inside a new file in a separate sub-directory called `inc`, indicating that it holds additional functions; in our case, this function definition can be found in `inc\template-tags.php`):

```
function daily_cooking_custom_posted_on() {
  $time_string = '<time class="entry-date published updated"
  datetime="%1$s">%2$s</time>';
  if ( get_the_time( 'U' ) !== get_the_modified_time( 'U' ) ) {
    $time_string = '<time class="entry-date published"
    datetime="%1$s">%2$s</time><time class="updated"
    datetime="%3$s">%4$s</time>';
  }

  $time_string = sprintf( $time_string,
    esc_attr( get_the_date( 'c' ) ),
    esc_html( get_the_date() ),
    esc_attr( get_the_modified_date( 'c' ) ),
    esc_html( get_the_modified_date() )
  );

  $posted_on = sprintf(
    _x( 'Posted on %s', 'post date', 'daily-cooking-custom' ),
    '<a href="' . esc_url( get_permalink() ) . '" rel="bookmark">'
```

```
    . $time_string . '</a>'
  );

  $byline = sprintf(
    _x( 'by %s', 'post author', 'daily-cooking-custom' ),
    '<span class="author vcard"><a class="url fn n" href="' .
    esc_url( get_author_posts_url( get_the_author_meta( 'ID' ) )
    ) . '">' . esc_html( get_the_author() ) . '</a></span>'
  );

  echo '<span class="posted-on">' . $posted_on . '</span><span
  class="byline"> ' . $byline . '</span>';
}
```

As you can see, this is quite a long function, but the thing to remember is that it's just meant to display the date of when the post was published and the byline of the author. Also, there are language functions (_e() and _x()) used here to fetch translated data from the database. You can learn more about these functions at https://codex.wordpress.org/ Function_Reference/_e and https://codex.wordpress.org/Function_Reference/_x.

Going back to our content.php file, we have the following:

```
<div class="entry-content">
  <?php
  the_content(sprintf(
    __('Continue reading %s <span class="meta-nav">&rarr;</span>',
     'daily-cooking-custom'),
    the_title('<span class="screen-reader-text">"', '"</span>', false)
  ));

  wp_link_pages(array(
    'before' => '<div class="page-links">' . __('Pages:', 'daily-
    cooking-custom'),
    'after'  => '</div>',
  ));
  ?>
</div>
```

The first part (`the_content()`) takes care of displaying the contents of the current post, along with a `Continue reading` link. This is actually the most important part of the whole file. Next, the second part (`wp_link_pages()`), is meant to display page links for paginated posts (WordPress allows you to divide your content into individual subpages; this can be useful when dealing with an overly long piece of text). Finally, we have the code for the footer section of the entry, as follows:

```
<footer class="entry-footer">
  <?php daily_cooking_custom_entry_footer(); ?>
</footer>
```

There's another call to a custom-made function there. Here's what the function looks like:

```
function daily_cooking_custom_entry_footer() {
  // Hide category and tag text for pages.
  if ( 'post' == get_post_type() ) {
    $categories_list = get_the_category_list( __( ', ',
     'daily-cooking-custom' ) );
    if ( $categories_list && daily_cooking_custom_categorized_blog() ) {
      printf( '<span class="cat-links">' . __( 'Posted in %1$s',
        'daily-cooking-custom' ) . '</span>', $categories_list );
    }

    $tags_list = get_the_tag_list( '', __( ', ', 'daily-cooking-custom'
      ) );
    if ( $tags_list ) {
      printf( '<span class="tags-links">' . __( 'Tagged %1$s',
        'daily-cooking-custom' ) . '</span>', $tags_list );
    }
  }

  if ( ! is_single() && ! post_password_required() &&
  (comments_open() || get_comments_number() ) ) {
    echo '<span class="comments-link">';
    comments_popup_link(__('Leave a comment', 'daily-cooking-custom'),
     __('1 Comment', 'daily-cooking-custom'), __('% Comments',
    'daily-cooking-custom'));
    echo '</span>';
  }

  edit_post_link( __( 'Edit', 'daily-cooking-custom' ),
  '<span class="edit-link">', '</span>' );
}
```

All this code handles the post details, such as the categories, tags, and the comment links (which other visitors can click to submit their opinions about the post). One interesting thing I'd like to point out here is the call to the `comments_popup_link()` function, as follows:

```
comments_popup_link(__('Leave a comment', 'daily-cooking-custom'), __('1
Comment', 'daily-cooking-custom'), __('% Comments', 'daily-cooking-
custom'));
```

Here, you can see that there are three arguments passed, separated by commas:

- The first one tells WordPress the text that it has to display when there are no comments.
- The second one tells WordPress the text that it has to display when there is just one comment.
- The third one tells WordPress the text that it has to display in case there's more than one comment. The percent symbol (`%`) gets replaced with the actual number of existing comments.

This is it regarding a basic understanding of the loop. Of course, its structure allows you to do many more things and include many custom features. However, for now, we are good with what we have here. Once you save your `index.php` and reload your website, you will see your new theme in action.

 This version of the `index.php` file is available in the code bundle for this chapter, inside a sub-directory called `phase 2`. Our theme files will go through a couple of phases before we have the final version.

Later in the chapter, I will show you how to create a custom page template, which will take advantage of the loop and use it for a slightly different purpose.

Creating template files within your theme

You've now got a functional, basic template for your theme. It works great on the main blog page and successfully loads content for anything you can click on within your site. However, we want slightly different templates for other types of content on our site. For example, a single post page needs to have a comment form where visitors can post comments; the page doesn't need to show the date, category, or tags; and the category page should show the category name.

Before we can create other templates, we need to break up the main `index.php` file into parts so that these different templates can share the common elements. I've mentioned the importance of the header, sidebar, and footer many times. We're going to break them up now. First, let's take a quick look at how it works.

Understanding the WordPress theme structure

Usually, WordPress themes are composed of a number of template files. This allows the different parts of the site (such as the frontend, blog archive, pages, single posts, and search results) to have different purposes. Breaking the `index.php` file into template files allows us to not only share some common parts of the design, but also to have different code in different parts. As I mentioned earlier, we'll soon be breaking up the four main pieces of the design (the header, sidebar, main column, and footer) so that WordPress can make good use of them. While the header and footer are probably shared by all pages, the content in the main column will be different. Also, you may want the sidebar on some pages, but not on others. We'll first create these template files, and then move on to the other, more optional template files.

Breaking it up

We're going to break up the `index.php` file by removing some of the code into three new files, as follows:

- `header.php`
- `footer.php`
- `sidebar.php`

The header.php file

First, we will create a header file. You can do so with the following steps:

1. Cut out the entire top of your `index.php` file. This means cutting the `doctype` declaration, the `<head>` tag, any miscellaneous opening tags, and the `<header>` tag. In my case, I'm cutting out all the way from this initial line:

   ```
   <!DOCTYPE html>
   ```

2. I'm cutting through to, and including, these lines:

```
</header><! -   #masthead   - >
<div id="content" class="site-content">
```

3. Paste all these lines into a new file named `header.php`, which you created within your theme directory.

4. Now, at the very top of the `index.php` file (that is, where you just cut the header text from), type in the following line of WordPress PHP code:

```
<?php get_header(); ?>
```

5. This is a WordPress function that includes the `header.php` file you just created.

If you save everything and reload your website now, nothing should change. The important part here is to make sure that the call to the preceding PHP function sits right at the very top of your `index.php` file.

The footer.php file

Next, we will create the footer file. You can do so in the following steps:

1. Cut out everything at the very bottom of the `index.php` file from the following code:

```
</div><! -   #content   - >
<footer id="colophon" class="site-footer" role="contentinfo">
```

2. Cut all the way through to the `</html>` tag. Paste the text you just cut into a new `footer.php` file. Save it in your theme directory.

3. Now, at the very bottom of the `index.php` file (from where you just cut the footer text), type in the following line of WordPress PHP code:

```
<?php get_footer(); ?>
```

4. This is a special WordPress function that includes the `footer.php` file you just created. Again, you should save everything and reload your website to make sure nothing changes.

The sidebar.php file

There is just one more essential template file to create. For this one, carry out the following steps:

1. Cut out the entire `div` element containing your sidebar. In my case, it's the following line:

```
<div id="secondary" class="widget-area" role="complementary">
    <?php if(is_active_sidebar('sidebar-1'))
dynamic_sidebar('sidebar-1' ); ?>
    </div>
```

2. Paste this line into a new file in your theme directory and save it as `sidebar.php`.

3. Now, in `index.php`, add this function call in place of the lines you've just cut, as follows:

```
<?php get_sidebar(); ?>
```

This will include the sidebar.

Your four template files

You now have four template files in your theme directory, namely, `header.php`, `footer.php`, `sidebar.php`, and the now much shorter `index.php`. By the way, my `index.php` file now has only a handful of WordPress functions and the main loop. The following code shows the entire file:

```
<?php get_header(); ?>

    <div id="primary" class="content-area">
        <main id="main" class="site-main" role="main">

        <?php if (have_posts()) : ?>

            <?php /* Start the Loop */ ?>
            <?php while (have_posts()) : the_post(); ?>

                <?php
                get_template_part('content', get_post_format());
                ?>

            <?php endwhile; ?>
```

```
        <?php daily_cooking_custom_paging_nav(); ?>

    <?php else : ?>

        <?php get_template_part('content', 'none'); ?>

    <?php endif; ?>

    </main><! -  #main   - >
  </div><! -  #primary   - >

<?php get_sidebar(); ?>
<?php get_footer(); ?>
```

This whole cutting-and-pasting process to create these four files was just to set the scene for the real goal of making alternative template files.

> This version of the index.php file, as well as header.php, footer.php, and sidebar.php, is available in the code bundle for this chapter, inside a sub-directory called phase 3.

Archive template

WordPress is now using the index.php template file to display every type of web page that's a part of your site. Let's make a new file—one that will be used when viewing the monthly archive, category archive, and tag archive.

> To learn more about how WordPress utilizes different files to display content, feel free to read the guide at https://www.codeinwp.com/blog/wordpress-theme-heirarchy/.

To create your archive template, make a copy of index.php and rename it archive.php. Now, navigate to see your monthly archive on the site by clicking on either of the months in the sidebar. At this point, the page you'll see should look exactly like the main listing—the one handled by index.php.

Let's make one change to the archive template. I'd like it to display a message that lets users know what type of archive page they are on. Currently, the archive looks the same as the main index listing, and this isn't the most optimized situation. To fix this, just add the following code the `<?php if (have_posts()) : ?>` line:

```
<header class="page-header">
  <?php
  the_archive_title('<h1 class="page-title">', '</h1>');
  the_archive_description('<div class="taxonomy-description">', '</div>');
  ?>
</header>
```

If I go to see my monthly archive now—or the category/tag archive—I'll get a new heading at the top of the page that lets me know where I am, as shown in the following screenshot:

This version of the `archive.php` file is available in the code bundle for this chapter, inside a sub-directory called `phase 4`.

Single template

The next template we need to create is the single post view. Right now, the single post looks like the site's front page (because it's using `index.php`)—except it populates the page with the contents of just one post.

To get started, make another copy of `index.php`, and name it `single.php`. This is the template that WordPress will look for when serving a single post. If it doesn't find `single.php`, it'll use `index.php`.

Without further delay, here's my `single.php` file. You should notice that the file features almost exactly the same elements as `index.php`. The only difference is that the `get_template_part()` function call fetches a different element. In this case, it's `single`, as demonstrated in the following code:

```php
<?php get_header(); ?>

  <div id="primary" class="content-area">
    <main id="main" class="site-main" role="main">

    <?php while (have_posts()) : the_post(); ?>

      <?php get_template_part('content', 'single'); ?>

      <?php daily_cooking_custom_post_nav(); ?>

      <?php
      if (comments_open() || get_comments_number())
        comments_template();
      ?>

    <?php endwhile; // end of the loop. ?>

    </main><! -  #main  - >
  </div><! -  #primary  - >

<?php get_sidebar(); ?>
<?php get_footer(); ?>
```

The aforementioned `get_template_part('content', 'single')` call will fetch the `content-single.php` file. Here's what the file looks like:

```php
<article id="post-<?php the_ID(); ?>" <?php post_class(); ?>>
  <header class="entry-header">
    <?php the_title('<h1 class="entry-title">', '</h1>'); ?>

    <div class="entry-meta">
      <?php daily_cooking_custom_posted_on(); ?>
    </div>
  </header>

  <div class="entry-content">
    <?php the_content(); ?>
    <?php
      wp_link_pages( array(
        'before' => '<div class="page-links">' . __( 'Pages:',
        'daily-cooking-custom' ),
```

```
          'after'  => '</div>',
       ) );
     ?>
   </div>

   <footer class="entry-footer">
     <?php daily_cooking_custom_entry_footer(); ?>
   </footer>
</article><! -  #post-##  - >
```

This file's structure is almost exactly the same as the one we discussed a couple of pages ago—content.php. The following are three specific things that are worth pointing out:

- The presence of the `<article>` tag. The individual post's content is displayed inside this tag.
- The call to the `the_content()` function. This time, we're displaying the whole content of the post, not just an excerpt.
- The call to the `comments_template()` function in `single.php`. This displays the comment form and the individual comments that have been submitted for this post.

 These versions of the `single.php` file and the `content-single.php` file are available in the code bundle for this chapter, inside a sub-directory called `phase 4`.

Page template

The last template we're going to create is for the static page view. On my food blog site, this would be the sample page, for example. The easiest way to go about this is to start with the `single.php` file this time. So, just make a copy of that file and rename it `page.php`. Now, we'll be simplifying the file, so that only the essential information about a given page is displayed. In the end, my `page.php` file will look like the following:

```php
<?php get_header(); ?>

  <div id="primary" class="content-area">
  <main id="main" class="site-main" role="main">

    <?php while (have_posts()) : the_post(); ?>

      <?php get_template_part('content', 'page'); ?>
```

```
        <?php endwhile; // end of the loop. ?>

    </main><! - #main - >
    </div><! - #primary - >

<?php get_sidebar(); ?>
<?php get_footer(); ?>
```

I made just a few modifications here. They are as follows:

- I changed the last parameter of the `get_template_part()` function to `page`, instead of `single`.
- I erased the call to `daily_cooking_custom_post_nav()`, which handled the display of post navigation.
- I erased the whole block of code that handled the comments. We don't need those on pages.

Next, we need a custom `content-page.php` file. The easiest way to build this is to make a copy of the `content-single.php` file and tune it up a bit. Here's my final `content-page.php` file:

```
<article id="post-<?php the_ID(); ?>" <?php post_class(); ?>>
    <header class="entry-header">
        <?php the_title('<h1 class="entry-title">', '</h1>'); ?>
    </header>

    <div class="entry-content">
        <?php the_content(); ?>
        <?php
            wp_link_pages(array(
                'before' => '<div class="page-links">' . __( 'Pages:',
                'daily-cooking-custom' ),
                'after'  => '</div>',
            ));
        ?>
    </div>

    <footer class="entry-footer">
    </footer>
</article><! - #post-## - >
```

Here's what I did here in terms of simplifying the file:

- I got rid of the whole code displaying metadata.
- I erased the entry footer, which was meant to display categories and tags. We don't use those with WordPress pages.

Now, my sample page looks much cleaner, as can be seen in the following screenshot:

These versions of the `page.php` file and the `content-page.php` file are available in the code bundle for this chapter, inside a sub-directory called `phase 4`.

Generated classes for body and post

As you're modifying your theme to accommodate different types of pages, you should also know about the CSS classes that WordPress will put into your theme. If you look carefully at the code we've been using, you'll see these two functions:

- `body_class()`: For example, in the `header.php` file, the exact line is `<body <?php body_class(); ?>>`
- `post_class()`: For example, in the `content-page.php` file, the exact line is `<article id="post-<?php the_ID(); ?>" <?php post_class(); ?>>`.

The `body_class()` function adds a whole bunch of classes to the body tag, depending on the page you're viewing. For example, the main page of my site has the following classes in the body:

```
<body class=" home blog custom-background">
```

My **Some Spanish Dishes** single post page's body tag looks like the following:

```
<body class=" single single-post postid-41 single-format-standard custom-
background">
```

If I wanted to style anything differently on any of my pages, I could do it largely via CSS, without having to create another template.

The `post_class()` function does something similar with the individual post's `div`, giving it different classes depending on the characteristics of the post itself. For example, my **Some Spanish Dishes** post's tag has the following class:

```
<article id="post-41" class="post-41 post type-post status-publish
format-standard hentry category-uncategorized">
```

Further more, my sample page post tag has the following class:

```
<article id="post-2" class="post-2 page type-page status-publish hentry">
```

Using these classes in my style sheet, I could style each post differently depending on its category, tag, post type, and so on. Keep this in mind as you design your theme. This becomes extremely important when working with theme frameworks further down the road. Although modifications inside PHP files are allowed, most of the time, you can customize the design of your whole site just by working in the CSS and tweaking various classes (both the native ones in WordPress and the new ones that the framework uses). Situations where a whole new site working on a theme framework gets built purely in CSS files are not uncommon.

Other WordPress templates

In addition to `archive.php`, `single.php`, and `page.php`, there are a number of other standard template files that WordPress looks for before using `index.php` for particular views. We're not going to create these files here, but you should feel free to experiment on your own WordPress installation. To learn about the complete file hierarchy for WordPress themes, feel free to visit `https://www.codeinwp.com/blog/wordpress-theme-heirarchy/`. There's a great graph there that presents the hierarchy visually. It's very easy to follow and does a much better job at explaining this than I would do here with word alone. In addition, when you browse the official code bundle for this chapter, you'll see that many additional files have been created and are actually available inside the bundle. We cover them here, however, as it would probably be too much information at this point.

Learning more
You can also find a detailed flowchart of the template hierarchy at
`https://developer.wordpress.org/themes/basics/template-hierarchy/.`

In this chapter, we've experimented with the uses of quite a number of WordPress template tags. In `Chapter 13`, *Creating a Non-Blog Website Part Two – E-Commerce Websites and Custom Content Elements,* I list more of the most useful template tags.

Next, we'll explore making custom templates for pages.

Creating and using a custom page template

WordPress allows you to create custom templates. These can only be used for pages (not for posts). A custom template allows you to display content differently and to easily use built-in WordPress functions within a template.

Just to give you a good example of what custom page templates are and how they can benefit your site (no matter what theme you're using), let's create a custom version of the archives template. This is also what we will use to create a custom archives page that should be much more useful to our readers than the standard one. The following screenshot shows what the **ARCHIVES** page looks like on my blog right now:

There are just a couple of small links in the sidebar that redirect visitors to a standard monthly archive. Of course, later on, when there are more posts on your site, there will be many more links shown (exactly one link for each month of your site's existence).

Now, as far as the idea of *archives* goes, I have to admit, somewhat reluctantly, that WordPress has never been good at this. One of the few problems with the platform as a web publishing solution is the fact that posts usually have very short life spans. Whenever you publish a post, it sits on the front page for a while, and then it vanishes in the archives, never to be seen again, irrespective of whether it's still relevant or not. In the end, it's really hard for a new visitor to find these old posts on your site.

One of the few chances you have of reviving those old posts is mastering the art of SEO, and driving some new traffic to your old posts through your SEO efforts alone (this the most popular solution). But luckily, it's not the only way to fix this issue. Again, custom page templates are an interesting remedy here.

In the preceding screenshot, you can see that the default version of the archives is just a sidebar widget with some links to individual months. The problem with such content organization is that it provides a rather bad user experience. Archives, in general, are not about listing everything in one place; they are about providing a hub where the visitor can go and find a specific piece of content. For example, think about how archives work in your local library. This is what you want to eventually have on your site as well. So, what we're going to do here is say *no* to the traditional archives template in WordPress and create a custom page template to handle archives manually. Then, we're going to link to this archive from one of the menus. Here's how to do it.

On our new archives page, we want to achieve the following things:

- **Display a piece of custom text**: For instance, as a form of introduction or a notification message explaining what's in the archives.
- **Display a categories archive**: This is a list of all of the categories in use on the site.
- **Display a tag cloud**: This is a form of tag archive where all of the tags in use on the site are displayed one after the other (inline, not in a list format), and the font size increases for the tags that have been used more often than others.
- Display a list of the 15 latest posts, or whatever other number you wish.
- **Display a monthly archives block**: The fact that it's displayed at the bottom is not accidental, as this block is not particularly useful for a typical visitor.

To do this, we need to create a template. The following demonstrates the steps that we'll take:

1. Create the template file. Make a copy of `page.php` and give it a new name. I like to prepend all of my custom template files with `tmpl_`, so that they are sorted separately from all of the WordPress template files that I will create. I'll name this file `tmpl_archives.php`. In order for WordPress to be able to identify this file as a template file, we need to add a specially styled comment to the top of the page (just as we did with `style.css`). The comment needs to be formatted as follows:

```php
<?php
/* Template Name: Blog Archives Custom */
?>
```

In the `wp-admin` panel, the template will be identified by this template name, so make sure the name signals to you what the template is used for.

2. Add WordPress functions. This is a crucial part of the process, but thankfully not a complicated one at this stage. Look over your new template file and find the occurrence of this line:

```php
<?php get_template_part('content', 'page'); ?>
```

3. Now, erase it and put the following code in its place:

```php
<?php get_template_part('content', 'tmpl_archives'); ?>
```

This is the result we're after; the middle part of your `tmpl_archives.php` file should now look like the following:

```php
<?php while (have_posts()) : the_post(); ?>
<?php get_template_part( 'content', 'tmpl_archives' ); ?>
<?php endwhile; // end of the loop. ?>
```

4. Next, create a completely new file called `content-tmpl_archives.php` and add the following code:

```php
<article id="post-<?php the_ID(); ?>" <?php post_class(); ?>>
  <header class="entry-header">
    <?php the_title('<h1 class="entry-title">', '</h1>'); ?>
  </header>

  <div class="entry-content">
    <?php the_content(); ?>

    <div style="float: left; width: 50%;">
      <h2>Categories</h2>
      <ul>
      <?php wp_list_categories('orderby=name&title_li='); ?>
      </ul>
    </div>
    <div style="float: left; width: 50%;">
      <h2>Tags</h2>
      <?php wp_tag_cloud('smallest=8&largest=20'); ?>
    </div>
    <div style="clear: both;"></div><! - clears float - >

    <?php
    $how_many_last_posts = 15;
    echo '<h2>Last '.$how_many_last_posts.' Posts</h2>';
    $my_query = new WP_Query('post_type=post&nopaging=1');
```

```
        if($my_query->have_posts()) {
          echo '<ul>';
          $counter = 1;
          while($my_query->have_posts() &&
            $counter<=$how_many_last_posts)
          {
            $my_query->the_post();?>
            <li><a href="<?php the_permalink() ?>"
              rel="bookmark" title="Permanent Link to <?php
              the_title_attribute(); ?>"><?php the_title();
              ?></a></li>
            <?php
            $counter++;
          }
          echo '</ul>';
          wp_reset_postdata();
        }
        ?>

        <h2>By Month</h2>
          <p><?php wp_get_archives('type=monthly&
            format=custom&after= |');
          ?></p>
      </div>

      <footer class="entry-footer">
      </footer>
    </article><! -  #post-##  - >
```

The code includes some additional functionality for our new archives template. In fact, because we are creating a custom template, we can add any of the WordPress functions we discovered earlier in the chapter, as well as any other WordPress function in existence (see Chapter 13, *Creating a Non-Blog Website Part Two – E-Commerce Websites and Custom Content Elements*).

Here are some of the more interesting parts of the code, starting with the following:

```
<div style="float: left; width: 50%;">
  <h2>Categories</h2>
  <ul>
  <?php wp_list_categories('orderby=name'); ?>
  </ul>
</div>
```

It's about adding a complete list of categories that are present on the site. The `div` elements are responsible for displaying this block on the left-hand side and allowing the next block, tags, to be placed next to it (it's a more effective way of achieving such an effect than using HTML tables, because it's a more cross-device-friendly approach).

The next part of the code is the following:

```
<div style="float: left; width: 50%;">
  <h2>Tags</h2>
  <?php wp_tag_cloud('smallest=8&largest=20'); ?>
</div>
<div style="clear: both;"></div><! - clears float - >
```

It has a very similar purpose, only this time we're displaying the aforementioned tag cloud. The last `div` element visible here is meant to clear the `float` parameter used in the previous `div` elements.

Next, we have the part responsible for displaying the latest posts, as follows:

```
<?php
$how_many_last_posts = 15;
echo '<h2>Last '.$how_many_last_posts.' Posts</h2>';
$my_query = new WP_Query('post_type=post&nopaging=1');
if($my_query->have_posts()) {
  echo '<ul>';
  $counter = 1;
  while($my_query->have_posts() && $counter<=$how_many_last_posts) {
    $my_query->the_post();
    ?>
    <li><a href="<?php the_permalink() ?>" rel="bookmark"
      title="Permanent Link to <?php the_title_attribute();
      ?>"><?php the_title(); ?></a></li>
    <?php
    $counter++;
  }
  echo '</ul>';
  wp_reset_postdata();
}
?>
```

Currently, the code displays the 15 latest posts, but this can be adjusted if you just change the value of the `$how_many_last_posts` variable.

Finally, there's the block that displays a traditional monthly archive, where every month is represented as a standard link, as follows:

```
<h2>By Month</h2>
<p><?php wp_get_archives('type=monthly&format=custom&after=
   |'); ?></p>
```

At this point, you can save the file and proceed to the next step, which is to apply the template to a page.

Leave your HTML editor and log into your `wp-admin`. You need to create the page in which you want to use this template. In my case, I'll name my new page **Archives**, to make its purpose clear. While working on the page, switch to the **Document** tab and scroll down to the **Page Attributes** section. This is where you'll find the **Template** setting, as demonstrated in the following screenshot:

Change it from **Default template** to **Blog Archives Custom** and save the draft or publish it right away. Now, in order to see the page somewhere, you have to add it to one of the menus. We already covered menus in `Chapter 4`, *Pages, Media, and Importing/Exporting Content*, so I'm sure you can get it done quickly. Once you have this handled, you can return to the frontend of your website and click on the **Archives** page. However, because your site is not that content-heavy at this point, you won't get a staggering effect, but there'll still be a nice presentation of the most recent posts, as shown in the following screenshot:

There is no limit to the number of custom templates that you can make for your WordPress theme.

 These versions of the `tmpl_archives.php` file and the `content-tmpl_archives.php` file are available in the code bundle for this chapter, inside a sub-directory called `phase 5`.

Making your theme widget-friendly

If you want to be able to use widgets in your theme, you will need to make your theme widget-friendly (also known as *widgetizing* your theme). Widgetizing is actually pretty easy, and to be honest with you, we already took care of that when constructing our sidebar. Let's now go back to this and explain how widgetizing works.

Going back to our sidebar

Back in the old days, it was very common for a WordPress site to use statically placed content blocks in the sidebar. In other words, the only way to place dynamic content in the sidebar of our sites was to use handmade code that would fetch whatever data we wanted and then display it. This solution wasn't very usable for everyday users who might not be familiar with the PHP source code. A better solution needed to be found. Hence, widgets.

Widgets give us the ability to set the sidebars in a way so that they fetch the data that's been set in **Appearance** | **Widgets**. Therefore, the only thing the user has to do is go to **Appearance** | **Widgets** and pick whatever content they want to feature in the sidebar (or any other widget area for that matter; it could be in the footer as well).

Just to give you an example of old versus new, here's what a standard piece of code might look like that handles displaying blog archives the old way (this can be placed in sidebar.php):

```
<div id="secondary" class="widget-area" role="complementary">
  <aside>
    <h1>Archives</h1>
    <ul>
      <?php wp_get_archives(); ?>
    </ul>
  </aside>
</div><! -  #secondary  - >
```

However, this code is not customizable in any way, so a much better solution to display the archives is to use the code that we already have in our `sidebar.php`, which is as follows:

```
<div id="secondary" class="widget-area" role="complementary">
  <?php if(is_active_sidebar('sidebar-1')) dynamic_sidebar(
    'sidebar-1' ); ?>
</div><! -  #secondary  - >
```

Then, just assign a new **Archives** widget to this sidebar in the **Appearance** | **Widgets** section of `wp-admin`.

Working with the functions.php file

Let's examine how all this actually works. As I said earlier, the `functions.php` file can contain many different elements, so now, it's about time to focus on how to enable dynamic sidebars, also known as widgets. In the `functions.php` file, we can place the following code:

```
function daily_cooking_custom_widgets_init() {
  register_sidebar(array(
    'name'          => __('Sidebar', 'daily-cooking-custom'),
    'id'            => 'sidebar-1',
    'description'   => '',
    'before_widget' => '<aside id="%1$s" class="widget %2$s">',
    'after_widget'  => '</aside>',
    'before_title'  => '<h1 class="widget-title">',
    'after_title'   => '</h1>',
  ));
}
add_action('widgets_init', 'daily_cooking_custom_widgets_init');
```

In this code, I'm using one new function to register a new widget area. As you can see, the widget area is simply called `Sidebar` (the `name` parameter).

Now, the final `add_action('widgets_init',`
`'daily_cooking_custom_widgets_init')`
function call is what actually registers the widget areas (it's the most important line of code here; it lets WordPress know when to enable the widget areas).

Adding some widgets

At this point, your theme is ready for widgets! You can now go to `wp-admin`, navigate to **Appearance | Widgets**, and add widgets. For example, as you can see in the following screenshot, I've added four widgets to one of the widget areas:

Be sure to click on **Save**, and then return to your website and reload the page. The default items you placed in the sidebar will have been replaced with widgets, as shown in the following screenshot:

Additional widgetizing options

What we've just covered is the simplest way to widgetize a theme. There are actually a lot of other possibilities that you could utilize when adding the code to your `sidebar.php` and `functions.php` files. For example, there are options that allow you to do the following:

- Widgetize more than one sidebar, giving each a name
- Widgetize a part of your sidebar, but leave in some default items
- Widgetize the footer
- Customize the search form widget, and much more

Learning more

To learn about the variety of options available and how to take advantage of them, take a look at the following resource in the Codex: `https://codex.wordpress.org/Widgetizing_Themes`.

Enabling a menu in your theme

The good news I have for you right now is that menus are already enabled in the structure of the theme we're creating here. Because we used the `wp_nav_menu()` function in the header of the site (in the `header.php` file), if the user creates a menu in **Appearance** | **Menus**, and then assigns it to the area indicated as **Primary Menu**, it will show up on the site, as demonstrated in the following screenshot:

Menu Settings

Auto add pages	☐ Automatically add new top-level pages to this menu
Display location	☑ Primary Menu

If you want to have more than one navigation menu in your theme, you can register multiple navigation menu locations, let the user create multiple menus, and choose which menu goes in which location. To learn more about this, check out the Codex at `https://codex.wordpress.org/Navigation_Menus`.

Learning more

The wp_nav_menu() function is quite powerful, and can take a number of parameters that will let you control the classes and IDs, the name of the menu, and more. Take a look here: https://developer.wordpress.org/ reference/functions/wp_nav_menu/.

Making your theme editable in the WordPress Customizer

WordPress Customizer is a relatively recent addition to the WordPress ecosystem. In short, it's a framework meant for live-previewing any changes that the user makes to their website. The Customizer's interface allows for the modification of various aspects of a theme's and website's appearance, starting from the name of the site, the tagline, all the way to the colors used, layouts, widgets, menus, and more. We talked about the Customizer from the user's point of view back in Chapter 8, *Customizing Your Website Appearance/Design*.

Now, from a developer's perspective, when you're building your WordPress theme, there are a couple of things that you should do in order to make it compatible with the Customizer. Luckily, the starter theme that we're using in this chapter as the foundation of our theme, the **_S** theme, already comes with some basic Customizer integrations. Let's go over them one by one, and at the same time, see how we can expand our theme's functionality further.

First, let's look at the following line of code. It should be placed at the end of your functions.php file:

```
require get_template_directory() . '/inc/customizer.php';
```

This definition simply includes an additional file that takes care of the Customizer integration itself. Even though we could do everything right in the functions.php file, having the Customizer handled in a separate file makes for a theme structure that's easier to grasp.

That new `customizer.php` file is where we're going to add all of our new code. The core of the Customizer integration is done via the `customize_register` hook. It allows us to define new Customizer panels, sections (the main elements of navigation within the Customizer), settings (the data that our theme can accept), and controls (the visual UI elements that allow us to tweak our settings).

In order to register all of our new Customizer elements, we can use the following function:

```
function daily_cooking_custom_customize_register( $wp_customize )
{ /* */ }
add_action( 'customize_register', 'daily_cooking_custom_customize_register'
);
```

Within this function is where creating new sections, settings, and controls is done. However, as you'll notice, we already have this function in the `customizer.php` file created. This is, again, a result of building our theme on top of the _**S** starter theme. We've opted for this approach since it allows us to get started with theme development a lot quicker than building things from scratch.

Our current `daily_cooking_custom_customize_register()` function already features the following lines:

```
$wp_customize->get_setting( 'blogname' )->transport = 'postMessage';
$wp_customize->get_setting( 'blogdescription' )->transport = 'postMessage';
```

This code capitalizes on some Customizer abilities that are available for WordPress themes by default. Namely, those two enable us to modify the title and blog description.

Now it's time to add something new to the Customizer. Firstly, adding a new section is very simple. Let's start by including the following function call inside our main `daily_cooking_custom_customize_register()` function:

```
$wp_customize->add_section();
```

The function can take two arguments—the first one is the identifier for your new section, and the other is an array of additional options. Here's what we're going to do:

```
$wp_customize->add_section( 'menu_bar_colors' , array(
  'title' => 'Menu Bar Colors',
  'priority' => 30) );
```

This creates a new section titled `Menu Bar Colors` and identified by `menu_bar_colors`. Now, let's add a new setting. Settings provide a way to communicate with WordPress and let it know that we're using a value that the user can modify. New settings can be added via the `$wp_customize->add_setting()` function call. We can handle this as follows (as you can see, I'm adding not one, but two new *settings*):

```
$wp_customize->add_setting( 'menu_bar_color1' , array(
  'default' => '#69CACA') );
$wp_customize->add_setting( 'menu_bar_color2' , array(
  'default' => '#279090') );
```

Once the settings are in place, the last elements of the puzzle are some new controls. Controls tie the two together; they let WordPress know which sections work with which settings. This is done via the `$wp_customize->add_control()` function call, as follows:

```
$wp_customize->add_control( new WP_Customize_Color_Control( $wp_customize,
'menu_bar_color1', array(
  'label' => 'Menu Bar Color 1',
  'section' => 'menu_bar_colors',
  'settings' => 'menu_bar_color1') ) );
$wp_customize->add_control( new WP_Customize_Color_Control( $wp_customize,
'menu_bar_color2', array(
  'label' => 'Menu Bar Color 2',
  'section' => 'menu_bar_colors',
  'settings' => 'menu_bar_color2') ) );
```

As you can see, each of our settings gets its own *control*. At this stage, when you save the file and go to the Customizer from the WordPress dashboard (**Appearance** | **Customize**), you'll see the new section in the sidebar. Inside it, you'll also see that the elements are all operational. Although, they don't have much impact on the appearance of the theme yet. We'll handle that next. Take a look at the following screenshot:

The first thing we need to do now is alter the CSS of the theme based on what the user has set in the Customizer. To make that happen, let's add the following code at the end of the `customizer.php` file:

```
function daily_cooking_customizer_menu_css()
{
  ?>
  <style type="text/css">
  .site-header .site-branding { background: <?php echo
    get_theme_mod('menu_bar_color1', '#69CACA'); ?>; }
  .main-navigation ul li { border-bottom: 1px solid <?php echo
    get_theme_mod('menu_bar_color1', '#69CACA'); ?>; }
  .site-header { background: <?php echo
    get_theme_mod('menu_bar_color2',
    '#279090'); ?>; }
  </style>
  <?php
}
add_action( 'wp_head', 'daily_cooking_customizer_menu_css');
```

This new function hooks up to `wp_head` and alters the CSS of the website. The most important instructions in it are those three inline PHP echo blocks. Here's one of them:

```
echo get_theme_mod('menu_bar_color1', '#69CACA');
```

The `get_theme_mod()` function allows you to grab the current theme's settings and indicate the name of the specific setting that you need in the first parameter (the second one is the default value). When you save your file now, the new color selection options should be fully enabled. Refer to the following screenshot:

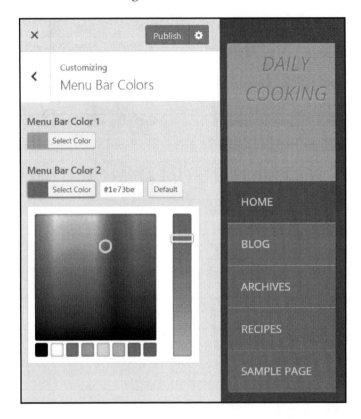

We have only scratched the surface here in terms of what's possible in the Customizer, but it's still given you a good overview, and has also proven that the Customizer is actually a very developer-friendly environment to work in. Always try putting as many of your theme's settings as possible in the Customizer module; the end user will thank you for it!

If you want to learn more about how to work with the Customizer and uncover some of its other features (such as working with JS files for dynamic live previews, for example), then don't hesitate to visit either of these resources:
`https://codex.wordpress.org/Theme_Customization_API` and `https://developer.wordpress.org/themes/customize-api/`.

Creating a child theme

If you've found an existing theme or theme framework that you like, and you just want to adjust it a bit to fit your requirements perfectly, you can create a child theme on top of it. A child theme uses a parent theme as a starting point and, without changing the theme itself, alters just the bits you *want to* alter.

As a matter of fact, using child themes is the recommended way of making modifications to any theme. The rule of thumb is simple—if you want to change anything at all about a stock theme (either inside the source code, graphics, or template files), do it through a new child theme.

In plain English, a child theme inherits the functionality and features of the parent theme. The biggest value of creating child themes is that you can introduce any bells and whistles you wish without altering the structure of the parent theme. I know that this sounds like some additional work, because if you just want to change a couple of lines of code, then it's always going to be quicker to do it directly within the theme. However, taking the longer *child theme* route has its benefits, such as the following:

- The main benefit is that if you were to modify the original theme directly, all your modifications would vanish the minute you updated the theme. However, if you're using child themes, you can take full advantage of any updates that the original theme's authors release. Let me say this again: preserving your modifications after performing a theme update is impossible unless you're using a child theme.
- You have a very clear view of the modifications that you've introduced into your theme. Basically, every new thing that you implement through a child theme has to be placed in a new file, so even when you come back to review your child theme after a while, you can still easily identify every piece of your work.

- The final benefit—actually, there's probably a lot more of them—is that it's very easy to revert any modification you've introduced through a child theme. In short, if something is causing any serious problems and you have to fix your site quickly, then you can simply delete the files responsible. If you were modifying your original theme directly, going through every file individually would surely take more time and would make any sort of quick recovery very difficult to achieve.

Let's take a quick look at how to make a child theme.

Creating the new theme directory

Just to make things easier to understand here, we'll take the theme that we've been creating in this chapter and build a child theme for it. The starting point is really simple. Create a new directory in `wp-content/themes/` and name it `daily-cooking-child`.

Creating the style sheet

The only file you need to start with in this directory is the style sheet (`style.css`). The style sheet needs the usual header, plus a new line, as follows:

```
/*
Theme Name: Daily Cooking Child Theme
Description: Child theme for the Daily Cooking Custom theme.
Theme URI: http://nio.tips/
Author: Karol K
Author URI: http://karol.cc/
Template: daily-cooking-custom
*/
```

The key line in this preceding code is `Template: daily-cooking-custom`. This instructs WordPress that your new theme is a child theme of `daily-cooking-custom`. Just to emphasize, that one line is really crucial. Then, to make your child theme start out with the CSS from the parent theme, add the following code after the comment:

```
@import url("../daily-cooking-custom/style.css");
```

If you don't use the preceding line, your child theme will begin its existence on a blank style sheet. In most cases, this is not a desirable scenario.

Using your child theme

That's it! Your new theme now shows up on the **Appearance** page, as shown in the following screenshot:

Granted, the theme is not really useful at this point, but it does exist and you can use it as the base for further modifications. By default, it will use all of the main theme's styles, template files, functions, and everything else. If you activate it, it will present your site as if you were using your main theme.

If you want to change anything, do so in your child theme's directory. You will override the main theme's original template file if you create a new template file (for example, `single.php`, `index.php`, and `archive.php`). The `functions.php` file works a little differently, however. If you create a new `functions.php` file, it will be executed in addition to the main theme's original `functions.php` file. In fact, your new file will be loaded first, right before the original one. If you want to override a specific function in the original `functions.php` file, just create a function with the same name. You can also create completely new functions that are not present in the parent theme.

Like I said, every other template file you create inside the child theme (such as, `page.php` and `single.php`) will override its namesake, so it's the perfect method to include a new, slightly different design or some new features. Apart from replacing the existing template files, you can add new ones that are not present in the parent (including custom page templates).

In the end, the whole topic of child themes is quite an easy one to grasp once you spend a little time trying out different things, and checking how your site reacts to the elements you include in the child theme.

Learning more
The WordPress Codex has a page devoted to learning about child themes, at https://codex.wordpress.org/Child_Themes.

Sharing your theme

If you want to turn your template into a package that other people can use, you just have to take the following steps:

1. Make sure you have the rights to redistribute images, icons, photos, and so on, that you've included in your theme.
2. Remove all unnecessary files from your theme's directory. Be sure you don't have backup versions or old copies of any of your files. If you do delete any file, be sure to test your theme to ensure you didn't accidentally delete something important.
3. Make sure the comment at the top of the style.css file is complete and accurate.
4. Create a Readme.txt file. This is a good place to let future users know which version of WordPress your theme is compatible with, and whether it has any special features or requirements.
5. Zip the directory and post your theme's ZIP file on your own website for people to download, or submit it directly to the WordPress **Theme Directory** at https://wordpress.org/themes/. Keep in mind, though, that the review process there tends to take a while. So be ready for a 3-6 month wait before you see your theme online.

Even though the preceding looks like a standard step-by-step process, it's actually nothing like it. To be honest, your theme has to be a really high quality one if it's to be allowed into the directory. Every theme undergoes a human review, which often results in themes not passing. In that case, you just have to make the requested changes, resubmit your work, and keep trying until you get in.

Then, there's also the issue of licensing. By default, WordPress is available under the **GNU General Public License (GPL)**. In plain English, this means that WordPress (the platform) is free, and every derivative work that is built on top of it has to be filed under GPL too—this includes themes. In short, every piece of PHP code you find inside WordPress, various themes, or plugins is GPL (that includes premium themes and plugins). When it comes to artwork and CSS, GPL might not apply. If you want to learn more about the GPL licensing, it's best if you go straight to the official documentation at `https://wordpress.org/news/2009/07/themes-are-gpl-too/`.

Now, apart from the official directory, you can share your theme through other channels. First of all, you have to decide whether you want your theme to be available for free or not. In the case of the former, you can reach out to some popular blogs about WordPress and WordPress design, and simply let them know that you have a theme that you'd like to share. Most of the time (if the theme looks attractive), they will have no problem notifying their community that there's a cool new free theme.

If you want to make your theme a premium one, you can go to **ThemeForest** (`https://themeforest.net/`) and try submitting it there. The only challenge is that your theme must really be a high quality one.

I'm not forcing you to share your theme with the community right away, but once you build some expertise and build your themes to be really cool and useful, you really should reach out to people and share your work. Finally, if you're interested in making an impact in the community, consider launching a website dedicated to it. This website would be a place where you could publish a demo version, deliver some documentation, and provide support forums and other things to deliver a great user experience.

 The final versions of all of the theme files (including the child theme) are available in the code bundle for this chapter, inside a sub-directory called `final`.

Summary

You have now crossed to the other side of the WordPress themes world—you have learned how to make your own theme. With just basic HTML and CSS code, you can create a design and turn it into a fully functional WordPress theme.

In this chapter, we looked at how to turn your HTML build into a basic theme, creating WordPress templates to influence the display of a variety of views on your site, creating custom templates to be applied to pages within your site, making your new theme widget-ready, creating a child theme, making a theme compatible with the WordPress Customizer, and share your theme with everyone in the WordPress community.

In the next chapter, we'll discuss social media integration, podcasting, and HTTPS (Hypertext Transfer Protocol Secure). This information will allow you to expand your blogging habits, and make your work more diverse and more noticeable on the web.

10
Social Media Integration, Podcasting, and HTTPS

Social media has grown a lot in importance over the last few years. Basically, if you don't have your profile on at least a couple of the most popular social networks, then you might as well not exist at all, right? Well, no matter if you agree with this or not, it certainly rings true for your website. In other words, if you hope to attract any kind of audience and somehow convince them to keep coming back to your website, you absolutely have to (*have to!*) integrate it with social media.

Luckily, WordPress lets you do this in a more or less easy-to-grasp way. Even though social media integration is not a built-in feature per se, it can still be enabled via different plugins or other mechanisms. In this chapter, you will learn all about these features. We'll cover things such as how to enable simple social media share buttons on your website, how to work with social media APIs and integrations, and how to publish your blog content to social media automatically.

But wait, that's not all! We're also going to cover podcasting (which, for some website owners is an important element of their online presence), and a relatively new topic in the WordPress realm—**HTTPS (Hypertext Transfer Protocol Secure)**, which is all about making your website more secure by adding an additional level of encryption to the browser-website communication. An important thing worth pointing out here is that Google now expects all websites to have HTTPS encryption enabled. If your website fails to comply, Google might decide to lower your search engine rankings, and thus make your website less visible compared to your competition.

In short, the topics we will explore in this chapter include the following:

- Integrating social media
- Podcasting
- HTTPS—what, why, and how?

Integrating social media

We've briefly mentioned the topic of social media integration in Chapter 5, *Plugins – What They Are and Why You Need Them,* when discussing the plugins that are worth having on your WordPress site. So now, let's take a moment to expand on this and list some more ways in which you can make your website social-media friendly, as well as understand why you'd want to do this in the first place.

Let's start with the *why*. In this day and age, social media is one of the main drivers of traffic for many websites. Even if you just want to share your content with friends and family, or you have some serious business plans regarding your website, you need to have at least some level of social media integration.

Even if you only install simple social media share buttons, you are effectively encouraging your visitors to pass your content onto their followers, thus expanding your reach and making your content more popular.

Making your blog social media friendly

There are a handful of ways to make your website social media friendly. The most common approaches are as follows:

- Setting up social media share buttons, which allows your visitors to share your content with their friends and followers
- Setting up social media APIs integration, which make your content look better on social media (design-wise)
- Setting up automatic content distribution to social media
- Setting up social media metrics tracking

Let's discuss these one by one.

Setting up social media share buttons

This is something we talked about in Chapter 5, *Plugins - What They Are and Why You Need Them,* when discussing plugins. There are hundreds of social media plugins available out there that allow you to display a basic set of social media buttons on your website. The one we advise you to use is called **Simple Social Media Share Buttons** (this plugin is available at https://wordpress.org/plugins/simple-social-buttons/). Its main advantage is that it allows you to display buttons for all of the most popular social media networks, and you can also choose where and how you want these buttons displayed.

You can find a full description, plus a tutorial on how to set everything up, in `Chapter 5, `
Plugins – What They Are and Why You Need Them.

Setting up social media APIs integration

The next step worth taking to make your content appear more attractive on social media is to integrate it with a number of social media APIs; particularly, that of Twitter. What exactly Twitter's API is and how it works isn't very relevant to the WordPress discussion that we're having here. So instead, let's just focus on what the outcome of integrating your website with this API is.

The following screenshot shows what a standard tweet mentioning a website usually looks like (pay attention to the overall design, not the text content itself):

Here's a different tweet, mentioning an article from a website that has Twitter's (Twitter Cards) API enabled:

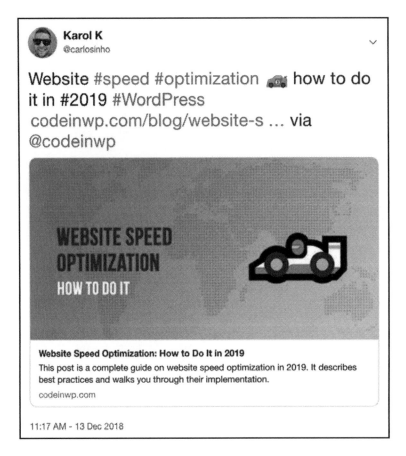

This looks much better. Luckily, having this level of Twitter integration is quite easy. All you need is a plugin called **JM Twitter Cards** (this is available at `https://wordpress.org/plugins/jm-twitter-cards/`). After installing and activating it, you will be guided through the process of setting everything up and approving your website with Twitter (which is a mandatory step).

Setting up automatic content distribution to social media

The idea behind the automatic social media distribution of your content is that you don't have to remember to do so manually whenever you publish a new post. Instead of copying and pasting the URL address of your new post by hand to each individual social media platform, you can have this done automatically.

This can be done in numerous ways, but let's discuss the two most usable ones: the *Jetpack* and *Revive Old Posts* plugins.

The Jetpack plugin

The **Jetpack** plugin is available at `https://wordpress.org/plugins/jetpack/`. We talked about the Jetpack plugin and its many modules in Chapter 5, *Plugins – What They Are and Why You Need Them*. One of these modules can be found by navigating to the **Jetpack** | **Settings** section of `wp-admin`, and then to the **Sharing** tab:

Here, you will be able to enable the feature labeled **Automatically share your posts to social networks** (this is visible in the preceding screenshot).

After doing so, click on the new link that will appear, labeled **Connect your social media accounts**. This will allow you to integrate with the available social media platforms, as demonstrated in the following screenshot:

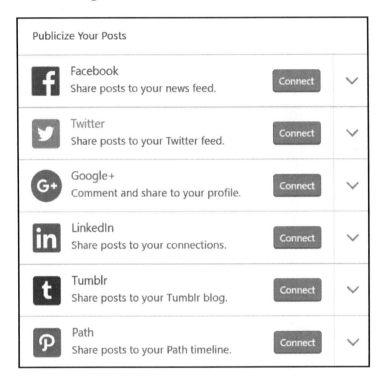

After going through the process of authorizing the plugin with each service, your website will be fully capable of posting each of your new posts to social media automatically.

The Revive Old Posts plugin

The **Revive Old Posts** plugin is available at `https://wordpress.org/plugins/tweet-old-post/`. While the **Jetpack** plugin takes the newest posts on your website and distributes them to your various social media accounts, the **Revive Old Posts** plugin does the same with your archived posts, ultimately giving them a new life—hence the name, **Revive Old Posts**.

After downloading and activating this plugin, go to the **Revive Old Posts** section in `wp-admin`. Then, switch to the **Accounts** tab. Here, you can enable the plugin by adding your social media accounts and authorizing them. The plugin will take you through the steps required to enable everything properly. These individual steps depend on the social media platform that you want to enable and change frequently over time, but you can always count on **Revive Old Posts** to be in tune with the most recent requirements:

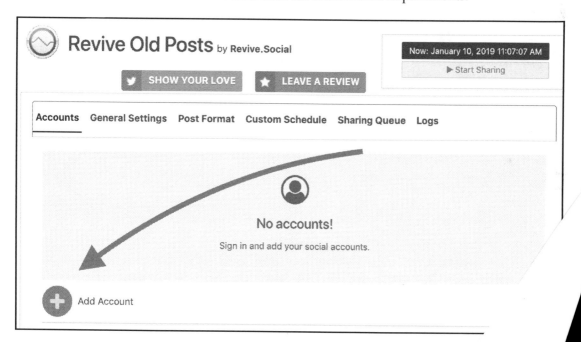

Next, go to the **General Settings** tab and handle the time intervals and other details of how you want the plugin to work with your social media accounts, as demonstrated in the following screenshot. When you're done, just click on the **Save** button:

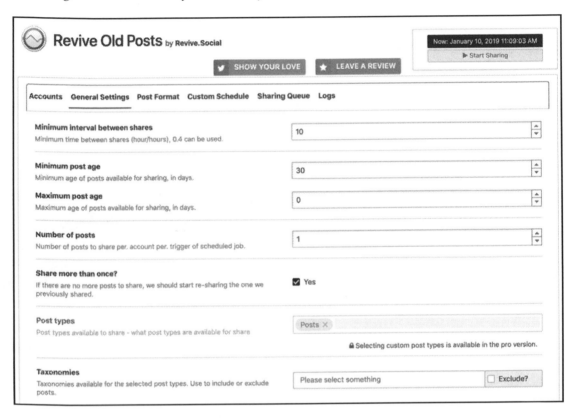

At this point, the plugin will start operating automatically and distribute random archived posts to your social media accounts.

Note that it's probably a good idea to not share things too often if you don't want to anger your followers and make them unfollow you. For that reason, I would advise against posting more than once a day.

Setting up social media metrics tracking

The final element of our social media integration puzzle is to set up some kind of tracking mechanism that will tell us how popular our content is on social media (in terms of shares).

Granted, you can do this manually by going to each of your posts and checking their share numbers individually. However, there's a quicker method, and it involves another plugin. This one is called **Social Metrics Tracker**, and you can download it at `https://wordpress.org/plugins/social-metrics-tracker/`.

In short, this plugin collects social shares data from a number of platforms and displays it to you in a single readable dashboard view. After you install and activate the plugin, you'll need to give it a couple of minutes to crawl through your social media accounts and get the data. Soon after that, you will be able to visit the plugin's dashboard by going to the **Social Metrics** section in `wp-admin`:

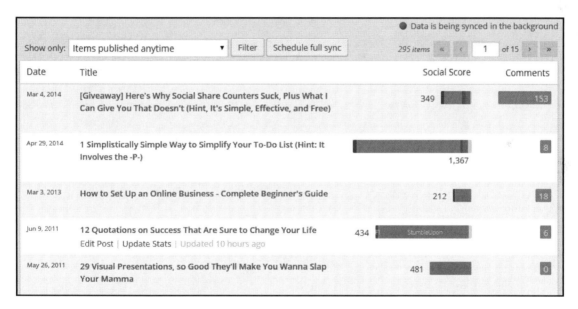

For some web hosts and setups, this plugin might end up consuming too much of the server's resources. If this happens, consider activating it only occasionally to check your results and then deactivate it again. Doing this even once a week will still give you a great overview of how well your content is performing on social media.

This ends our short guide on how to integrate your WordPress site with social media. I'll admit that we're just scratching the surface here, and there's a lot more that can be done. There are new social media plugins being released almost every week, and describing every single one of them would fill a book of its own. That being said, the methods described here are more than enough to make your WordPress site social media friendly and enable you to share your content effectively with your friends, family, and audience.

Podcasting

Podcasting has become very popular in the last couple of years. Right now, there are thousands of podcasts available on the web, touching upon any topic or niche imaginable. Basically, a podcast is like a radio show or program, but run on entirely the internet. Under the hood, however, a podcast is just an audio recording. It can be episodic or serial, depending on your preference and the way you want to make it. The main idea with podcasts is that people can subscribe to them and they are notified whenever a new episode becomes available. Basically, your subscribers, instead of reading your posts on their computers, can listen to your content through their headphones at any time.

Adding a podcast to your WordPress blog is quite easy. From a technical point of view, the *subscription* mechanism of a podcast is handled by **Really Simple Syndication** (**RSS**) feeds. RSS is a web technology that allows you to deliver (or consume) content structured in an XML format. RSS feeds are usually organized with the most recent information at the top. The way WordPress works with RSS feeds by default, is that it enables feeds for your most recent posts, as well as for the most recent comments. Whoever wants to stay up to date with your content can use one of the popular feed aggregators and connect to your website's RSS feed. For example, **Feedly** (`https://feedly.com`) is a popular solution.

Using an RSS feed is also how podcast distribution is handled in WordPress. While generating your blog's RSS feeds, WordPress automatically adds all the required tags if an audio file is linked within that post. These tags are read by podcast clients/tools (such as iTunes). Therefore, all you need to do is create a post, and WordPress will handle the rest for you.

Creating a podcast

For basic podcasting, there are just two steps you need to take, as follows:

- Recording yourself
- Making a post

Let's look at these steps in detail.

Recording yourself

By using any commercial or free software, you can record your voice, a conversation, music, or anything else you'd like to podcast, and then save it as an MP3 file. You may also find that you need to do some editing afterward.

Some examples of good software to consider using are as follows:

- I recommend using **Audacity**, which is a free, cross-platform sound recorder and editor. You can download Audacity from `https://sourceforge.net/projects/audacity/`. You may have to do a bit of extra fiddling around to get the MP3 part working, so pay attention to the additional instructions at that point. If you don't want to learn the basics of audio compression and equalization, you may also want to use a leveling tool, such as the **Levelator**, which can be found at `http://www.conversationsnetwork.org/levelator/`. Although it has not been updated since the end of 2012, it still works well if you want to level the volume in a simple audio file.
- Alternatively, you can use **OBS Studio**, which can be found at `https://obsproject.com/download`. It's another cross-platform solution, it's open source, and some users find it superior to other tools in the market.
- If you are working on macOS and want some free software, take a look at *Garage Band*. It comes with the OS, so it will already be installed on your computer.
- If you want to examine some advanced pieces of audio software, called **Digital Audio Workstations** (**DAWs**), and are used by professional podcast producers and musicians, then look into **Sonar X2**, **Studio One**, **Logic**, or **ProTools**.

To learn more about the basics of audio recording and production for podcasters, and to make your podcasts sound professional, feel free to check the in-depth tutorial at `https://www.hongkiat.com/blog/audio-production-for-podcasters/`.

Making a post

Now that you've created an MP3 file and it's sitting on your computer, you're ready to create a WordPress post that will be the home for the first episode of your podcast. Take a look at the following steps:

1. In `wp-admin`, go to **Posts** | **Add New** like you normally would. Enter some initial text into your post if you want to provide a description for the episode. Also, at this point, add a new category called **Podcast** to your blog.

2. Just so you can learn the basics of including media files, let's upload your media file to your WordPress media library. Later on in this chapter, I will explain why this is not always the most effective approach. However, for now, we're here to learn. Start by adding a new block to the page, called **Audio**. Next, pick an audio file from your desktop and upload it, as shown in the following screenshot:

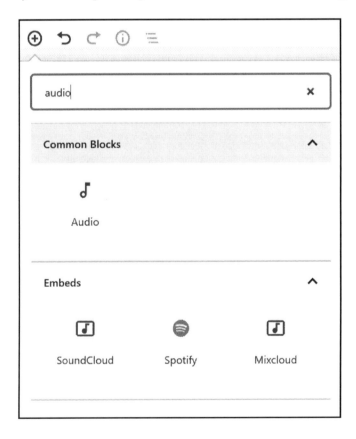

3. When the upload finishes, you'll see your audio file right in the post itself (remember that audio files are bigger than images, so uploading will always take a little longer), as shown in the following screenshot:

My new podcast episode

▶ 0:00 / 1:50 ●━━━━━━━━━━━━━━━━━━━━━ 🔊 ⋮

4. Make any other changes or additions you want, and publish the post.

That's it! Your website's RSS feed can now be used by podcast clients to pick up your podcast. You can use your own podcast client to subscribe right away. If you are using iTunes, navigate to **Advanced | Subscribe to podcast,** and paste the RSS feed URL of the new podcast category you've just set (for example, `http://yoursite.com/category/podcast/feed/`). At this point, you (and your visitors) can enjoy the new podcast that you've just created.

This is just how *you* can add your podcast to *your own* iTunes. If you want to make the podcast searchable via iTunes for the public, you need to go through the submission process, as described at `https://itunespartner.apple.com/en/podcasts/overview`.

Podcasting plugins

You have just learned that it's quite easy to add a podcast to your WordPress website. However, if you want additional features, you may want to use a podcasting plugin. Some additional features could be as follows:

- Automatic feed generation and configurable RSS feeds to optimize your podcast even further for clients, such as iTunes, Google Play, or Stitcher
- A preview of what your podcast will look like in iTunes
- Downloading statistics and tracking the number of listeners you're getting
- New custom post types to handle your podcasts in a more specialized way
- Running multiple podcasts from the same website

- Shortcodes for displaying your podcast episode lists, single episodes, and playlists
- Easy settings to host your episodes on another server

There are quite a number of podcast-related plugins available in the WordPress plugin repository. The three most popular ones are as follows:

- **PowerPress Podcasting plugin by Blubrry** (`https://wordpress.org/plugins/powerpress/`)
- **Seriously Simple Podcasting** (`https://wordpress.org/plugins/seriously-simple-podcasting/`)
- **Podlove Podcast Publisher** (`https://wordpress.org/plugins/podlove-podcasting-plugin-for-wordpress/`)

For an in-depth guide on how to use the PowerPress plugin (which is my favorite one from the preceding list) and how to configure it correctly, watch this 30-minute video tutorial by Pat Flynn at `https://www.youtube.com/watch?v=Ei67QMWD4MA#!`. In this tutorial, you'll learn how to optimize your podcast and set it up properly, so that it can be picked up by iTunes and then shared with the community.

There are hundreds of other similar plugins available. You can find them by looking at all the plugins tagged `podcasting` (`https://wordpress.org/plugins/tags/podcasting`) in the official plugin directory at WordPress.org. Don't forget to read the plugin descriptions and user reviews to decide which of these might be the best match for you.

Using a service to host audio files for free

As I mentioned earlier, the old-school approach of uploading your podcast straight to your blog has its flaws, which doesn't make it the most effective way to handle things these days. First of all, if you want to host the media file on your main server (the one where your website is hosted), you can quickly encounter serious bandwidth problems, especially if your podcast becomes popular. Also, there's a problem with the maximum upload size in WordPress. Depending on your web host, you might not be able to upload files larger than 2 MB, 8 MB, or 16 MB (you can contact your web host's support to clarify this for you). This is what the problem looks like in the uploader:

> **Error** 3. H.I.M - T...nterlude.mp3
>
> 3. H.I.M - The interlude.mp3 exceeds the maximum upload size for
> this site.

Therefore, if you anticipate having a large number of subscribers, or if you plan to produce such a large volume that you'll run out of space on your server, you can use an external hosting service that will host your audio files, either for a fee or free of cost. Some options to consider are as follows:

- **Libsyn**: This company provides effective and affordable podcast hosting. Go to `https://www.libsyn.com/`.
- **Blubrry**: This is another great host for podcasts. What makes their offer particularly interesting is that they integrate with WordPress very well. They even have their own plugin, which I mentioned earlier in this chapter. Go to `https://create.blubrry.com/resources/podcast-media-hosting/`.
- **PodBean**: This company offers free podcast hosting for a period of time. Go to `https://podbean.com/`.

Working with each of the companies mentioned is slightly different. However, the main thing that you always need to do is to upload your media file to your chosen company's servers, rather than to your own media library in WordPress. In return, you'll get a direct URL pointing to your podcast file, which you can then use however you wish. For instance, you can insert the URL into your WordPress post using one of the plugins mentioned earlier.

HTTPS – what, why, and how?

Surprisingly, the story of HTTPS starts somewhere else—it starts with **HTTP (Hypertext Transfer Protocol)**. HTTP is a web protocol, through which information is sent online between the user's web browser and the website they're trying to visit. HTTP defines the structure of this data and the way it's being sent. This topic is highly technical, and we certainly don't need to understand it from top to bottom just for the purpose of what we're discussing in this chapter.

Overall, the current way in which HTTP is implemented doesn't allow for very secure connections. For the most part, with HTTP, data is transmitted in plain text, which means that if someone were to intercept the communication, they would be able to see everything that's being transmitted. Now, this may not seem like much of a problem at first, but imagine what could happen when dealing with sensitive information. For example, when you're submitting your credit card information at an online checkout, you really don't want it to be intercepted by anyone. Unfortunately, HTTP doesn't give you any sort of protection in that area. This is where HTTPS comes into play.

What is HTTPS?

HTTPS, which stands for **Hypertext Transfer Protocol Secure** , is basically an upgraded version of HTTP. Under the hood, the main mechanisms that make it work are kind of the same; but instead of using its own layer protocol for sending data, HTTPS uses additional protocols, secure ones, called a **Secure Sockets Layer (SSL)**, and **Transport Layer Security (TLS)**. SSL encrypts the information that's being sent, which means that even if someone intercepts it, they won't be able to decode it anyway. The true meaning of the data is not visible without the encryption/decryption key.

So, how do you know if a website has HTTPS? Finding this out is very simple. Basically, your web browser will let you know. When you're visiting a website that has HTTPS enabled (and properly integrated), you'll see a green padlock icon next to the website's address. Additionally, you should also see `https://` in the address bar. The following screenshot shows an example of this from PayPal:

Why HTTPS is important for a modern WordPress site

While HTTPS is not a requirement per se, it's still a great step towards a safer web overall. Every website that supports HTTPS is simply safer to use, especially when dealing with any sort of user input. Quite naturally, people are not happy about submitting their personal information anywhere, particularly if they're not sure whether this information is going to be taken care of properly. These days, we're constantly hearing about hacks and security breaches, even at some of the most respectable web properties. With that in the picture, the public becomes more concerned with data security and privacy every year.

That said, modern WordPress sites need to embrace the idea to the fullest. There really is no downside to having HTTPS enabled on your website, and the process of doing it is not too difficult either. Added to this, in 2014, Google announced that HTTPS was officially a ranking factor for Google search. What this means is that you have a better chance of getting your website ranked, and thus found by potential visitors, if you have HTTPS integrated.

How to set up HTTPS

Setting up HTTPS on WordPress is a two-part process, as follows:

- First, you need to have an SSL certificate assigned to you, which you can then use on the website
- Second, you need to integrate this SSL with your WordPress site

Let's start with getting the SSL certificate itself. The thing with this is that they often come with a price tag. A good certificate can cost you anywhere from a couple of dollars to as much as $600 per year. This probably doesn't sound too attractive, but luckily for everyone, there are also good, free SSL options out there. Particularly, one called **Let's Encrypt** (`https://letsencrypt.org/`). Let's Encrypt is a free, automated, and open **Certificate Authority** (**CA**). It has been found to popularize SSLs and make them affordable for all websites, thus increasing the number of websites worldwide with encrypted connections.

The way you can get started with Let's Encrypt depends on the web host of where your WordPress website is hosted. Usually, at least with most hosts, you can enable a Let's Encrypt certificate straight from your hosting control panel. Showing the exact steps of how that's done would be difficult to do, since each host has their own control panel and their own way of letting you enable a Let's Encrypt certificate. Therefore, the first step is to actually contact your host and ask them to help you enable the certificate.

Before you do that, you can consult the official documentation at Let's Encrypt and make sure that your host does indeed support Let's Encrypt certificates. This documentation can be found at `https://community.letsencrypt.org/t/web-hosting-who-support-lets-encrypt/6920`.

After you go through your host's process, which shouldn't be too complicated, you can finish up the integration in your WordPress dashboard. In order to make your website fully integrated, you're going to need an additional plugin. This plugin is called **Really Simple SSL** (`https://wordpress.org/plugins/really-simple-ssl/`) and it's going to do two main things for you:

- It will update the URL of your website to HTTPS and overwrite the previous settings in the WordPress database
- It will add a permanent 301 redirect to your non-HTTPS URLs so that all your visitors, as well as search engines, will be forwarded to the new HTTPS versions of your content (such as posts and pages)

The plugin is very simple to use. All you need to do is install and activate it, and then you can go into the plugin's settings in **Settings** | **SSL**. Once there, just click on the main **Go ahead, activate SSL!** button, as demonstrated in the following screenshot:

The plugin will then work its magic in the background, and once it's done, it will log you out of the admin panel. This is normal, so you don't need to be worried here. When you try logging back in, you'll notice that you've been redirected to the HTTPS version of the admin panel. Just to make sure that everything is working, you can try visiting your website at `http://YOURSITE.com`, and see if you get automatically redirected to `https://YOURSITE.com`. At this stage, your WordPress site is fully integrated with HTTPS!

Summary

There was a lot going on in this chapter. First, we focused on social media integration—the bread and butter of all modern websites. Next, there was the topic of podcasting and a brief guide to getting started (how to configure your feeds, what plugins to use, and so on). Finally, we talked about HTTPS and SSL certificates—what they are, their importance for your website's security (and the security of your visitors' personal information), and how to enable them.

In the next chapter, we'll discuss the topic of developing your own plugins and widgets, including what the basics are and how to get your head around them. We'll also introduce you to the REST full API.

11
Developing Plugins, Widgets, and an Introduction to REST API

Plugins are a way to add to or extend WordPress' built-in functionalities. In Chapter 5, *Plugins – What They Are and Why You Need Them,* you learned how to install them. There are thousands of useful plugins (at the time of writing, the official counter at https://wordpress.org/plugins/ shows over 55,000 plugins) available from the online WordPress community, and they all perform different kinds of functions. In the earlier chapters, we installed plugins that catch spam, back up your website, and give you basic SEO features. You can also get plugins that manage your podcasts, track your stats, translate your content into other languages, and much more.

Sometimes, however, you'll find yourself in a situation where the plugin you need just doesn't exist. Luckily, it's quite easy to write a plugin for WordPress that you can use on your own website and share with the larger community if you want to. All you need is some basic **Hypertext Preprocessor (PHP)** knowledge, and you can write any plugin you want.

This chapter is divided into four major parts, as follows:

- In the first part, we'll create two plugins using an easy-to-follow, step-by-step process.
- In the second part, we'll create a widget using the built-in WordPress widget class.
- In the third part, you will learn what shortcodes are and how to use them.
- In the fourth part, we'll discuss the topic of the REST API.

Plugins

In this section, we'll create a plugin via a simple step-by-step process. We'll first see what the essential requirements are, then try out and test the plugin, and then briefly discuss the PHP code involved. That said, you should already have a basic background in PHP before going into this chapter.

Building plugins from scratch

First of all, we're here to learn about WordPress, so in this particular case, we will indeed build things from scratch. This is always the best approach to get an in-depth look into how a particular technology works.

However, later on, once you're working with WordPress on a regular basis, and managing your own or other people's websites, I advise you to always look for an already existing plugin before deciding to write a new one yourself. As I mentioned earlier, there are around 55,000 plugins in the official directory alone, not to mention all the premium plugins available all over the web. In short, if you need some functionality, most likely, there's a plugin for it, so you can just go out and get it.

Why is this the recommended approach? If I'm correct, you've chosen to use WordPress because you wanted to make your website as functional as possible, with the least amount of effort possible. Following this line of thought, using an existing plugin simply requires much less effort than building one. Also, many existing plugins are already used by thousands of other people and have large communities supporting them. Choosing a high-quality plugin is, therefore, a safer path to take.

I feel that I should emphasize this clearly because experience tells me that many young WordPress developers tend to press their peers to create things from scratch just for the heck of it, despite the fact that there are other, better solutions available.

Moreover, remember that everything that's a derivative work based on WordPress is available under the **GNU General Public License (GPL)**. So, there's nothing stopping you from taking an existing plugin, building upon it, making it better, and then re-sharing your version with the world. That way, we all win and there's no redundant work.

However, before we can do that, we indeed must learn the craft by constructing something of our own from start to finish. Onward, then!

Plugin code requirements

Just as there were requirements for a theme, there are requirements for a plugin. At the very least, your plugin must satisfy the following:

- It must be placed in the `wp-content/plugins` directory (inside the root directory of WordPress)
- It must have a PHP file with a unique name (that is, a name not used by any other plugin in the main `wp-content/plugins` directory)
- It must have a specially structured comment at the top of the file (see `https://codex.wordpress.org/File_Header` for more information)

Then, of course, you must have some functions or processing code; but WordPress will recognize any file that meets these requirements as a plugin.

If your plugin is a simple one, then you can just place a unique PHP file straight in your `wp-content/plugins` directory, so it can sit next to the default **Hello Dolly** plugin that WordPress comes with. However, a much better practice is to create a subdirectory (again, with a unique name) and place your PHP file there. It makes the `wp-content/plugins` directory seem much more organized. Plus, you never know when your plugin is going to need some additional files (it's always easier to simply add new files to a previously existing `plugin` directory, than to restructure the plugin from scratch).

A basic plugin – adding link icons

As a demonstration, we will create a simple plugin that adds icons to document links within WordPress. For example, if you create a new post and add a link to an MP3 file in it, it'll look something like the following screenshot:

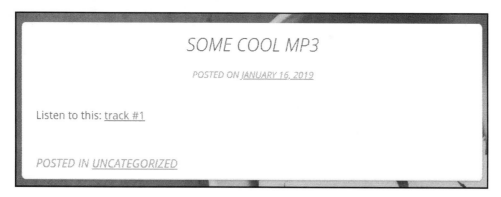

Once this plugin is complete, the link will look like the following screenshot instead:

To accomplish this, we have to do the following:

1. Provide images of the icons that will be used
2. Have a PHP function that identifies the links to documents and adds a special CSS class to them
3. Have a style sheet that creates the CSS classes for displaying the icons
4. Tell WordPress that whenever it prints the content of a post (that is, using the `the_content()` function), it has to run the PHP function first
5. Tell WordPress to include the new styles in the `<head>` tag

Keep this list in mind as we move forward. Once all of these five requirements are met, the plugin will be done. So, let's get started!

Naming and organizing the plugin files

Every plugin should have a unique name, so that it does not come into conflict with any other plugin in the WordPress universe. When choosing a name for your plugin and the PHP file, be sure to choose something unique. You may even want to do a Google search for the name you choose in order to be sure that someone else isn't already using it.

Apart from the main plugin file itself, your plugin can contain any number of other files and subdirectories. If the situation calls for it, you can even use media files, such as audio and video, to go along with your plugin. Of course, additional CSS or JS files (or even full libraries) are allowed as well.

In this case, as my plugin will be composed of multiple files (a PHP file, a style sheet, and some image files), I'm going to create a directory to house my plugin. I'll name the plugin **Add Document Type Styles New,** and place it in a directory called add_doctype_styles_new. The PHP file, doctype_styles_new.php, will live in this directory. I've also collected a number of document type icons (provided by https://www. freepik.com/ via https://www.flaticon.com/).

The directory I created for my plugin now looks like the following:

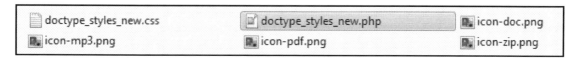

 It is best practice to also create directories, such as images, css, and js inside your plugin's directory if what you're building will consist of more files.

Now that I've got the images in my directory, I've taken care of the *first* requirement in the list of requirements my plugin has to meet.

 If your plugin has any unusual installation or configuration options, you may also want to include a readme.txt file in its directory that explains this. This README file will be useful, both as a reminder to you, and as an instructional document to others who may use your plugin in the future. If you plan to submit your plugin to the WordPress plugin directory, you will be required to create a README file. To get the template for such a file, visit https://wordpress.org/plugins/developers/.

As mentioned earlier, your plugin has to start with a special comment that tells WordPress how to describe the plugin to users on the plugins page. Now that I've got my directory and a blank PHP file created, I'll insert the special comment. It has to be structured like the following (this really is fundamental and is explained in more detail at https://codex.wordpress.org/File_Header):

```php
<?php
/*
Plugin Name: Add Document Type Styles New
Plugin URI: http://nio.tips/
Description: Detects URLs in your posts and pages and displays nice
document type icons next to them. Includes support for PDF, DOC, MP3, and
ZIP.
Version: 1.1
```

```
Author: Karol K
Author URI: http://karol.cc/
Text Domain: add_doctype_styles_new
License: GNU General Public License v2 or later
*/
```

Another good piece of information to have in your plugin is about licensing. Most plugins use GPL. This license essentially means that anyone can use, copy, and enhance your code, and that they are not allowed to prevent anyone else from redistributing it. I've also added a note about the GPL to my plugin's PHP file. Remember that all PHP code you encounter in any WordPress plugin is GPL by default. However, graphic files, CSS, JavaScript, and other elements might have a different license, so be careful when copying other people's work and making it part of your own. You can read more about the license at `https://www.gnu.org/copyleft/gpl.html`.

That's all about the introductory code. Now, we can add the *meat!*

Writing the plugin's core functions

The core of any plugin is the unique PHP code that you bring to the table. This is the part of the plugin that makes it what it is. Since this plugin is so simple, it only has a few lines of code in the middle.

The *second* requirement the plugin has to meet is to have a PHP function that identifies links to documents and adds a special class to them. The following function does just that. Note that in keeping with my efforts to ensure that my code is unique, I've prefixed both of my functions with `doctype_styles_new`:

```
function doctype_styles_new_regex($text) {
    $text = preg_replace('/href=([\'|"][[:alnum:]|
        [:punct:]]*)\.(pdf|doc|mp3|zip)([\'|"])/', 'href=\\1.\\2\\3
        class="link \\2"', $text);
    return $text;
}
```

When the function is given some `$text`, it will perform a search for any HTML anchor tag linking to a PDF, DOC, MP3, or ZIP file, and replace it with a class to that anchor. Then, the function returns the altered `$text`.

The *third* requirement the plugin has to meet is to have a style sheet that creates classes for displaying the icons. The following function fetches our style sheet:

```
function doctype_styles_new_styles() {
  wp_register_style('doctypes_styles', plugins_url
    ('doctype_styles_new.css', __FILE__));
  wp_enqueue_style('doctypes_styles');
}
```

As you can see, this function uses the same enqueue mechanism that we used in Chapter 9, *Developing Your Own Theme,* when registering the style sheets for our custom theme. Here's the CSS file that the preceding function fetches (inside `doctype_styles_new.css`):

```
.link {
  background-repeat: no-repeat;
  background-position: left center;
  padding: 0 0 0 18px;
}
.pdf { background-image: url(icon-pdf.png); }
.doc { background-image: url(icon-doc.png); }
.mp3 { background-image: url(icon-mp3.png); }
.zip { background-image: url(icon-zip.png); }
```

Indeed, a very simple file, containing just a handful of styles and icons to distinguish our document links!

Adding hooks to the plugin

We get our code to actually run when it is supposed to by making use of WordPress **hooks**. The way in which plugin hooks work is as follows: at various times while WordPress is running, they check to see whether any plugins have registered functions to run at that time. If there are, the functions are executed. These functions modify the default behavior of WordPress.

There are two kinds of hooks, as follows:

- **Actions**: Actions are the hooks that the WordPress core launches at specific points during execution, or when specific events occur. Your plugin can specify that one or more of its PHP functions are executed at these points, using the Action API.
- **Filters**: Filters are the hooks that WordPress launches to modify the text of various types before adding it to the database or sending it to the browser screen. Your plugin can specify that one or more of its PHP functions is executed to modify specific types of text at these times, using the Filter API.

This means that you can tell WordPress to run your plugin's functions at the same time, when it runs any of its built-in functions. In our case, we want our plugin's first function, `doctype_styles_new_regex()`, to run as a filter along with WordPress' `the_content()` function (this is the *fourth* requirement a plugin has to meet).

Now, add the following code to the bottom of the plugin:

```
add_filter('the_content', 'doctype_styles_new_regex');
```

This uses the `add_filter` hook that tells WordPress to register a function named `doctype_styles_new_regex()` when it is running the function called `the_content()`. By the way, if you have more than one function that you want to add as a filter to the content, you can add a third argument to the `add_filter()` function. This third argument will be a number representing the load priority (the default value is 10, the highest priority is 1, and there are no particular limits for the lowest priority—you can even assign values such as 100 or 999), and WordPress will run your functions in ascending order.

All that's left in our list of requirements that a plugin has to meet is the *fifth* requirement—that is, to tell WordPress to include the new styles in the <head> tag. This is actually done the same way that it's done for themes, which is through the following hook using `add_action()` with the `wp_enqueue_scripts` handle:

```
add_action('wp_enqueue_scripts', 'doctype_styles_new_styles');
```

Here is the complete plugin PHP file:

```php
<?php
/*
Plugin Name: Add Document Type Styles New
Plugin URI: http://nio.tips/
Description: Detects URLs in your posts and pages
and displays nice document type icons next to them.
Includes support for PDF, DOC, MP3 and ZIP.
Version: 1.1
Author: Karol K
Author URI: http://karol.cc/
Text Domain: add_doctype_styles_new
License: GNU General Public License v2 or later
*/

// this function does the magic
function doctype_styles_new_regex($text) {
  $text = preg_replace('/href=([\'|"][[:alnum:]|
    [:punct:]]*)\.(pdf|doc|mp3|zip)([\'|"])/',
    'href=\\1.\\2\\3 class="link \\2"', $text);
```

```
    return $text;
}

// this functions adds the stylesheet to the head
function doctype_styles_new_styles() {
    wp_register_style('doctypes_styles',
    plugins_url('doctype_styles_new.css', __FILE__));
    wp_enqueue_style('doctypes_styles');
}

// HOOKS =============

add_filter('the_content', 'doctype_styles_new_regex', 9);
add_action('wp_enqueue_scripts', 'doctype_styles_new_styles');
```

Make sure that there are no blank spaces before `<?php`. If there are any spaces, the PHP code will break, complaining that headers have already been sent. This is quite a common mistake that developers stumble into during their initial attempts with WordPress plugins. It's also a generally good idea to not use the PHP closing tags (`?>`) at the end of your PHP files. It saves you from some of the most unfortunate execution errors.

Make sure you save and close this PHP file. You can now do one of two things, as follows:

- Using your FTP client, upload `add_doctype_styles_new/` to your `wp-content/plugins/` directory
- Zip up your directory into `add_doctype_styles_new.zip`, and use the plugin uploader in `wp-admin` to add this plugin to your WordPress installation

This version of the plugin is available in the code bundle for this chapter, inside a subdirectory called `phase 1`. Our plugin files will go through a couple of phases before we have the final version.

Once the plugin is installed, it will show up on the plugins page, as shown in the following screenshot:

Plugin	Description
Add Document Type Styles New Activate | Delete	Detects URLs in your posts and pages and displays nice document type icons next to them. Includes support for: PDF, DOC, MP3 and ZIP. Version 1.0 | By Karol K | Visit plugin site

Now, you can activate it and test it out.

Trying out the plugin

If you go to view the same post that we created at the beginning of this chapter, you'll see the plugin in action. Here's the same screenshot again:

You can also try adding a new post with links to PDF, ZIP, or DOC files. Then, when you view the post, you'll see that even more icons have been added to it by our plugin.

Now that you've learned about a basic plugin that uses hooks to piggyback on the existing WordPress functionality, let's enhance this plugin by giving the user some controls.

Adding an admin page

Some plugins add a page to `wp-admin` where you or the user can edit plugin options. We've seen this with W3 Total Cache, Yoast SEO, and more. Now, let's modify our plugin to give the user some control over which document types are supported. The following screenshot shows what the new management page will look like when we are done:

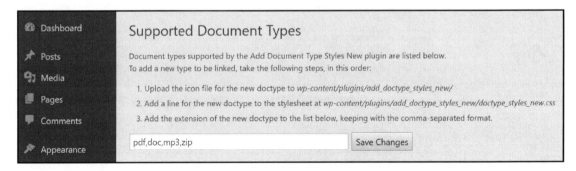

First, deactivate the plugin we just wrote. We'll make changes to it and then reactivate it. The following list details the steps we'll carry out to modify the plugin in order to make this new page possible:

1. Add functions that create an admin page and save the user's input in a new option
2. Modify the `doctype_styles_new_regex()` function so that it retrieves the user's input
3. Add hooks for the admin page functions

Let's get started!

Adding management page functions

The management page that we will create is going to add an option to `wp-admin`. This uses the existing space in the WordPress `options` table in the database, so no database modifications are required. The name of this new option must be unique. I'm going to call the new option `doctype_styles_new_supportedtypes`.

There are six functions we need to add to the plugin, so that an admin page can be added to `wp-admin`. Let's take a look at the functions, one by one:

1. The *first* function adds the new `doctype_styles_new_supportedtypes` option when the plugin is activated, and sets the default value as follows:

   ```
   function set_supportedtypes_options() {
       add_option("doctype_styles_new_supportedtypes",
           "pdf,doc,mp3,zip");
   }
   ```

2. The *second* function removes the new option when the plugin is deactivated, as follows:

   ```
   function unset_supportedtypes_options () {
     delete_option("doctype_styles_new_supportedtypes");
   }
   ```

3. Let's look at the new *third* function, as follows:

   ```
   function modify_menu_for_supportedtypes() {
     add_submenu_page(
     'options-general.php',    //The new options page will be added as
                               //a submenu to the Settings menu.
     'Document Type Styles',   //Page <title>
   ```

```
        'Document Type Styles',     //Menu title
        'manage_options',           //Capability
        'add_doctype_styles_new',   //Slug
        'supportedtypes_options'    //Function to call
        );
    }
```

This function adds a new item to the **Settings** menu in `wp-admin` using the `add_submenu_page()` function call. This takes six arguments, namely: where the options page should be placed, page title, menu link text, the user at the maximum level who can access the link, what file to open (none, in this case), and the function to call, `supportedtypes_options()`.

4. The `supportedtypes_options()` function is, in fact, the *fourth* new function we are adding:

```
function supportedtypes_options() {
  echo '<div class="wrap"><h2>Supported Document
    Types</h2>';
  if (isset($_POST['submit'])) {
    update_supportedtypes_options();
  }
  print_supportedtypes_form();
  echo '</div>';
}
```

This function actually displays our new page. It prints a title and checks to see whether someone has clicked on the `submit` button; if the `submit` button has been clicked on, the `supportedtypes_options()` function updates the options and then prints the form.

5. The new *fifth* function we have to add is responsible for updating options if the `submit` button has been clicked on, as follows:

```
function update_supportedtypes_options() {
  $updated = false;
  if ($_POST['doctype_styles_new_supportedtypes']) {
    $safe_val = addslashes(strip_tags($_POST
      ['doctype_styles_new_supportedtypes']));
      update_option('doctype_styles_new_supportedtypes',
      $safe_val);
    $updated = true;
  }
  if ($updated) {
    echo '<div id="message" class="updated fade">';
    echo '<p>Supported types successfully updated!</p>';
```

```
    echo '</div>';
  } else {
    echo '<div id="message" class="error fade">';
    echo '<p>Unable to update supported types!</p>';
    echo '</div>';
  }
}
```

6. The last function we need to add, which is the new *sixth* function, prints the form that the users will see. Make sure there are no spaces before or after the closing tag (EOF;), as follows:

```
function print_supportedtypes_form() {
  $val_doctype_styles_new_supportedtypes =
    stripslashes(get_option('
    doctype_styles_new_supportedtypes'));
  echo <<<EOF
<p>Document types supported by the Add Document Type Styles New
plugin are listed      as follows.<br />To add a new type to be linked,
take the following steps, in this order:
  <ol>
    <li>Upload the icon file for the new doctype to <i>wp-
      content/plugins/add_doctype_styles_new/</i></li>
    <li>Add a line for the new doctype to the stylesheet at
      <i>wp-content/plugins/add_doctype_styles_new/
      doctype_styles_new.css</i></li>
    <li>Add the extension of the new doctype to the following list,
keeping with the comma-separated format.</li>
  </ol>
  </p>
  <form method="post">
    <input type="text" name=
      "doctype_styles_new_supportedtypes" size="50"
      value="$val_doctype_styles_new_supportedtypes" />
    <input type="submit" name="submit" value="Save Changes"
    />
  </form>
  EOF;
  }
```

These six functions together take care of adding a link in the menu, adding the management page for this link, and updating the new option.

Modifying the doctype_styles_new_regex() function

Now that the users are able to edit the list of supported document types by appending the document types they want, we should have a way of telling the `doctype_styles_new_regex()` function to use the user's list instead of the built-in list. To do so, we need to use `get_option('doctype_styles_new_supportedtypes')` in our `doctype_styles_new_regex()` function. The `get_option()` function will retrieve the value that the user has saved in the new option we just created. Modify your `doctype_styles_new_regex()` function so that it looks like the following:

```
function ahs_doctypes_regex($text) {
  $types = get_option('doctype_styles_new_supportedtypes');
  $types = preg_replace('/,\s*/', '|', $types);

  $text = preg_replace('/href=([\'|"][[:alnum:]|
     [:punct:]]*)\.('.$types.')([\'|"])/i', 'href=\\1.\\2\\3
     class="link \\2"', $text);

  return $text;
}
```

Adding hooks

We have added our management page functions, but now we have to tell WordPress to use them. To do so, we just need to add the following three new hooks:

```
add_action('admin_menu', 'modify_menu_for_supportedtypes');
register_activation_hook(__FILE__, "set_supportedtypes_options");
register_deactivation_hook(__FILE__,
   "unset_supportedtypes_options");
```

The first hook tells WordPress to add our link to the menu when it creates the menu with `admin_menu()`. The next two hooks tell WordPress to call the activation and deactivation functions when the plugin is activated or deactivated.

 This version of the plugin is available in the code bundle for this chapter, inside a subdirectory called `final`. It is the final version of our plugin.

Trying out the plugin

We have added all of the new functions. Now it's time to save the file and see what happens. You can go ahead and reactivate the plugin. Now, when you look at the **Settings** menu, you will see that a new link has been added, as demonstrated in the following screenshot:

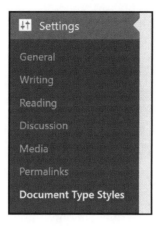

Click on the new link to see the management page, as shown in the following screenshot:

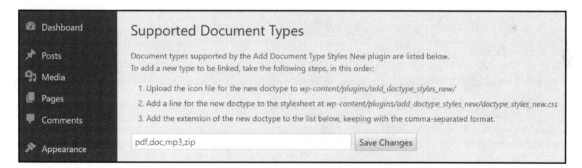

If you follow the three steps shown in the preceding screenshot on the management page (upload the file icon, add a new style to the style sheet, and add the extension to the option), then the new document type will be supported.

There are already a number of ways in which this plugin could be improved. Some of them are as follows:

- Instead of forcing the user to upload their new icons using FTP, the plugin could allow the user to upload icons directly via the **Settings** page.
- The plugin could display the icons for the supported document types on the **Settings** page so that the users see what they look like.
- The plugin could check to make sure that for every document type in the option field there is an existing icon, otherwise, it will display an error.

Perhaps you'd like to try to make these changes yourself!

Testing your plugins

We've tried out our new plugin, so it's probably a good moment to say a word or two about testing your plugins and making sure that they don't cause any problems for regular users in general.

Our particular plugin is a very simple one; the only thing it does is process each link it finds inside any post or page's content, and adds a custom icon next to it. However, even such a simple plugin can be a possible security breach point. For example, the only place where the user can input anything is the plugins section in `wp-admin` (the field handling the supported file types). Now, there is a possibility that someone might use this field to input a piece of specific PHP code instead of a standard file type; for instance, code that is meant to perform a specific action on the server side, and which could result in a serious security breach. That is why our `update_supportedtypes_options()` function has the following two lines:

```
$safe_val = addslashes(strip_tags($_POST
    ['doctype_styles_new_supportedtypes']));
update_option('doctype_styles_new_supportedtypes', $safe_val);
```

Thanks to them, everything that the user inputs will have all of the PHP and HTML tags stripped by `strip_tags()`, and then every character that needs to be quoted in database queries will be handled by `addslashes()`. Using such functions is a just-in-case practice, but it tends to be something that eventually pays off.

Apart from testing our work against some of the common hacking practices, such as code injection or SQL injection, we also need to handle all kinds of unconventional uses we can think of. For instance, would anything bad happen if someone put a value that's not a standard file type? Or, what if the CSS file goes missing all of a sudden? These are just some of the questions a good testing session should answer.

Another good way of testing plugins is to hand them over to a few trusted users and ask for feedback. Someone who's entirely new to your plugin will usually do a way better job of testing it than you, the author.

Of course, this short section here only scratches the surface of plugin testing and code testing in general, so I encourage you to give it a closer look on your own. There are many great resources on the web and in your nearest bookstore.

A plugin with database access – capturing searched words

We're going to leave the document types plugin behind now, and create a new one, featuring active use of a database. Let's create a simple plugin that stores all the words that visitors search for (when using the blog's search feature).

Overall, this plugin is very basic, and doesn't require its own directory like the previous plugin that we worked on. That's why this whole plugin will be done inside one file: `capture_searches_new.php`. I'm calling the plugin `Capture Searched Words New`.

The database table structure for this plugin will be as follows. The table name is `wp_searchedwords`:

Field	Type	Null	Key	Default	Extra
Id	INT	NOT NULL	PRI	-	auto_increment
Word	VARCHAR(255)	-	-	NULL	-
created	DATETIME	NOT NULL	-	Today 00:00:01	-

Now, let's write the plugin code.

 Even though I say that the table is named `wp_searchedwords`, it won't always be the case. It's all based on the table prefix that's set for your website (the default one is indeed `wp_`). Here, I'm going to refer to the table as `wp_searchedwords` anyway, for convenience.

Getting the plugin to talk to the database

The first part of this plugin should only be run when the plugin is activated. This will be the initialization function. One of its tasks is to create or update the database table (the table will only be created if it hasn't been created before):

```
function searchedwords_init($content) {
  global $wpdb;
  $sw_table_name = $wpdb->prefix.'searchedwords';

  //creating the table (if it doesn't exist) or updating it if
  // necessary
  if(isset($_GET['activate']) && 'true' == $_GET['activate']) {
    $sql = 'CREATE TABLE `'.$sw_table_name.'` (
      id INT NOT NULL AUTO_INCREMENT,
      word VARCHAR(255),
      created DATETIME NOT NULL DEFAULT \''.date('Y-m-d').'
        00:00:01\',
      PRIMARY KEY  (id)
    )';

    require_once(ABSPATH.'wp-admin/includes/upgrade.php');
    dbDelta($sql);
  }

  // in case a search has just been performed, store the searched
  // word
  if (!empty($_GET['s'])) {
    $current_searched_words = explode(" ",urldecode($_GET['s']));
    foreach ($current_searched_words as $word) {
      $wpdb->query($wpdb->prepare("INSERT into `$sw_table_name`
        VALUES(null,'%s','".date('Y-m-d H:i:s')."')", $word));
    }
  }
}
```

This function connects to the database using various function calls, such as dbDelta(), $wpdb->query(), and $wpdb->prepare(). The dbDelta() function takes care of creating the table or updating it (it does whatever is needed at the time; you can find out more at https://codex.wordpress.org/Creating_Tables_with_Plugins). Apart from this, when dealing with the WordPress database, you can utilize any database-related PHP function in existence. Or, you can use WordPress' class member function: $wpdb->get_results(). The function we're using here also stores the searched word in the database table if a search has just been performed. This is done through the $wpdb->query() and $wpdb->prepare() functions.

Adding management page functions

We now need a familiar-looking function that adds a management page to `wp-admin`. In this case, we use `add_management_page()` instead of `add_submenu_page()`, because this plugin is more of a tool than something that requires settings:

```
function modify_menu_for_searchedwords() {
  $page = add_management_page(
    "Capture Searched Words",
    "Capture Searched Words",
    'manage_options',
    'capture_searches_new',
    'searchedwords_page'
  );
}
```

For this plugin, we're not going to load any custom styling or CSS files. The purpose here is to just showcase how database connection can be done, so we're going to keep everything else ultra-simple and minimal. Therefore, the only thing we have to do at this point is to write a function that retrieves the information from the database and displays it on the new management page (again, everything is done through the `$wpdb` object—it's a class defined by WordPress that contains a set of functions that you can use to interact with the database):

```
function searchedwords_page() {
  global $wpdb;
  $sw_table_name = $wpdb->prefix.'searchedwords';

$searched_words = $wpdb->get_results("SELECT COUNT(word) AS
  occurrence, word FROM `$sw_table_name` GROUP BY word ORDER BY
  occurrence DESC");
  ?>
<div class="wrap" style="max-width: 600px;">
<h2>Searched Words</h2>
<table class="wp-list-table widefat">
<thead>
  <tr>
    <th scope="col">Search Words</th>
    <th scope="col"># of Searches</th>
  </tr>
</thead>
<tbody>
  <?php
  if($searched_words !== NULL) {
    foreach($searched_words as $searched_word) {
      echo '<tr valign="top"><td>'.$searched_word-
        >word.'</td><td>'.$searched_word->occurrence.'</td></tr>';
```

```
    }
    $searched_perfomed = true;
  }
  else {
    echo '<tr valign="top"><td colspan="2"><strong>No searches
      have been performed yet</strong></td></tr>';
  }
  ?>
</tbody>
</table>
</div>
  <?php
}
```

That's it. The previous plugin had more functions because data was being captured from the user and then saved. Here, that's not necessary.

Lastly, we just need to add two hooks, as follows:

```
add_filter('init', 'searchedwords_init');
add_action('admin_menu', 'modify_menu_for_searchedwords');
```

The first hook tells WordPress to run the initialization function when the plugin is activated, or when a search is performed. The second hook modifies the admin_menu to add a link to the new management page.

 This version of the plugin is available in the code bundle for this chapter, inside a subdirectory called final. It is the first and final version of the plugin.

Trying out the plugin

As with the last plugin, you can now either upload your plugin using FTP to wp-content/plugins, or turn it into a ZIP file and add it using the uploader to wp-admin.

Once you've installed it, activate it. Then, look at the menu under **Tools** and you'll see a link to the new management page, as demonstrated in the following screenshot:

When you click on **Capture Searched Words**, you'll see a new page that the plugin has created, as shown in the following screenshot:

Searched Words

Search Words	# of Searches
spanish	2
podcast	1
chili	1

As you can see, I did perform some searches beforehand just to have something to show on this new page. You can do the same by placing a search field widget in your sidebar (as shown in the following screenshot), and then experimenting with different search words and phrases. The plugin will pick them all up and display the most searched ones in its section in `wp-admin`:

Building a plugin for the block-based editor

As you know by now, there's a new content editor in WordPress that's been introduced in the 5.0 version of the platform. Essentially, it does away with the previous single editing window and instead, allows the user to work with individual content blocks, placing them one after another. When put together, all those blocks construct the final blog post. That's all fine and dandy for the user, but what does it mean for the plugin developer? A handful of things!

Firstly, building a plugin for a block-based editor is very different from building standard plugins like we've been doing in this chapter. While you can build those classic plugins with just a basic knowledge of PHP and HTML, building for the block-based editor is a bit more complex. It involves setting up and mastering additional web technologies. You need things such as **npm**, **Node.js**, and **webpack**, not to mention that you also need to be comfortable working with JavaScript in general. Teaching all of this is a large-enough topic for its own book. So, instead of doing that, I'm going to point you to some external sources where you can begin your adventure with the block-based editor. However, before I do that, let's summarize briefly what the general idea of building for the editor is and what is possible.

The new editor accepts two main types of elements, as follows:

- Blocks
- Sidebar sections

In other words, as a plugin developer, you can either create new blocks to be included in the editor, or new sidebar entries to customize the fine details about your plugin's functionality, or both.

I'm sure you know what a block is at this point, so let me show you an example of a good sidebar use in the new editor. It comes from the **Yoast SEO** plugin (`https://wordpress.org/plugins/wordpress-seo/`; we discussed this in `Chapter 5`, *Plugins - What They Are and Why You Need Them*). If the user has the plugin enabled on their site, and they proceed to work on a new blog post, they'll see this new sidebar section in the top-right corner of the editor, as demonstrated in the following screenshot:

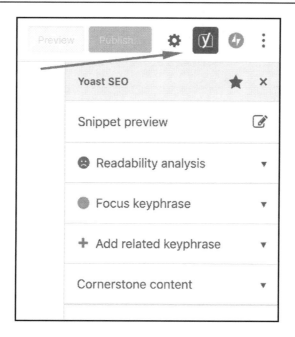

It allows the user to tune up the SEO parameters of their post. The thing worth noticing is how well the plugin's block integrates with the rest of the editor's user interface. This seamless integration is the whole goal of building plugins with the block-based editor in mind.

The same thing goes if you want to build a plugin that enables new blocks. They also need to use the same interface conventions as the default blocks that come with WordPress built in. Here's an example of a plugin that does exactly that. It's called **Otter** blocks (`https://wordpress.org/plugins/otter-blocks/`).

When you install and activate it, you'll get a whole set of new blocks, and the best part is that they blend in with the default blocks perfectly. For example, one of the blocks included is the **Sharing Icons** block. The following screenshot shows what it looks like:

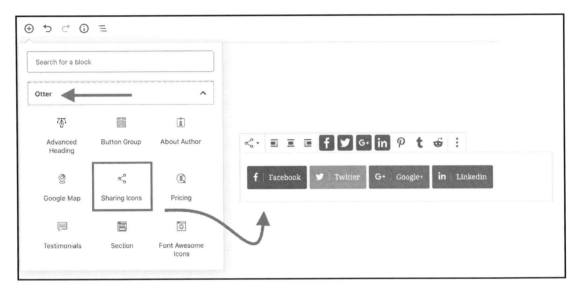

As you can see, it has the same controls and similar options to all of the other blocks. Of course, this plugin is a fairly complex creation, built by a team of developers, and you surely don't have to make your first block plugin similarly impressive.

That said, you might be notice one thing in particular as it relates to the block-based editor; that is, what if your plugin doesn't require creating any new blocks or sidebar elements? In such a case, you don't need to trouble yourself with the editor at all. The two plugins we've created in this chapter so far don't use the editor in any way, so making your plugin compatible with the editor certainly isn't a must.

To begin your adventure with the block-based editor, read this two-part guide on how to adapt your plugin for the block editor: part 1 can be found at `https://www.codeinwp.com/blog/adapt-your-plugin-for-gutenberg-block-api/` and part 2 is available at `https://www.codeinwp.com/blog/make-plugin-compatible-with-gutenberg-sidebar-api/`.

Additionally, you can experiment with the free Gutenberg Boilerplate plugin (`https://github.com/HardeepAsrani/gutenberg-boilerplate`), which delivers the minimal block editor development setup and examples inside a single package. There's one example block, and one example sidebar included. You can build upon these elements when creating your own block-ready plugin.

Learning more

There are hundreds of hooks available in WordPress—way too many to cover in this book. You can learn more about them by going online. Start out at these online reference sites:

- The *Plugin API* article contains very thorough information about writing plugins and using hooks, at: `https://codex.wordpress.org/Plugin_API`.
- For a complete list of action hooks, visit `https://codex.wordpress.org/Plugin_API/Action_Reference`.
- For a complete list of filter hooks, visit `https://codex.wordpress.org/Plugin_API/Filter_Reference`.
- You may also want to take a step back and look at the general *Plugin Resources* page in the WordPress Codex at `https://codex.wordpress.org/Plugin_Resources`.
- Another page that you might find very helpful is the new *Code Reference* for developers: `https://developer.wordpress.org/reference/`.
- A key resource to bookmark if you want to build plugins for the new block-based editor is the *Gutenberg Handbook*, available at `https://wordpress.org/gutenberg/handbook/`.
- If you want to submit your plugin to the WordPress plugin repository, you'll need to take steps similar to those that you took when preparing a theme, and you'll also need to get hooked up to the WordPress SVN repository. Learn more about how to submit a plugin to the WordPress plugin repository at `https://developer.wordpress.org/plugins/wordpress-org/`.

Widgets

Writing a widget bears some similarities to writing a plugin. In some ways, it's even easier because there is a widget class that you can leverage for some of the functionalities. In other ways, it's also a bit more time-consuming as there's a lot of mandatory code that every widget has to feature.

Custom tag cloud widget

In this section, we'll see how to write a widget that displays a custom tag cloud that we can then place in the sidebar. There will also be the possibility to change the title of the widget, and although this is a tag cloud widget, we'll be able to switch tags to categories and display them using a tag-cloud-like style as well. In its final form, the widget will look like the following screenshot:

Just as a comparison, here's what the standard tag cloud widget (the native one in WordPress) looks like:

Let's get started!

Naming our widget

In this case, we're going to create the widget as a standalone plugin. So, just like any other plugin, it needs a unique name and a unique appearance in the `wp-content/plugins` directory.

I encourage you to search the web whenever you're creating a new widget or plugin, just to make sure that there's nothing out there going by the same name. On top of that, use a namespace as a prefix with every filename (and function name) that you're creating. For example, mine is kk_.

I'll name the new plugin file (which holds the widget) kk_tag_cloud_widget.php, and put it in its own kk_tag_cloud_widget directory inside wp-content/plugins.

This main PHP file starts just like any other plugin, with the following declaration:

```php
<?php
/*
Plugin Name: Karol K's Tag Cloud Widget
Description: Displays a nice tag cloud.
Plugin URI: http://nio.tips/
Version: 1.1
Author: Karol K
Author URI: http://karol.cc/
License: GNU General Public License v2 or later
*/
```

The widget structure

When you are building a widget using the widget class, your widget needs to have the following structure:

```php
class UNIQUE_WIDGET_NAME extends WP_Widget {

  public function __construct() {
    $widget_ops = array();
    $control_ops = array();
    parent::__construct('base id', 'name', $widget_ops,
      $control_ops);
  }

  public function widget($args, $instance) {
    // used when the sidebar calls the widget
  }

  public function form($instance) {
    // prints the form on the widgets page
  }

  public function update($new_instance, $old_instance) {
    // used when the user saves his/her widget options
```

```
        }
    }

    // initiate the widget

    // register the widget
```

My unique widget name for this project is `KK_Widget_Tag_Cloud`. Now, let's go over each of the preceding functions one by one and understand what's going on.

The widget initiation function

Let's start with the widget initiation function. Before we add anything to it, it looks like the following:

```
public function __construct() {
    $widget_ops = array();
    $control_ops = array();
    parent::__construct('base-id', 'name', $widget_ops,
        $control_ops);
}
```

In this function, which is the constructor of the class, we initialize various things that the `WP_Widget` class is expecting. The first two variables, to which you can give any name you want, are just a handy way to set the two array variables expected by the third line of code.

Let's take a look at these three lines of code, as follows:

- The `$widget_ops` variable is where you can set the class name, which is given to the `div` widget itself, and the description, which is shown in `wp-admin` on the widgets page.
- The `$control_ops` variable is where you can set options for the control box in `wp-admin` on the widgets page, such as the width and height of the widget, and the ID prefix used for the names and IDs of the items inside. For my basic widget, I'm not going to use this variable (as it's optional).
- When you call the parent class's constructor, `WP_Widget()`, you'll tell it the widget's unique ID, the widget's display title, and pass along the two arrays you created.

For this widget, my code now looks like the following:

```
public function __construct() {
  parent::__construct(
    'kk-tag-cloud',
    'KK Tag Cloud',
    array(
      'description' => 'Your most used tags in cloud format; same
        height; custom background'
    )
  );
}
```

The widget form function

The widget form function has to be named `form()`. You may not rename it if you want the widget class to know what its purpose is. You also need to have an argument in there, which I'm calling `$instance`, which the class also expects. This is where the current widget settings are stored. This function needs to have all of the functionalities to create the form that users will see when adding the widget to a sidebar. Let's look at some abbreviated code and then explore what it's doing, as follows:

```
public function form($instance) {
  $instance = wp_parse_args((array) $instance,
  array('template' => ''));
  $current_taxonomy = $this->_get_current_taxonomy($instance);
  ?>
  <p>
    <label for="<?php echo $this->get_field_id('title');
      ?>">Title</label>
    <input type="text" class="widefat" id="<?php echo $this-
      >get_field_id('title'); ?>" name="<?php echo $this-
      >get_field_name('title'); ?>" value="<?php if
      (isset($instance['title']))
      {echo esc_attr($instance['title']);}
  ?>" />
  </p>
  <p>
    <label for="<?php echo $this->get_field_id('taxonomy');
      ?>">Taxonomy</label>
    <select class="widefat" id="<?php echo $this-
      >get_field_id('taxonomy'); ?>" name="<?php echo $this-
      >get_field_name('taxonomy'); ?>">
    <?php foreach(get_object_taxonomies('post') as $taxonomy) :
      $tax = get_taxonomy($taxonomy);
      if(!$tax->show_tagcloud || empty($tax->labels->name))
```

```
        continue;
    ?>
    <option value="<?php echo esc_attr($taxonomy) ?>"
    <?php selected($taxonomy, $current_taxonomy); ?>>
    <?php echo $tax->labels->name; ?></option>
<?php endforeach; ?>
</select>
</p>
<?php
}
```

First, you use a WordPress function named `wp_parse_args()`, which creates an `$instance` array that your form will use. What's in it depends on what defaults you've set and what settings the user has already saved. Then, you create form fields. Note that for each form field, I make use of the built-in functions that will create unique names and IDs and input the existing values, as follows:

- `$this->get-field_id()` creates a unique ID based on the widget instance (remember, you can create more than one instance of this widget).
- `$this->get_field_name()` creates a unique name based on the widget instance.
- The `$instance` array is where you will find the current values for the widget, whether they are defaults or user-saved data.

All the other code in there is just regular PHP and HTML. Note that if you give the user the ability to set a title, name that field `title`, and WordPress will show it on the widget form when it's minimized. The widget form this will create will look like the following:

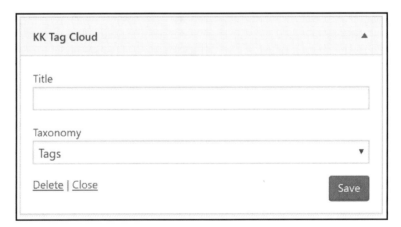

The widget save function

When a user clicks on the **Save** button on the widget form, WordPress uses AJAX to run your save function. You need to be sure to save whatever the user types in, which is all we're doing in this case, but you can put other functionalities here if it's appropriate for your widget (for example, database interactions, conversions, calculations, and so on). The final code for this function is as follows:

```
public function update($new_instance, $old_instance) {
  $instance['title'] = $new_instance['title'];
  $instance['taxonomy'] = stripslashes($new_instance['taxonomy']);
  return $instance;
}
```

Be sure this function is named `update()` and is prepared to accept two instances, one with the old data and one with the just-submitted data. You can write your code to check `$new_instance` for problems, and thus, return `$old_instance` if the new one isn't valid. The `$instance` data you return will be what's shown in the update widget form.

The widget print function

The third main function in your widget class is the one that is called by the sidebar when it's time to actually show the widget to people visiting the website. It needs to retrieve any relevant saved user data and print out information for the website visitor. In this case, our final print function looks like the following:

```
public function widget($args, $instance) {
  extract($args);
  $current_taxonomy = $this->_get_current_taxonomy($instance);
  if(!empty($instance['title'])) {
    $title = $instance['title'];
  }
  else {
    if('post_tag' == $current_taxonomy) {
      $title = 'Tags';
    }
    else {
      $tax = get_taxonomy($current_taxonomy);
      $title = $tax->labels->name;
    }
  }
  $title = apply_filters('widget_title', $title, $instance, $this-
    >id_base);
  $before_widget = '<div class="widget-container kk_widget_tag_cloud">';
  $after_widget = '</div>';
```

```
$before_title = '<h1 class="widget-title">';
$after_title = '</h1>';

echo $before_widget;
if ( $title )  echo $before_title . $title . $after_title;
echo '<div class="kk_tagcloud">';
wp_tag_cloud(apply_filters('widget_tag_cloud_args',
    array('taxonomy' => $current_taxonomy)));
echo "</div>\n";
echo $after_widget;
}
```

The preceding function calls one more helper function responsible for fetching the current taxonomy. It is a very simple one, though, as follows:

```
function _get_current_taxonomy($instance) {
  if ( !empty($instance['taxonomy']) &&
    taxonomy_exists($instance['taxonomy']) )
    return $instance['taxonomy'];
  return 'post_tag';
}
```

The first thing I do in the main function is to extract the data in the instance, which contains the information the website administrator had saved when filling out the widget form. Then, the widget takes a look into the selected taxonomy (tags or categories) and displays all of the individual items as a simple one-line list.

Custom widget styles

Our small widget has its own style sheet that needs to be included in the current theme's head section, like any other style sheet.

The file is named kk_tag_cloud_widget.css and contains the following:

```
.kk_widget_tag_cloud .kk_tagcloud {
    line-height: 1.5em;
}

.kk_widget_tag_cloud .kk_tagcloud a {
    display: inline-block;
    margin: 3px 2px;
    padding: 0 11px;
    border-radius: 3px;
    -webkit-border-radius: 3px;
    background: #eee;
    color: #279090;
```

```
    font-size: 12px !important;
    line-height: 30px;
    text-transform: uppercase;
}

.kk_widget_tag_cloud .kk_tagcloud a:hover {
    color: #f2f2f2;
    background: #404040;
}
```

Nothing fancy, just a set of classes that will make sure that the widget looks great. The only thing we have to do with this style sheet is enqueue it through a standard WordPress hook. Place the following code in your plugin's main file:

```
function kk_tag_cloud_widget_styles_load() {
  wp_register_style('kk_tag_cloud_widget_styles',
     plugins_url('kk_tag_cloud_widget.css', __FILE__));
  wp_enqueue_style('kk_tag_cloud_widget_styles');
}
add_action('wp_enqueue_scripts',
   'kk_tag_cloud_widget_styles_load');
```

Initiating and hooking up the widget

That's it for widget functionality! Now, you just need to add a little piece of code that will hook the widget up to the rest of WordPress, as follows:

```
function KK_Widget_Tag_Cloud_Reg() {
  register_widget('KK_Widget_Tag_Cloud');
}
add_action('widgets_init', 'KK_Widget_Tag_Cloud_Reg');
```

This tells WordPress that when it initiates widgets, it should be sure to register our new widget.

> This version of the widget is available in the code bundle for this chapter, inside a subdirectory called `phase 1`. We'll still be adding one more feature before we can call it the final version.

Trying out the widget

Your widget is ready to go! Let's try this widget we have created now:

1. Save all your changes, and upload your widget to the `wp-content/plugins` directory.

2. Go to the **Plugins** section and you'll see your widget waiting to be activated, as usual.

3. After you click on the **Activate** button, you can navigate to **Appearance** | **Widgets**. You'll see the widget waiting to be added to a sidebar, as demonstrated in the following screenshot:

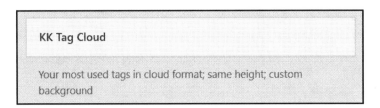

4. Drag the widget to a sidebar, and then click on the little downward arrow to edit it. You'll see the options slide down, as shown in the following screenshot:

5. You can enter a **Title** or leave it blank for the default, and choose the **Taxonomy** that you want to display.

6. Then, click on **Save** as you would with any widget.
7. When you return to the frontend of the site and reload, the new tag cloud will be right there, as shown in the following screenshot:

Learning more

You can browse the following online reference sites to learn more about widgets:

- The WordPress *Widgets API* is located at `https://codex.wordpress.org/Widgets_API`.
- WordPress lists a number of widgets at `https://codex.wordpress.org/WordPress_Widgets`.
- If you want to find more widgets to install on your website, visit the widgets section of the plugin repository at `https://wordpress.org/plugins/tags/widget`.

Bundling a widget with an existing plugin

If you're writing a plugin and you'd like to make a widget available with it, you don't have to create a separate widget plugin. Just include all of the widget code—similar to what we created in the preceding section—in with your plugin's PHP file. When the user activates the plugin, the widget will automatically show up on the widgets page in `wp-admin`. There's no need for a separate file!

Shortcodes

Shortcodes are a handy way to let a non-technical person, such as an editor of a website, include dynamic content within pages and posts, without having to actually use any PHP, complex HTML structures, or custom JavaScript. In other words, shortcodes are handy reusable pieces of code, yet they don't require any actual coding experience or knowledge on the end user's part.

Shortcodes and the way they work

The way a shortcode works is that you tell WordPress to look at the text within square brackets (`[]`) and evaluate it by running a PHP function. That PHP function can live in the `functions.php` file of your theme, or in a plugin file, or in a widget file. Let's create a simple shortcode and include it with our most recent widget plugin.

Types of shortcodes

Shortcodes are a pretty simple concept by definition, but we can still distinguish three main types, as follows:

- **Single-tag shortcodes**: These shortcodes are executed with just a single tag, for example, `[my_first_shortcode/]`.
- **Double-tag shortcodes**: These shortcodes are executed with opening and closing tags, for example, `[my_2nd_shortcode]some text here[/my_2nd_shortcode]` (notice that the closing tag has an additional /). As you can see, there's also some content within the tags. This content can be processed by the shortcode function.
- **Shortcodes with attributes**: These shortcodes can have one or two tags and also a number of attributes we can use to customize the output, for example, `[my_3rd_shortcode name="Karol" twitter="carlosinho"]some text here[/my_3rd_shortcode]`.

Creating a simple shortcode

Let's create a simple shortcode that will make it possible to use our widget's output inside any given post or page. This is going to be a double-tag shortcode with one additional attribute, which we'll use to indicate whether the output should be formatted using our custom CSS or WordPress' native styling:

1. Let's start by creating a new function at the bottom of our `kk_tag_cloud_widget.php` file, and then we'll go through each individual line, as follows:

```php
function kk_tag_cloud_handler($atts, $content=null) {
  extract(shortcode_atts(array(
    'use_css' => '1',
    'taxonomy' => 'post_tag'
  ), $atts));

  $tax = 'post_tag';
  if(taxonomy_exists($taxonomy)) $tax = $taxonomy;

  $result = '';

  if ('0' != $use_css) {
    $result .= '<div class="kk_widget_tag_cloud"><div
      class="kk_tagcloud">';
  }
  if (null != $content) {
    $result .= addslashes(strip_tags($content)).' ';
  }
  $result .= wp_tag_cloud(apply_filters(
    'widget_tag_cloud_args',
    array('taxonomy' => $tax, 'echo' => false)
  ));
  if ('0' != $use_css) {
    $result .= '</div></div>';
  }

  return $result;
}
```

First of all, note that this function does not *echo* or *print* anything. It just returns a string. If you let your function print, it won't look correct on the website.

Inside our function, the first line handles the custom attributes that the shortcode receives (in this case, just the `use_css` parameter for indicating whether the styles should be used or not, and the `taxonomy` parameter to indicate the taxonomy that should be shown in the shortcode). WordPress will hand off the `$atts` argument automatically, and we only have to use the `extract()` function to turn the attributes the user submits into variables available in the function. The values in the array passed to the `extract()` functions set the defaults, in case the user chooses no options. In general, there is no limit to the number of options that you can make available to the shortcode users.

The next line extracts the taxonomy identifier and tries to turn it into a valid taxonomy. In case the user's input is not valid, the default `post_tag` taxonomy will be used. The final part of the function handles the display based on the state of the `use_css` attribute. It's pretty basic at this point! There's also a possibility to include custom text as the main content of the shortcode. This can be useful in some situations.

2. What we have to do now is tell WordPress that this function is a shortcode, and we do so using a hook. Be sure to choose something unique. I've chosen `kk_tag_cloud` as the name for this shortcode, so the hook looks like the following:

```
add_shortcode('kk_tag_cloud', 'kk_tag_cloud_handler');
```

3. To use this shortcode in our content, all we have to do is edit any given post or page and insert a line such as the following:

```
[kk_tag_cloud taxonomy="category"] Select the category you'd like
    to read next:[/kk_tag_cloud]
```

4. Such usage will have the following effect:

5. We can also use the shortcode such as the following:

```
[kk_tag_cloud use_css="0" taxonomy="category"]Select the category
    you'd like to read next:[/kk_tag_cloud]
```

6. This will disable the custom styles and produce the following effect:

Select the category you'd like to read next: Food Talk Podcast Recipes
Uncategorized

7. To display the tag cloud in its default form (showing the tags and using the custom style sheet), all we have to do is execute the shortcode, as follows:

```
[kk_tag_cloud][/kk_tag_cloud]
```

The effect is shown in the following screenshot:

FOOD   ITALIAN   MEXICAN

There are very few limitations regarding what you *can* and *cannot* do with shortcodes.

This version of the widget is available in the code bundle for this chapter, inside a subdirectory called `final`. It is the final version of our widget.

The WordPress REST API

The WordPress REST API is a relatively new addition to the WordPress platform. Before it was added to core, the REST API was available as a standalone mechanism via a separate plugin. You could get everything and also learn how to work with the package from the project's official website at `http://v2.wp-api.org/`.

However, the REST API was included in the WordPress core package in WordPress version 4.7. This means that you no longer need any additional plugins or tools to make it work. Basically, as long as you're on the most recent version of WordPress, you have the REST API installed and enabled by default. Which is great news! But let's get a bit deeper.

What is the REST API?

Under the hood, the REST API—officially called the WordPress REST API—is just another layer of technology that allows you to interact with your WordPress site, as well as the sites of other people. Chiefly, the REST API allows you to separate the presentation layer of a WordPress site from the mechanism of how WordPress operates in the background. In other words, with specific REST API calls, you can perform actions on the contents of a WordPress site without having to enter the `wp-admin` of the site, or even visit it via a web browser at all.

Why use WordPress REST API?

The introduction of the REST API opens up a lot of new possibilities as to *what you can do* with a WordPress site and *what you can use it for*. For instance, via the REST API, you can interact with WordPress content remotely, add new content, erase content, or perform any other operation. Just to name one major possibility, this makes it easy to create a mobile app for your website, and have the app communicate with the website via the REST API. In other words, if you want to communicate with a WordPress site via any other way than by visiting the site directly, then you can do that with the REST API.

How to get started with the REST API

We're only scratching the surface here, and the description provided in this chapter is by no means exhaustive. The REST API is a rather advanced piece of technology that lets you do a multitude of things—sometimes via rather complex code structures. So, the only thing we want to achieve here is to help you get started by giving you a foundation that you can then explore further as you're learning about the REST API elsewhere. A great place to get started if you want to truly master the REST API is the official developer manual at `https:/ /developer.wordpress.org/rest-api/`. With that said, what follows are the basics of how to begin with the REST API.

The REST API allows you to interact with any WordPress site via the means of sending *requests* and receiving *responses* through the WordPress HTTP API. To make a valid request, you need to reference the following: the *base URL path* of the REST API, the *route*, and the *endpoint*.

The base URL path is similar for all WordPress websites: `http://YOURWEBSITE.com /wp-json/wp/v2/`.

The route defines the exact part of the website's content that you want to communicate with. For example, you can use `posts/` in order to communicate with the site's posts. In that case, the full URL would be `http://YOURWEBSITE.com/wp-json/wp/v2/posts/`.

Endpoints are specific functions available through the REST API. For example, if you expand the route to target a specific post by ID, such as `http://YOURWEBSITE.com/wp-json/wp/v2/posts/123`, then this allows you to call one of three endpoints:

- `GET` returns the post data
- `PUT` updates the post data and returns that updated post data
- `DELETE` deletes the post and returns the now-deleted post data

Apart from the default endpoints, you can also create your own, depending on what you want to be able to do with your content through the REST API. This, however, is perhaps a topic for a more in-depth REST API manual. For the purpose of this book, let's just do a simple demonstration and create a plugin that will communicate with an external WordPress website via the REST API.

Creating a plugin that uses the REST API

You've already learned how to create basic WordPress plugins in this very chapter, so now, let's combine this knowledge with the new addition of the REST API. The plugin we're building is going to simply display a list of posts from another blog based on a shortcode.

Let's have a look at the full code of this plugin—all contained within a single file named `kk_rest_demo.php`, as follows:

```
function kk_rest_handler($atts, $content=null) {
  extract(shortcode_atts(array(
    'website_domain' => 'newinternetorder.com',
    'how_many' => '3'
  ), $atts));
  $response = wp_remote_get( 'http://' . $website_domain . '/wp-
json/wp/v2/posts/' );

  if( is_wp_error( $response ) ) {
    $error_string = $response->get_error_message();
    return 'Error occurred: <em>' . $error_string . '</em>';
  }
  $posts = json_decode( wp_remote_retrieve_body( $response ) );
  if( empty( $posts ) ) { return 'No posts found'; }
  else {
    $result = '<ul>';
    $post_count = 0;
```

```
    foreach( $posts as $post ) {
      $post_count++;
      if ($post_count <= $how_many) {
        $result .= '<li><a href="' . $post->link. '">'
        . $post->title->rendered . '</a></li>';
      }
    }
    $result .= '</ul>';
    return $result;
  }
}
add_shortcode('kk_rest', 'kk_rest_handler');
```

The first function call, extract(), is something we know from the previous shortcode plugin/widget. It extracts the attributes given to the shortcode. In our case, the shortcode works with two optional attributes, as follows:

- website_domain: This indicates the domain name of the WordPress site that the plugin should communicate with (defaults to newinternetorder.com).
- how_many: This indicates how many posts should be fetched (defaults to 3).

The next function call is where the main REST API communication happens. This call references a given route and fetches blog posts using the GET endpoint (by default), as follows:

```
$response = wp_remote_get( 'http://' . $website_domain . '/wp-
json/wp/v2/posts/' );
```

After that, we just need to check there weren't any errors, and if so, halt the function. The next function call decodes the response and allows us to reference individual posts one by one later on, as follows:

```
$posts = json_decode( wp_remote_retrieve_body( $response ) );
```

The final foreach loop and if clause go through each post and retrieve their title and URL, which then get added to a standard HTML-unordered list and returned by the shortcode. At this point, and once I activate this plugin on my test site, I can create a new post and add the following shortcode to it:

```
[kk_rest website_domain="newinternetorder.com" how_many="2"]
[/kk_rest]
```

This tells the plugin to communicate with newinternetorder.com and fetch the two most recent posts. The following screenshot shows the result of this as visible on the frontend:

MY FAV CONTENT

POSTED ON JANUARY 25, 2019

- GetResponse vs MailChimp vs SendinBlue vs Sendy vs MailPoet
- 13 Successful Entrepreneurs Share How to Gain Confidence When Starting an Online Business

POSTED IN UNCATEGORIZED

Of course, the plugin we've built here is very simple, and it does not do anything in terms of making sure that the domain provided is valid, or anything else security-related. However, the purpose of this demo is only to show you the simplest way of working with the REST API, and nothing else. Once again, I strongly encourage you to review some of the official resources, such as the *REST API Handbook* at `https://developer.wordpress.org/rest-api/`.

> This version of the plugin is available in the code bundle for this chapter, inside a subdirectory called `final`.

Summary

In this chapter, you learned everything you need to know about creating basic plugins and widgets. Now you know how to structure the plugin's PHP files, where to put your functions, and how to use hooks. You also learned about adding management pages, enabling plugins and widgets to have database access, and how to create shortcodes.

On top of all of this, you learned how to work with the REST API and perform basic communication with other WordPress websites. With your existing knowledge of PHP and HTML, you have the tools to get started writing any plugin and/or widget your heart may desire.

In the next chapter, we'll walk you through the process of creating a complete non-blog website from scratch.

Section 3: Non-Blog Websites 3

This section is the last step in your WordPress journey. Here, you'll learn how easy it is to use WordPress as the central pillar of a non-blog website.

This section will cover the follow chapters:

- Chapter 12, *Creating a Non-Blog Website, Part One – The Basics*
- Chapter 13, *Creating a Non-Blog Website, Part Two – E-Commerce Websites and Custom Content Elements*

12
Creating a Non-Blog Website
Part One - The Basics

As you have seen while reading this book, WordPress comes fully equipped to power a blog, with all of the particular requirements of post handling, categorization, chronological display, and so on, that come with a blog. However, powering blogs is not WordPress' only purpose. Not anymore. In fact, there are millions of websites out there right now that run WordPress, but where blogging is not the primary focus of the website. I myself have built a number of such sites.

Just to give you a general idea of what's possible, the following is a list of some popular non-blog type websites that you can build and launch using WordPress (we will cover some of them in more detail later in this and the next chapter):

- **Static websites**: These feature just a handful of static subpages that are not meant to be updated very often; also, the main content is not organized chronologically like blog posts.
- **Corporate or business websites**: These are similar to the previous type, but usually a bit bigger in size and in the number of subpages; additionally, for most business sites, their design appears very official and toned down.
- **One-page websites**: These are websites that only have a single page of content; used mostly as a business card-type site, or used by businesses that don't have a lot of content to showcase on their site. Even though the whole site is comprised of just a page, the designs are usually attractive, with a lot of dynamic transition effects and parallax scrolling backgrounds.
- **E-commerce stores**: These are websites where anyone can browse through a number of products and then use a shopping cart to make a purchase. Apart from the shopping cart functionality, there's also online payment integration and often a backend inventory management system.

- **Membership websites**: A type of site where some of the content is available only to those users who have signed up for a membership and (often) paid a small fee for the privilege; such members-only areas can contain any type of content that the site owner finds suitable—WordPress doesn't limit this in any way.
- **Video blogs**: This is just like a standard blog, only instead of text-based posts, the blogger publishes video posts.
- **Photo blogs**: These are just like video blogs, only revolving around photos; they are a very common type of blog for photographers, graphic designers, and other people of similar professions.
- **Product websites**: In short, it's a type of site very similar to an e-commerce store, only this time, we're usually dealing with just a single product on sale. It's a very popular type of website for all kinds of web, iOS, Android apps.
- **Social networks**: Just like Facebook, only these are run on WordPress.
- **Niche business websites**: Some examples of such sites are local restaurant websites, hotel websites, coffee shop websites, personal portfolio websites, art gallery websites, and so on.

Again, if I were to explain, in brief, what a general non-blog website is, I'd say that it's any kind of website where the blog is not the main functionality used by the website owner. And of course, non-blog websites make up the majority of the internet as a whole. However, since we're discussing WordPress here, which many still believe to be a blog system only, I just want to assure you that this is no longer the case. These days, WordPress can be used for virtually anything.

In this chapter and the next, we will go through some of the types of websites we have just mentioned and present an effective way of building them with WordPress. We'll also use the knowledge that we've acquired in the previous chapters, so it's best that you get familiar with everything that's been going on so far, before consuming the information in the following pages.

Here are the types of websites that we're going to cover in depth:

- Static websites
- Corporate or business websites
- One-page websites
- E-commerce stores
- Video blogs and photo blogs
- Social networks

Also, there are a number of new pieces of functionality that we have not explored in the previous chapters, and this is what we will be focusing on. These include the following:

- Creating a custom post type with a custom taxonomy
- Altering the custom post type display in `wp-admin`

Let's get started!

The must-do tasks

Even though there are many different types of sites that one can build with WordPress, there are some steps that are mandatory for all of them.

For instance, no matter what type of website you want to launch, you always have to start by installing WordPress properly. This is exactly what we talked about in Chapter 2, *Getting Started with WordPress*. Virtually, nothing is different at this point. The installation process is the same, all of the steps are the same, and the final result is the same too—you end up with a clean, blank WordPress installation. Also, whenever installing specific themes and plugins, make sure to follow the same guidelines that we discussed in Chapter 5, *Plugins – What They Are and Why You Need Them*, and Chapter 7, *Choosing and Installing Themes*.

Last but not least, to ensure that your site is secure and has a good user management structure, you have to keep in mind all of the best practices revolving around user accounts and editorial workflow (publishing new content).

Basically, the only element that's different when building a non-blog website is the process of picking the theme and selecting the plugins for the site. Additionally, if you want to take it to the next level, you'll have to look into implementing various functionalities by hand, or getting a custom solution made for you by a professional.

Luckily though, the process itself is not much more difficult than working with a standard blog. So, once you have some experience with WordPress under your belt, you'll be able to get it done just as quickly.

Static websites

Let's start with static websites, as they are the simplest type of non-blog websites, and also the easiest ones to create (which shouldn't be surprising).

The best part about static websites is that building them doesn't require any specific themes or plugins. The secret is your mindset as the developer. In essence, to pull this off effectively, the only things you need to do are the following:

1. Utilize the page's functionality in WordPress
2. Tune up the default home page to create a more static experience

The process

Firstly, let's tackle one common misconception. The point of a static website isn't to make the content hard coded into the HTML or PHP files at all. The actual point is to abandon the standard chronological organization of content (to abandon the blog functionality) and to focus on building a site where pages exist on their own, independently of one another. So, in the end, we can still edit everything pretty easily through wp-admin, and the only difference is that we're not using the standard WordPress posts for anything. Instead, we're focusing on the WordPress pages.

During the setup process of a good static page, you'll have to do the following:

1. Pick a WordPress theme that fits your goals and looks attractive for your particular project (something we talked about in Chapter 7, *Choosing and Installing Themes*); this is a mandatory step for all types of non-blog websites. Quite simply, not every theme will fit every type of website. So, whenever picking a specific one, keep in mind what you want to use the website for—this is going to make your work easier as a developer and make the website better for future visitors once the site is launched.
2. Create a list of all of the static pages that you want to make a part of your website. For instance, for a local pet grooming service, the pages could be a gallery, offers and pricing, testimonials, a contact page, and a map.
3. Create each page in the wp-admin (through **Pages** | **Add New**).
4. Create one more page, call it **HOME**, and tweak it to provide a good home page experience. For instance, start by focusing on the elements that a first-time visitor would consider useful on your home page. A good home page should answer the question, *what is this site about?*
5. Create easy-to-grasp menus to make navigation a breeze.

Steps 1 to 3 are pretty straightforward, so let's just focus on the last two.

Building your home page

By default, WordPress takes the main blog listing (the chronological list of posts) and uses it as the home page. This is not the desired situation in our case, since there will be no posts. What we'll do instead is create a custom page and then use it as a static front page (home page).

We talked about how to do this in detail back in Chapter 4, *Pages, Media, and Importing/Exporting Content*. Therefore, let's just focus on a basic overview here, but feel free to go back to Chapter 4, *Pages, Media, and Importing/Exporting Content*, for a more hands-on tutorial.

To build a new home page, go to **Pages** | **Add New** and proceed as if you were working on any other page. You can call it **HOME** to make it clear what it is for. What you place on this page is up to you. Essentially, a home page should be a great starting page for anyone who visits a given site for the first time. For instance, you can go with a short introductory message, a list of some popular articles on your site, a contact form provided by the **Contact Form 7** plugin, and an interactive map by *Google Maps*. You can place all of those elements using the new block-editor that's in WordPress.

Once you have your page ready, the only thing you have to do is assign it as the *front page*. This can be done in **Settings** | **Reading**, as discussed in Chapter 4, *Pages, Media, and Importing/Exporting Content*.

If you want to make your home page more fancy, you can create a custom page template (described in Chapter 9, *Developing Your Own Theme*), which will allow you to include any design elements you might need, along with a wealth of custom functionality. Again, it all depends on the project.

Creating easy-to-grasp menus

The last element of this static-website puzzle is a proper menu (or menus). Because our home page is just like any other page that you can create in WordPress, it will appear in the default pages menu (pages widget), which isn't the most optimized situation.

Therefore, whenever working with static websites, make sure to use only custom menus created in **Appearance** | **Menus**. This gives you full control over what gets displayed in the header, the sidebar, and anywhere else on the site.

Corporate or business websites

When we look at the main purpose of corporate or business websites, it becomes apparent that their construction is very similar to static websites. The only difference is that they are much bigger (with more pages and more content), and their design seems much more official. Also, most businesses like to publish some occasional announcements, so a blog-like functionality is required too (but it still won't be the main element on the site).

In essence, creating a quality corporate site with WordPress is all about picking (or building) the right theme. If you do a quick bit of research on the web, you'll see that most corporate sites (at least the good ones) feature hardly any design. The thing that makes them stand out is their very subtle branding (through a certain color scheme or clever use of logos), and stellar navigation layout.

What this means is that the easiest way to build a great corporate site with WordPress is to do the following:

- Pick a clean theme with good content organization and featuring almost none of the design bells and whistles
- Include specific branding elements and pick the right color scheme
- Build a nice user-friendly navigation structure through custom menus
- Construct a custom home page
- Add one visual element in the form of a home page slider to make the site seem more alive (optional)

Let's go through this list one by one.

Picking a clean theme

This is something we talked about in the previous chapters, so let me just point you toward some of the top places where you can get WordPress themes real quick. They are as follows:

- The official directory (https://wordpress.org/themes/)
- ThemeIsle (https://themeisle.com/)
- Elegant Themes (https://www.elegantthemes.com/)
- ThemeForest (https://themeforest.net/category/wordpress)

The thing to keep in mind is to go straight to the business-related part of the theme directory you're browsing. For example, at ThemeForest, go straight to `https://themeforest.net/category/wordpress/corporate`. This will make the selection process a lot quicker.

> Keep in mind that if it's a free theme you're after, you should always get it from the official directory (we discussed this in `Chapter 7`, *Choosing and Installing Themes*).

The features to look for in a quality corporate theme include the following:

- A minimal design that lets you include branding elements
- An easy way of adding a logo and other graphics
- Custom header functionality
- Favicon support
- A responsive layout (meaning that it'll be equally as attractive on a desktop computer as on a mobile phone)
- Customizable sidebars
- Customizable layouts (for example, full-width, 1-sidebar, 2-sidebar, and so on)
- Multi-author support (there's usually a number of people taking care of a corporate site simultaneously)
- Built-in color schemes to choose from
- Be SEO-ready
- Custom page templates for the home page, contact page, FAQ, offers, gallery, team, testimonials, 404 errors, portfolio, and so on
- Be cross-browser compatible

Your theme doesn't have to do all of these things, but this list should be a good benchmark in determining how suitable the theme you're about to pick is when it comes to running a corporate site.

Branding elements

From a business point of view, branding is the most important parameter of a recognizable site. Therefore, make sure that both the logo and the corporate identity of the company match the color scheme of the theme. Also, as I mentioned in the previous section, a good theme should allow you to pick the color scheme from one of the predefined ones.

Finally, turn the logo into a favicon and upload it to the site too (this can be done through your theme's built-in favicon functionality, or via a plugin, such as **All In One Favicon**, available at `https://wordpress.org/plugins/all-in-one-favicon/`). This will give the site some additional visibility in the bookmarks menu (should the visitor choose to bookmark it).

Good navigation

This is probably the toughest part of the job when building a corporate site, mainly because we can never be sure how much content the site is eventually going to feature. There's always the danger that our navigation will either be too much for a handful of pages of content or too little for hundreds of pages. There are, however, some good practices that you can follow:

- Focus on providing an extensive menu in the footer. This will make sure that every visitor will be able to find what they're looking for once they scroll down to the bottom of the page. This is easily doable with footer widget areas, which every good corporate theme should provide you with. The following screenshot shows an example by Samsung:

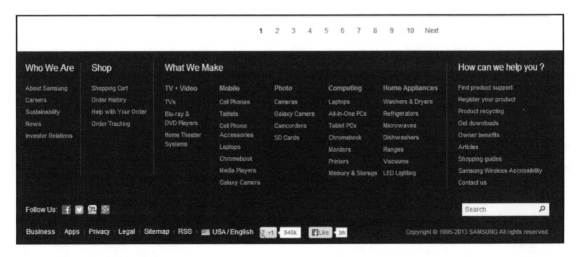

- Create a top menu with only a couple of the most essential pages. Sometimes, just four links will be enough. For example, the following screenshot demonstrates how Home Chef does this:

- Create a sidebar menu linking to the important areas of the site, such as specific categories, products, announcements, or other things the average visitor might find interesting.
- Use breadcrumbs: Breadcrumbs are small links that present the path of the visitor in relation to the home page. Most themes provide this functionality by default. It's best to place them just below the header. That way, the reader can easily go back to a more general page. An example of this is highlighted in the following screenshot:

- Display a visible search field. A large number of visitors coming to a corporate site are after a specific piece of information, so they naturally start looking for a search field right away. Making their life easier is a very good idea. A great placement for a search field is in the header and in the main sidebar (sidebar menu) for good visibility.

Custom home page

Just as with static websites, the default blog listing rarely makes a good home page for a corporate site. Going with a custom home page is always a better strategy, and gives us a more optimized way of presenting the company, its goals, and its field of expertise. To create such a home page, you can safely follow the instructions given earlier in this chapter, when we were discussing static websites.

Now, like I said, showing the default blog listing as the home page is not a good approach here. However, we should still provide at least some integration with the blog part of the website. The two most sensible solutions are to either link to the blog listing page in a visible place on the home page, or include a simplified listing as a widget in one of the available widget areas on the home page itself.

The latter can be done by the **Recent Posts** widget that's available in WordPress by default (we covered widgets and how to use them in Chapter 5, *Plugins – What They Are and Why You Need Them*). The former can be done as follows:

1. Create a new page (**Pages | Add New**) and call it **NEWS**. The page doesn't have to feature any content. It only needs to exist with a unique name. I'm suggesting **NEWS** because it gives a clear indication of what's going on.
2. Navigate to **Settings | Reading** and set your new page as the default **Posts page**, as shown in the following screenshot:

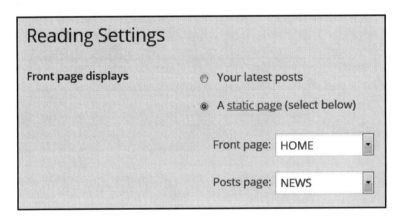

3. As you can see, there's also the old **HOME** page that's currently set as the **Front page**; we're going to leave it like that.

4. Place the link to the new blog section (**NEWS**) in the top menu (preferably). You can do it in **Appearance | Menus**.

5. Now, if you navigate to your new **NEWS** page (using something like `http://yoursite.com/news`), you will see the default blog listing, which the company (or the owner of the website) can use to publish various announcements, or whatever else they see fit.

Slider (optional)

The last element worth discussing here is a home page slider. Although most corporate websites are not about the graphics, this single visual element is often added. Animated sliders make any website seem more alive and attractive to the visitor. For a corporate site, the slider can present photos from events, individual announcements, product offers, or contact details, as well as a number of other things.

Some themes will come with a slider functionality built-in right from the get-go. If they don't, you can always get a plugin to handle the job. The only downside is that most slider plugins are not free. Among those that are free, I can point out these two, as follows:

- **Master Slider**: `https://wordpress.org/plugins/master-slider/`
- **Nivo Slider**: `https://wordpress.org/plugins/nivo-slider-lite/`

In general, sliders are not a mandatory thing for corporate websites, but they might improve user experience, so they're probably worth a try.

One-page websites

One-page websites are a relatively new invention in the online world. A couple of years ago, webmasters were not that keen on having just a single page to make up their entire website. It simply seemed like not working hard enough on your website's presence. These days, however, things have changed. It's no longer looked down on. In fact, single-page websites are the new trend.

In some way, a one-page or a single-page website is similar to a static website. You mostly get to work with WordPress pages rather than its blog functionality, and after you set that page in place, it will likely stay that way for a longer period of time—that is, it will remain static. On one-page websites, though, you simply get to work with only one page as opposed to having a number of them.

Just to give you a general overview of what a one-page site looks like, visit `http://karol.cc/`. It's my personal website, which I use to market my freelance writing services, and can be seen in the following screenshot:

As you can see, the website is built up of just a single page—the home page. However, each block on this page is visually separated from the previous and the next one. This visual separation is one of the most important aspects of single-page websites. So, as with many types of websites, creating a truly great-looking one-page site is about picking the right theme—something that your target audience will enjoy and appreciate. The easiest way to build a great one-page site with WordPress is to do the following:

- Pick a theme that's marketed explicitly as a one-page theme and has a clean design, with good-looking content blocks on the main page
- Include specific branding elements and pick the right color scheme
- Make sure to prepare a number of high-quality images that you can use in the background

Let's go through this list one by one.

Picking a one-page theme

Just as with most other categories, one-page themes are now highly popular in theme stores across the web. The best places to go find them include, again, the official directory (`https://wordpress.org/themes/`), ThemeIsle (`https://themeisle.com/`), and ThemeForest (`https://themeforest.net/category/wordpress`). Not all of them, however, feature specialized categories for one-page themes, so you might have to use the search option to find something interesting. Searching for terms such as *single page* or *one page* should give you great results.

The features to look for in a quality one-page theme are as follows:

- A minimal design that lets you include your branding elements
- An easy way of adding a logo and other graphics
- Custom header functionality
- A parallax scrolling option (where the background images appear to move more slowly than the foreground)
- A responsive layout (meaning that it'll be equally as attractive on a desktop computer as on a mobile phone)
- Built-in color schemes to choose from
- Be SEO-ready
- Be cross-browser compatible

The more of these preceding features that your theme includes, the better. If anything is missing, you can always find a plugin that will fill the void. After all, there's a plugin for everything, remember?

Branding elements

Branding elements are particularly important with one-page sites because, by definition, you don't get much online real estate to work with, so to speak. If there's just one page on the site, you need to make sure that it's as in tune with your brand and identity as possible. Therefore, a good theme should allow you to place elements, such as your own logo, social media links, and custom graphics, in places such as the header, footer, and the background. Luckily, those sorts of features are considered the standard among modern WordPress themes, so you probably won't have to worry about this part at all.

High-quality images

One of the main flaws with one-page themes is that they often rely heavily on good visuals and high-quality images. The designs are often simple and very minimalist, and their attractive appearance is based on the images used in the background of the site. Unfortunately, finding such images is entirely up to you. Themes rarely come with unique images that you will be able to use on your site.

How to get those images? You can buy them in places such as `https://www.istockphoto.com/`, that's one solution. But you can also get a lot of great images for free in places such as `https://unsplash.com/`. The last solution is, of course, to take your own photos and use them on your site.

As an example, I will get one of the most popular one-page themes in the WordPress directory right now—**Hestia** (available at `https://wordpress.org/themes/hestia/`), and do some basic tuning up around it to show you how one-page themes work.

Right after downloading and activating the theme (this is the standard procedure; see `Chapter 7`, *Choosing and Installing Themes,* for the how-to), you can go straight to WordPress Customizer at **Appearance | Customize**. You'll see a large customization panel there. With it, I can change the main headline on the site, the buttons, the appearance of individual blocks, and also the background image of the whole site, as demonstrated in the following screenshot:

After a handful of tweaks, I end up with a great-looking one-page site. You can see what my final header looks like in the following screenshot:

That's pretty much it when it comes to launching a nice one-page website with WordPress. The most remarkable thing here is how easy it is to actually do this. Just imagine how much time it would take to create something like this from the ground up, or the cost required to set it up. The possibilities that WordPress delivers these days are really incredible.

Summary

We covered a lot of excellent material in this chapter. We started by listing some of the popular types of non-blog websites that you can build successfully with WordPress. Then, we went through some of those websites individually and discussed the specific elements to focus on, in order to guarantee a quality final product.

The next chapter is part two of our guide to creating a non-blog website. In it, we'll go through some of the more user-centered types of websites, such as e-commerce stores, photo and video blogs, and finally, building your own social network.

13
Creating a Non-Blog Website Part Two - E-Commerce Websites and Custom Content Elements

In the previous chapter, you saw different types of non-blog websites. This chapter is a continuation of that topic, so let's do two things. First, let's go through some of the more trendy uses of WordPress and focus on a step-by-step process for reaching a great final result. Then, let's discuss some of the custom content elements you can create in WordPress, such as custom post types, custom taxonomies, and the process of customizing the admin display slightly. We will study the following topics in this chapter:

- E-commerce stores
- Video blogs and photo blogs
- Social networks
- Introducing custom post types

E-commerce stores

E-commerce stores, in general, are websites where anyone can browse through a number of products and then use a shopping cart to make a purchase. Also, most e-commerce stores offer some kind of online payment integration, which allows every visitor to make and complete a purchase quickly. Additionally, sometimes there's even a backend inventory management system (an online warehouse of sorts) to make backend business management easier and integrated with the website.

Is WordPress a good platform for an e-commerce store?

The best thing about e-commerce is that you can actually launch a fully functional online store with WordPress. This, in my opinion, is simply incredible! As a former website developer, I actually remember how expensive and time-consuming it was to build such a store from the ground up. And now, you can just install WordPress, get a proper theme, download a specialized e-commerce plugin, and you're good to go! This is a prime example of how technology helps you to run your business the modern way.

Okay, enough with the intro. Let's focus on the actual process of building a quality e-commerce store. First off, the thing with e-commerce stores on WordPress is that they are extremely plugin-driven, so to speak. What I mean is that if you want to launch such a website, you will need to get one main e-commerce plugin that's going to be responsible for the complete set of operations available in your store. In short, this plugin will run your store. For that reason, choosing the right plugin is extremely important, which is something I'm sure you understand.

Getting a good e-commerce plugin

There are numerous premium plugins on the market. They offer a ton of features and integrate with almost any online payment processing method available. But, what's actually quite surprising is that the most popular plugin of them all is 100% free. It's called **WooCommerce**, and it has become the *de facto* standard for running an e-commerce store on WordPress.

WooCommerce (available either at `https://woocommerce.com/` or `https://wordpress.org/plugins/woocommerce/`) is beautifully designed and offers a truly exceptional range of features, which I will get into in a minute. The main reason why I like the WooCommerce plugin so much is because it can be integrated with any theme. And I really do mean *any*. However, for a real-life business website (not just a test website, like the one we're going to build in a minute), I still think that you should use an optimized e-commerce theme. Again, feel free to visit one of the popular theme stores to get something of top quality. I listed a number of them in `Chapter 7`, *Choosing and Installing Themes*.

In short, a good e-commerce theme should achieve the following:

- Have a clear design
- Present the center content block in an attention-grabbing way (this is where the products are going to be displayed)
- Allow you to tune the number of sidebars you want to display
- Be responsive (that is, viewable on any device)
- Have a good navigation structure that's ready to house hundreds, if not thousands, of subpages (usually product pages)
- Handle multilingual content
- Provide some level of social media integration (to allow users to share product links on Twitter or Facebook)

Just to summarize this introduction, to give a head start in running an e-commerce store on WordPress, you need to pair the WooCommerce plugin with a good-looking WordPress theme that's optimized to work on an e-commerce website.

Plugin installation and initial setup

Now that we have our plugin chosen, perform the following steps to install and set it up:

1. To get WooCommerce, you can either go to `https://wordpress.org/plugins/woocommerce/`, or install it straight from the `wp-admin` panel when you go to **Plugins | Add New**.
2. Just input `WooCommerce` into the main search field. Most likely, the first plugin on the list is the one you're looking for.

3. Click on **Install Now** and when the process finishes, activate the plugin. The following screenshot shows what you'll see afterward:

4. WooCommerce shows you the main page of the onscreen setup wizard. The best thing about it is that you're being guided through the whole process step by step.

Setting up the main store pages

Among the first things that you need to do is create some of the mandatory pages that allow your website to transform into a fully-fledged e-commerce store. Luckily, WooCommerce takes care of this for you—all you have to do is click on the **Continue** button. You will get the following pages:

- **Shop**: Your main shop page—this is where your products are going to appear
- **Cart**: The shopping cart area of the store
- **Checkout**: The area where your customers can finalize their orders
- **My Account**: Profile pages for your registered customers

Your store location

The next step is setting up your store location. This is quite simple, since you only need to select where your store is based and which currency it will use. Additionally, if you're going to be charging sales tax, you can set that up there too, as shown in the following screenshot:

Shipping and payments

The next screen in the WooCommerce wizard is about setting up your shipping details, along with weight and dimension units. After that, you get to set the payment methods that your store will use. What you select there depends on your store type and the kinds of goods that you're going to be selling. The following screenshot shows what's available:

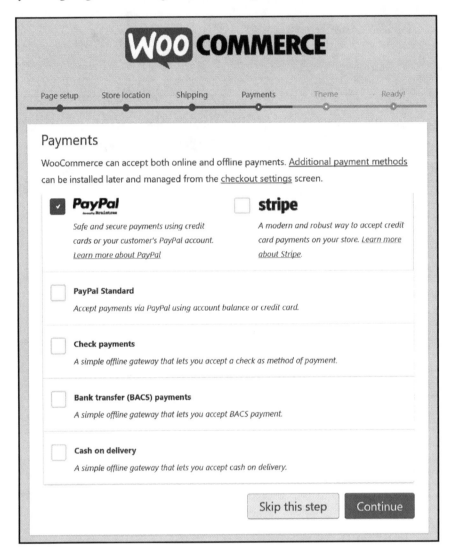

Usually, you will want to enable PayPal at the very least.

Adjusting your store design

The next step in the process, a very important step, is picking a design for your store. One of the best ways to get started here is to go with the official WooCommerce theme, called **Storefront**. This theme can be installed with a click on the right from the WooCommerce wizard, as shown in the following screenshot:

Once you get **Storefront** installed, the setup process is complete and the store is fully operational, as in, you can begin adding your first products.

Adding products

When it comes to products, WooCommerce follows the standard content organization method in WordPress. This means that you can manage products just like you'd manage any other piece of content (pages or posts). All you have to do is perform the following steps:

1. Go to **Products** | **Add New** and fill out the product fields. Notice that products also have their own categories and tags, as shown in the following screenshot:

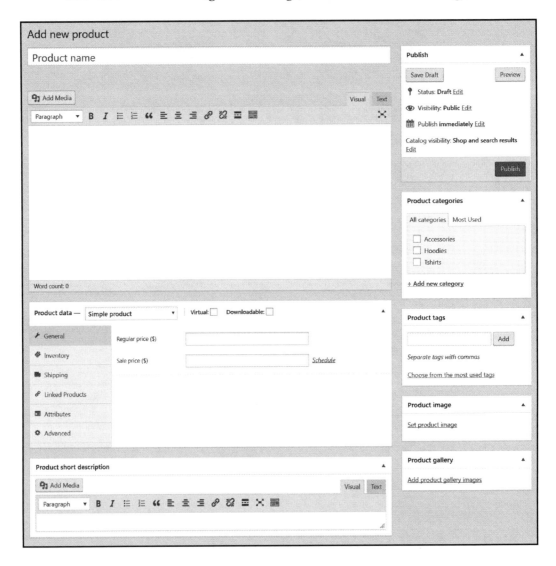

2. Once you have a handful of products added, the following screenshot shows what the **Products** | **All Products** section of your `wp-admin` panel is going to look like:

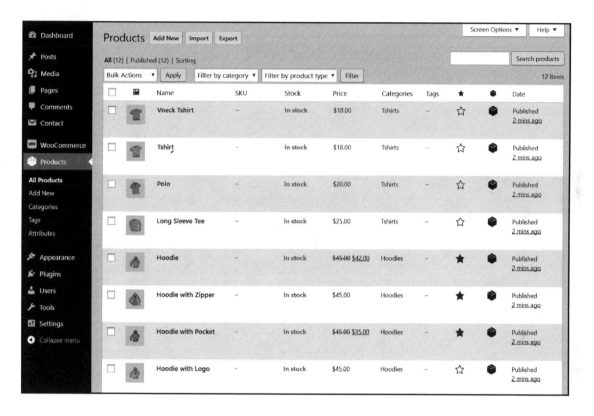

3. The following screenshot shows the main page of the store, with all the products available to your customers:

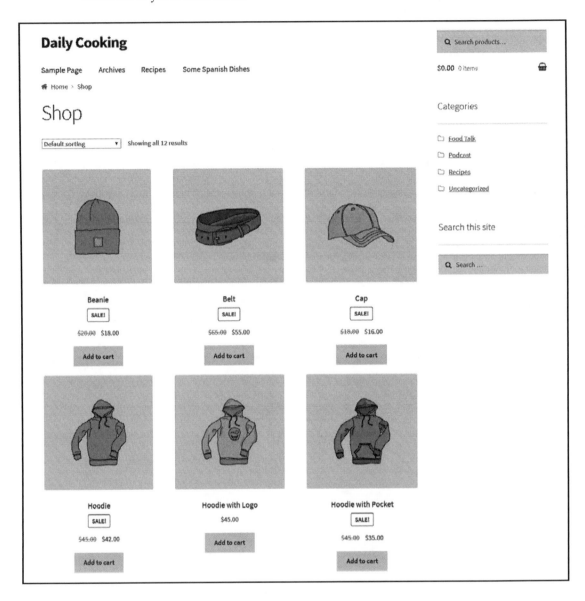

4. Each individual product also looks quite nice when you view it. An example is shown in the following screenshot:

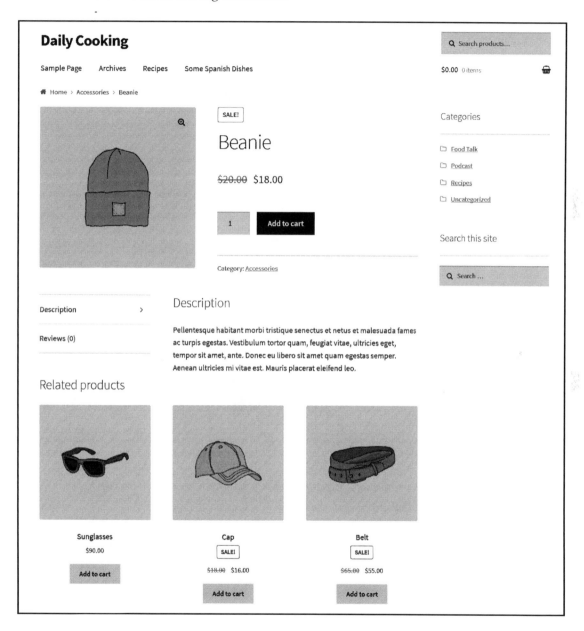

Stats – orders, coupons, and reports

The last element of the plugin worth discussing here for a minute is the management backend—the orders, coupons, and reports.

Orders can be found in **WooCommerce | Orders**. You can manage them just like any other piece of WordPress content. There are a number of additional fields and parameters, though, so there might be a slight learning curve. But it is still a very friendly and easy-to-use environment. An example of what orders look like is shown in the following screenshot:

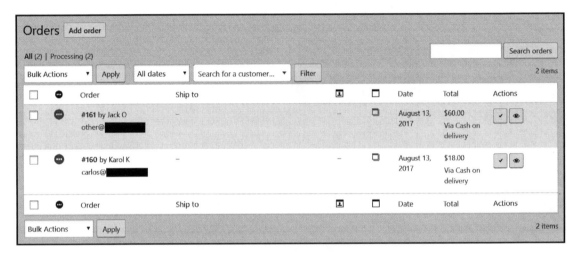

To view and create new coupon codes, navigate to **WooCommerce | Coupons**. Coupons are a great way to bring new people to your store. Everyone loves a bargain, don't they? Or, you can make your coupon codes publicly available on the internet as a promotional method.

Lastly, to view reports, navigate to **WooCommerce | Reports**. There's a nice graphical representation of what's been going on in your store. You can view sales, coupons used, customer activity, and your current stock. Right now, I don't have much going on in my store, so the graph looks like the following:

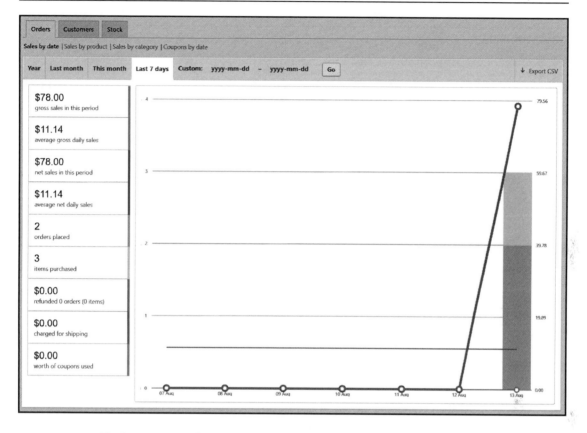

To learn more about managing orders and coupons, look at these official pages in the WooCommerce docs:

- https://docs.woocommerce.com/document/managing-orders/
- https://docs.woocommerce.com/document/coupon-management/

That's pretty much it on the topic of using WooCommerce and launching a nice e-commerce store on WordPress. The most remarkable thing here is how easy it is to actually do it. Just imagine how much time it would take to create something with similar functionality from the ground up. Or, better yet, the cost required to set it up. The possibilities that WordPress and various plugins deliver these days are really incredible. I'm sure that a couple of years ago, no one would even believe that launching a quality e-commerce store could be done this easily.

One last thing, WooCommerce is not entirely free all the time. If you want to install additional features, the official extensions are anything between $29 and $99. So, for some specific, real-world applications, investments might be required.

We've only scretched the surface here, and there's a lot more that WooCommerce can do. It is a truly impressive piece of software, and it's absolutely exceptional when it comes to giving you reliable e-commerce functionality that turns your otherwise standard WordPress website into a professional e-commerce store. If you want to learn more about building a store with WooCommerce from scratch, the best place to get your information is probably the official docs section at `https://docs.woocommerce.com/documentation/plugins/woocommerce/getting-started/`.

Video blogs and photo blogs

Let's cover these two types of WordPress sites together because the individual goals for each are often very similar (although their designs may still be a bit different). In short, a video blog is one where the author mainly publishes videos, instead of traditional text-based posts. A photo blog, on the other hand, is essentially the same thing, the only difference being it revolves around photos.

Now, why would you even bother with a customized setup for a video blog or a photo blog in the first place when you can just use a standard WordPress installation with a traditional blogging-optimized theme? Well, to be honest here, you can indeed go with a standard setup, and your video/photo blog will be just about *fine*. But with some additional work (not much) put into building something that's tailor-made for multimedia blogs, your site can gain a big advantage over your competition, mostly in terms of usability and content presentation.

For instance, let's focus on the following interesting features you can add to a video blog:

- A blog home page built on a grid layout with big thumbnails, so every visitor can see the snapshots of the videos right away
- Videos in the main listing presented as concise blocks containing the thumbnail and a small amount of text to convince people to click on the video
- A wide main blog listing with just a narrow sidebar on the left (or right)
- Integrated social media features (including YouTube subscription buttons)
- Social media comments fetched from the platform where the video was originally hosted

- A custom backend to host the videos on the blog (or on an external server)
- A shareable embed code, so your visitors can embed the videos easily
- A custom player to replace the native YouTube or Vimeo players

You can have the following interesting features on a photo blog:

- A custom home page featuring one main photo (*a photo of the day*)
- An automatic photo slider on the home page
- Lightbox functionality for viewing the photos in full size
- A wide main blog listing with integrated social media features
- Social media comments
- A custom backend to host photos
- A shareable embed code
- Custom photo controls (such as *save, view full size, share,* and so on)

As you can see, most of these features can work equally well on both video blogs and photo blogs. As usual with WordPress, you can get most of them either by obtaining a quality theme, or using some third-party plugins. Let's cover both of these approaches.

Exploring themes for video and photo sites

Being quite popular kinds of blogs, both video and photo blogs have a very wide range of themes available on the internet. But, be careful! Searching for a theme on Google can get you in trouble. Well, maybe not in *trouble* per se, but if you end up downloading a theme from a random site, you have no guarantee that it's a secure solution and that there's no malicious or encrypted code inside. A much better method is to either go to the official directory or to some of the recognized theme stores.

For starters, the following themes are available out there:

- **Shapely**, available at `https://wordpress.org/themes/shapely/`
- **TheMotion Lite**, available at `https://wordpress.org/themes/themotion-lite/`
- **RokoPhoto Lite**, available at `https://wordpress.org/themes/rokophoto-lite/`
- **Activello**, available at `https://wordpress.org/themes/activello/`

These are all free, but you can also get a premium theme. However, this will require an investment, so only do it if you're devoted to creating a really high-quality multimedia blog.

Getting plugins for video and photo blogs

As I said, apart from video and photo optimized themes, you can also get a number of plugins that will make your site more functional. The good news is that we're only going to focus on free plugins:

- **Optimole** (`https://wordpress.org/plugins/optimole-wp/`): This plugin doesn't present any particular output on the frontend of your site, because what it actually does is automatically optimizes your images in the background. This is a great plugin for saving your bandwidth, especially if you're publishing a lot of images. The installation process is quite standard. Once the plugin is activated and you've provided your free API key, it starts working in the background with no supervision required.

- **Simple Lightbox** (`https://wordpress.org/plugins/simple-lightbox/`): This plugin delivers a really good-looking lightbox functionality. The best thing about this plugin is that it's ultra easy to use. All you have to do is activate it, and it will immediately start taking care of the images you're displaying on your blog. The plugin will intercept image clicks and show the image file in a nice lightbox instead of loading them individually (on a blank page).

- **Envira Gallery** (`https://wordpress.org/plugins/envira-gallery-lite/`): This is one of the most popular gallery plugins for WordPress. It allows you to create responsive (optimized for desktop and mobile) photo and video galleries. The great thing about it is that you can build your galleries with drag and drop.

- **10Web Instagram Feed** (`https://wordpress.org/plugins/wd-instagram-feed/`): Instagram is now a crucial part of any photographer or videographer's presence on the web. This plugin offers you quick integration with everyone's favorite photo platform. Use it to showcase your Instagram feed as a widget.

Just to sum up the topic of multimedia blogs, I have to point out that this is a very crowded area among both theme and plugin developers. The plugins mentioned here will give you a good start, but having your finger on the pulse and paying attention to what's new on the market (as in, cool new plugins and themes) is actually the best way to keep your photo or video blog on top of its game. That being said, getting and testing every new plugin out there is not the recommended approach. Still, from time to time, you can find a true gem that's going to help you take your blog to the next level.

Social networks

Finally, it's time to discuss one of the most surprising topics in relation to building various types of websites with WordPress. As it turns out, the platform can be used very well to run a fully functional social network. In other words, you can have your own Facebook if you want to, at least when it comes to functionality.

And speaking of functionality, in short, a social network built with WordPress can offer the following features:

- Support for any number of user accounts
- Facebook-like publishing method for users (a *Wall* or an activity stream)
- Forums
- Blogs and microblogs
- Friends
- Groups
- Private messages
- Comments
- Photo and video content

That being said, building and then running a well-constructed social network, utilizing all of the available features, will require some serious work. This is way beyond the scope of this book. So, here, we're only going to focus on the basic setup process and getting started. If you're planning to launch an actual social network and make it available to the world, you should probably get more information, either by going to the official online documentation, or obtaining some more publications on the topic.

Essentially, social networking on WordPress works through one specific plugin—**BuddyPress**, although calling it just a plugin is a massive understatement. BuddyPress is a whole online publishing environment on its own, which integrates with WordPress. Unlike other plugins, it doesn't just display some custom content here and there. It actually changes the whole appearance (structure) of your WordPress site to make it look, and operate, like a social network.

Let's take the topic step by step, starting with installation.

Installing a social network

There's nothing fancy here, to install a social network all you have to do is perform the following steps:

1. Go to `https://buddypress.org/`, download the main plugin and then upload it to your WordPress site, or search for the plugin from within the `wp-admin` panel (**Plugins** | **Add New**) using the name `BuddyPress`.

2. The installation process of the plugin itself is quite standard, meaning that after getting it on your server, you only have to click on the **Activate** button.

3. When the process finishes, visit the settings section under **Settings** | **BuddyPress**. First, pick the components you'd like to use in your new social network. For testing purposes, I just enabled all of them, as shown in the following screenshot:

	Component	Description
☑	Extended Profiles	Customize your community with fully editable profile fields that allow your users to describe themselves.
☑	Account Settings	Allow your users to modify their account and notification settings directly from within their profiles.
☑	Friend Connections	Let your users make connections so they can track the activity of others and focus on the people they care about the most.
☑	Private Messaging	Allow your users to talk to each other directly and in private. Not just limited to one-on-one discussions, messages can be sent between any number of members.
☑	Activity Streams	Global, personal, and group activity streams with threaded commenting, direct posting, favoriting, and @mentions, all with full RSS feed and email notification support.
☑	Notifications	Notify members of relevant activity with a toolbar bubble and/or via email, and allow them to customize their notification settings.
☑	User Groups	Groups allow your users to organize themselves into specific public, private or hidden sections with separate activity streams and member listings.
☑	Site Tracking	Record activity for new posts and comments from your site.
☑	BuddyPress Core	It's what makes ~~time travel~~ BuddyPress possible!
☑	Community Members	Everything in a BuddyPress community revolves around its members.

4. The second tab on this settings page, titled **Options**, is where you can adjust some of the other standard settings, such as the presence of the top toolbar, various profile settings, and group settings.

5. Finally, the third tab, **Pages**, lets you assign the pages that will house some standard areas of your social network, such as the activity stream, user groups, and member profiles.

You can create new pages here or use the ones that BuddyPress created already during installation.

Designing your social network

In its current form, BuddyPress can work with any WordPress theme. That's right, you don't have to have an optimized social networking design if you don't want to. BuddyPress will manage to display its contents inside either the main content block of your current theme, or the widget areas you have available.

However, as usual, if you want to make your social network look more professional, then you should probably look around and get something that's specifically optimized for social networks. The best rule of thumb when you're searching for such themes, in my opinion, is to compare them against the biggest social network of them all—Facebook. Although some people don't enjoy the design that Facebook offers, it is still the most successful social network around, so they are clearly doing something right. Treating it as a benchmark of sorts is, therefore, a very good idea.

If you want to find a nice list of BuddyPress-compatible themes, the WordPress directory comes to the rescue yet again. When you go to `https://wordpress.org/themes/search/buddypress/`, you'll find a filtered list of themes that have been tested with BuddyPress and are optimized to work as a social network.

Once you've found yourself a nice-looking theme, you can go straight to working with your new social network without focusing any more on the setup. However, if you really want to get to know the platform and the way it's built, I advise you to go to the official documentation, which is one of the best BuddyPress resources available (`https://codex.buddypress.org/`). It's also where you can learn all the ins and outs of BuddyPress development, creating your own themes, or even BuddyPress extension plugins.

Extending the functionality

BuddyPress is constructed in a way that provides the basic social networking functionality and site organization. If you want to extend your social media site and give it some new features, you can install a number of BuddyPress plugins. You can find them at `https://wordpress.org/plugins/search/buddypress/`. Basically, they are just like other WordPress plugins (the installation process is the same), but instead of delivering some new functionality to WordPress itself, they focus more on BuddyPress.

There is a lot more waiting for you inside BuddyPress, and I actually encourage you to do some researching and learning on your own, especially if you're planning to launch a social network at some point. But for now, I think that we've got the topic covered, at least when it comes to giving you an introduction to social networking with WordPress and getting started with the best social networking plugin available.

Introducing custom post types

While building some of the sites described in the current and the previous chapters, you may stumble upon what're called custom post types. Or you may even decide to create them yourself for the purpose of your individual projects. But let's take it from the top. The most commonly known types of content in WordPress are *posts* and *pages*. However, if we feel that the situation/project calls for it, we can create any number of new post types by taking advantage of the custom post type functionality and its wide versatility.

The need for custom post types can appear in many scenarios. For instance, when a writer is building a personal portfolio site, they might need a custom post type named `book` to present their publications in an attractive way, instead of just using standard posts. This is exactly what we're about to do in this section of the chapter. So, gear up to learn how custom post types work by building a new one.

For this purpose, we'll go back to our main cooking blog theme—*Daily Cooking Custom*. In its default form, it doesn't feature any custom post types, and that's a good thing as we've got a blank canvas to work on. To specify that you'd like to have a custom post type in your theme, you can add some code to your theme's `functions.php` file. This is what we'll be doing. However, keep in mind that you can also attach the custom post type to a plugin or a widget if you don't want it to be tied to a particular theme.

Registering a new post type

To register a new post type, all you have to do is add some simple code to your theme's `functions.php` file. It's good practice to tie the creation of the new type to the `init` function of the theme so that it gets called at the right moment in the booting process. The following is the initial, blank, custom-post-type code:

```
function book_init() {
   register_post_type('book');
}
add_action('init', 'book_init');
```

The `register_post_type()` function takes an array as its second parameter, and in that array, you can specify whether the object is public or should be involved in rewriting the URL, what elements it supports on its editing page, and so on. Let's set up an array of all the arguments and then pass it to the function, as shown in the following code:

```
function book_init() {
   $args = array(
      'description' => 'A custom post type that holds my books',
      'public' => true,
      'rewrite' => array('slug' => 'books'),
      'has_archive' => true,
      'supports' => array('title', 'editor', 'author', 'excerpt',
      'custom-fields', 'thumbnail'),
      'show_in_rest' => true
   );
   register_post_type('book', $args);
   flush_rewrite_rules();
}
add_action('init', 'book_init');
```

I've chosen each of the following parameters because they make sense for the `book` custom post type:

- `description`: This one's pretty self-explanatory.
- `public`: This means that the post type is available publicly, just as posts and pages are—rather than being hidden behind the scenes. It'll get a user interface and can be shown in navigation menus, and so on.
- `rewrite`: This specifies that the post type can be used in the rewrite rules for pretty permalinks.
- `has_archive`: This enables post type archives (a classic index page, like we have for our standard posts).

- **supports**: This is an array of the capabilities that users see when they're creating or editing an item. For books, we're including six items.
- **show_in_rest**: This enables our new custom post type to work with the block editor introduced in WordPress 5.

The final function call, `flush_rewrite_rules()`, will allow us to show a standard archive listing of the books later on (just like a standard post listing, but for our custom post type).

 These are just some of the arguments you can pass. Read about the others in the codex at `https://codex.wordpress.org/Function_Reference/register_post_type`.

Now that we've got the basic post type set up, let's add some labels.

Adding labels

You can add labels to your custom post type so that WordPress knows what to say when talking about it. First, let's simply create an array of all the labels. Put this as the first thing inside the `book_init()` function, as shown in the following code:

```
$labels = array(
  'name' => 'Books',
  'singular_name' => 'Book',
  'add_new' => 'Add New',
  'add_new_item' => 'Add New Book',
  'edit_item' => 'Edit Book',
  'new_item' => 'New Book',
  'view_item' => 'View Book',
  'search_items' => 'Search Books',
  'not_found' =>   'No books found',
  'not_found_in_trash' => 'No books found in Trash'
);
```

Then, add a single line of code to the `$args` array telling it to use the labels, as shown in the following snippet:

```
$args = array(
  'labels' => $labels,
  'description' => 'A custom post type that holds my books',
/* the rest of the function remains the same */
```

The next step is to add messages, which is what WordPress tells the user when they are doing stuff with books.

Adding messages

Whenever a user updates, previews, or does anything with a book, you'll want them to see an accurate message. All we need to do is create an array of messages and then hook them to WordPress, as shown in the following code:

```
function book_updated_messages( $messages ) {
  $messages['book'] = array(
    '', /* Unused. Messages start at index 1. */
    sprintf('Book updated. <a href="%s">View book</a>',
    esc_url(get_permalink($post_ID))),
    'Custom field updated.',
    'Custom field deleted.',
    'Book updated.',
    (isset($_GET['revision']) ?
    sprintf('Book restored to revision from %s',
    wp_post_revision_title((int)$_GET['revision'], false)) : false),
    print('Book published. <a href="%s">View book</a>',
    esc_url(get_permalink($post_ID))),
    'Book saved.',
    sprintf('Book submitted. <a target="_blank" href="%s">
    Preview book</a>',
    esc_url(add_query_arg('preview', 'true',
    get_permalink($post_ID)))),
    sprintf('Book scheduled for: <strong>%1$s</strong>.
    <a target="_blank"
    href="%2$s">Preview book</a>',
    date_i18n('M j, Y @ G:i', strtotime($post-
    >post_date)), esc_url(get_permalink($post_ID))),
    sprintf('Book draft updated. <a target="_blank" href="%s">
    Preview book</a>',
    esc_url(add_query_arg('preview', 'true', get_permalink($post_ID))))
  );
  return $messages;
}
add_filter('post_updated_messages', 'book_updated_messages');
```

This code creates a function named `book_updated_messages()`, which sets up an array of messages and returns it. We call this using the filter for `post_updated_messages`.

Now, our custom post type is ready to use! Go to your `wp-admin` panel and reload it. You'll see that a new menu has appeared under **Comments**. It's called **Books**. Let's add a book, as shown in the following screenshot:

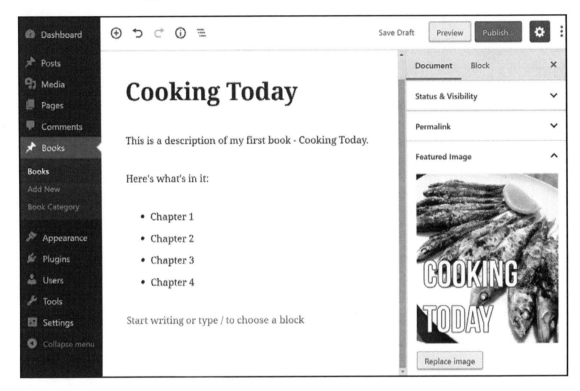

Note that I gave it a custom field named `book_author`, and I also uploaded a featured image for the book cover. Now, when you go to the main **Books** page, you'll see the book listed. If you click on the **View** link under the book's title, you'll see the book displayed using the `single.php` theme template, which won't be the most reader-friendly experience. Therefore, let's make some new template files to display our books.

Creating book template files

WordPress needs to know how to display your new post type. You have to create a template for a single book, and one for the listing of books. Perform the following steps to do this:

1. First, we'll make a book version of `single.php`. It must be named `single-POST_TYPE_NAME.php`, which in our case is `single-book.php`.

2. Using `page.php` as our starting point (as it's already the closest to what we'd like our book page to look like), we're going to add the display of the custom field, `book_author`, and the featured image.

3. So, let's start by taking our `page.php` file, making a copy of it, and renaming it `single-book.php`. Also, let's make a copy of `content-page.php` and call it `content-book.php`.

4. Next, it's time to include all the elements. Here's what the two files look like. First, `single-book.php` looks like this:

```php
<?php
/**
 * The template for displaying a single book.
 *
 * @package Daily Cooking Custom
 */
?><?php get_header(); ?>

<div id="primary" class="content-area">
  <main id="main" class="site-main" role="main">
    <?php while (have_posts()) : the_post(); ?>

      <?php get_template_part('content', 'book'); ?>

      <?php endwhile; // end of the loop. ?>

  </main><!-- #main -->
</div><!-- #primary -->

<?php get_sidebar(); ?>
<?php get_footer(); ?>
```

The only change that's been made to this file is the `get_template_part()` function call.

5. Next, the `content-book.php` file looks like the following:

```php
<?php
/**
 * The template used for displaying book content
 *
 * @package Daily Cooking Custom
 */
?>

<article id="post-<?php the_ID(); ?>" <?php post_class(); ?>>
  <header class="entry-header">
```

```
    <?php the_title('<h1 class="entry-title">', '</h1>'); ?>
  </header>

  <div class="entry-content">
    <?php if(has_post_thumbnail()) : ?>
      <div class="post-image alignleft">
      <?php echo get_the_post_thumbnail($post->ID, 'medium',
      array('style' => 'border: 1px solid black;')); ?></div>
    <?php endif; ?>
    <?php the_content(); ?>
  </div>

  <footer class="entry-footer">
  </footer>
</article><!-- #post-## -->
```

6. Now, let's take our custom field, `book_author`, and display it right below the featured image. We can do this by adding one new line of code in between the featured image code and the main content code, as shown in the following code snippet:

```
<?php if(has_post_thumbnail()) : ?>
  <div class="post-image alignleft">
  <?php echo get_the_post_thumbnail($post->ID, 'medium',
  array('style' => 'border: 1px solid black;')); ?></div>
<?php endif; ?>
<?php echo '<p><em>by '.get_post_meta($post->ID, 'book_author', true).
'</em></p>'; ?>
<?php the_content(); ?>
```

7. At this point, when you visit a single book page, the author's name is displayed and the book cover shows up automatically, as shown in the following screenshot:

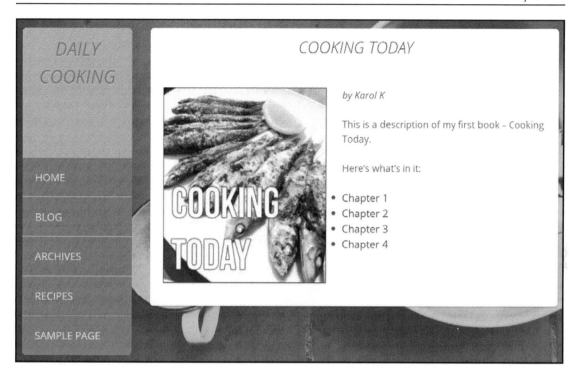

8. Our next task is a page that will show a listing of the books, like what `index.php` does for the posts. By default, WordPress uses the `archive.php` file to show the listing of every new custom post type.

We can customize this by creating a new template file and calling it `archive-book.php`. To be more exact, every template file controlling the archive for any new custom post type has to be named `archive-POST_TYPE.php`. The easiest way to create such file is by making a copy of the standard `archive.php` file or the `index.php` file, and renaming it to `archive-book.php`. Then, we can take it from there and modify the file to fit our requirements. So, what I'm going to do here is use my `index.php` as the template and do some tuning up around it.

9. Right now, my new `archive-book.php` file doesn't offer any custom way of displaying my books. What it looks like is shown in the following code:

```php
<?php
/**
 * The listing of books.
 *
 * @package Daily Cooking Custom
 */
?><?php get_header(); ?>

  <div id="primary" class="content-area">
    <main id="main" class="site-main" role="main">

    <?php if (have_posts()) : ?>

        <?php /* Start the Loop */ ?>
        <?php while (have_posts()) : the_post(); ?>
        <?php get_template_part('listing', 'book'); ?>
        <?php endwhile; ?>

        <?php daily_cooking_custom_paging_nav(); ?>

    <?php else : ?>

        <?php get_template_part('content', 'none'); ?>

    <?php endif; ?>

    </main><!-- #main -->
  </div><!-- #primary -->

<?php get_sidebar(); ?>
<?php get_footer(); ?>
```

10. As you can see, the actual display is done by the `get_template_part('listing', 'book')` function call. In order to make this line work, we have to create the listing file itself. The simplest way of doing this is by making a copy of `content.php` and modifying it slightly. First, rename it to `listing-book.php`.

11. Right away, I'm going to erase the unnecessary sections and leave only those that can be used to make our book listing look great.

12. Next, I will also include a thumbnail display. Quite frankly, I don't have to do this, but I believe that the book listing will look better with smaller thumbnails.

13. Finally, I will also display the author of each book. The following code shows how the finished file will look:

```php
<?php
/**
 * @package Daily Cooking Custom
 */
?>
<article id="post-<?php the_ID(); ?>" <?php post_class(); ?>>
  <header class="entry-header">
    <?php the_title(sprintf('<h1 class="entry-title"><a href="%s"
    rel="bookmark">', esc_url(get_permalink())), '</a>"</h1>'); ?>
  </header>

  <div class="entry-content">
    <?php if(has_post_thumbnail()) : ?>
      <div class="post-image alignleft">
        <?php echo '<a href="'.esc_url(get_permalink()).'"
        >'.get_the_post_thumbnail($post->ID, 'thumbnail').'</a>'; ?>
      </div>
    <?php endif; ?>

    <div class="entry clearfix">
      <p><em>by <?php echo get_post_meta($post->ID,
      'book_author', true); ?>
      </em></p>
      <?php the_content(sprintf(__('Continue reading %s
      <span class="meta-nav">&rarr;</span>', 'daily-cooking-custom'),
      the_title('<span class="screen-reader-text">"',
      '"</span>', false)));
      ?>
    </div>
  </div>

  <footer class="entry-footer">
  </footer>
</article><!-- #post-## -->
```

14. The following screenshot shows the final effect (I've added one more book just for demonstration purposes):

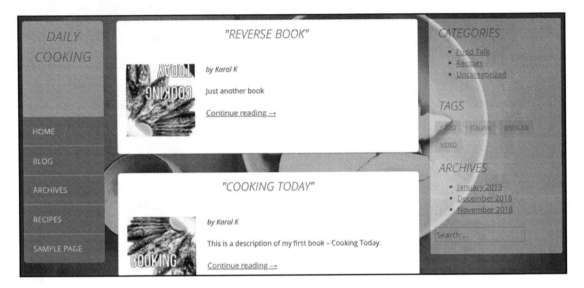

Registering and using a custom taxonomy

Just to follow the example given a while ago with our custom post type for books, let's now create a custom taxonomy. Why? You simply might not want to mix book categories and post categories, so we are going to create a custom taxonomy named **Book Categories**. Add the following code to your `functions.php` file:

```
function build_taxonomies() {
  register_taxonomy(
    'book_category',
    'book',
    array(
      'hierarchical' => true,
      'public' => true,
      'show_in_rest' => true,
      'label' => 'Book Category',
      'query_var' => true,
      'rewrite' => array('slug' => 'available-books')
    )
  );
}
add_action('init', 'build_taxonomies', 0);
```

Like the `register_post_type()` function, the `register_taxonomy()` function allows you to register a new taxonomy within WordPress. You can read up on the details of all of the parameters you can add in the codex (`https://codex.wordpress.org/Function_Reference/register_taxonomy`). For now, you can see that we're calling it `book_category`; it belongs to the `book` object type and is hierarchical, and you can query it, too. It needs to be included in the rewrite of URLs with a custom slug, `available-books`.

Next, we need to make this taxonomy available to books. Simply find the `$args` array we used while registering the book post type (the `book_init()` function) and add the `taxonomies` item to the array, as shown in the following code:

```
$args = array(
    'labels' => $labels,
    'description' => 'A custom post type that holds my books',
    'public' => true,
    'rewrite' => array('slug' => 'books'),
    'has_archive' => true,
    'taxonomies' => array('book_category'),
    'supports' => array('title', 'editor', 'author', 'excerpt',
    'custom-fields', 'thumbnail')
);
```

When you return to the `wp-admin` panel and edit a book, you'll see that the book categories have appeared on the right, as shown in the following screenshot:

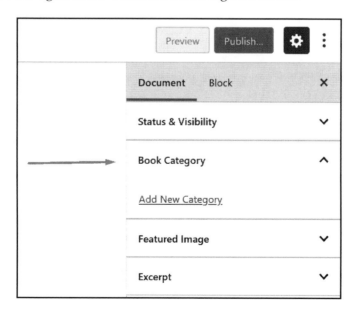

After you've added some categories and assigned them to the books, let's take a look at displaying those categories on the front of the website. First, we'll add them to the single book display. Open `content-book.php` and add the following code in at an appropriate place within the loop (for example, you can add it right after the `the_content()` function call):

```
<div class="entry-content">
  <?php if(has_post_thumbnail()) : ?>
    <div class="post-image alignleft">
    <?php echo get_the_post_thumbnail($post->ID, 'medium',
    array('style' => 'border: 1px solid black;')); ?></div>
  <?php endif; ?>
  <?php echo '<p><em>by '.get_post_meta($post->ID,
  'book_author', true).
  '</em></p>'; ?>
  <?php the_content(); ?>
  <?php echo get_the_term_list($post->ID, 'book_category',
  '<em>Categories: ', ', ', '</em>'); ?>
</div>
```

You're using the `get_the_term_list()` function , which takes the following arguments:

- The ID of the post (`$post->ID`)
- The name of the taxonomy (`book_category`)
- Print before the list (`<em>Categories:`)
- Separate items in the list with (`,`)
- Print after the list (`</em>`)

Also, now that you have categories, you can visit **Appearance** | **Menus** and add links to those categories to your header menu, and you can also create a custom menu with all the categories and add it to one of the sidebars.

> If you get a 404 error from WordPress at any point during the creation of your custom post type and custom taxonomy when you don't think you should, then navigate to **Settings** | **Permalinks** and just save the changes without actually changing anything. Sometimes, WordPress needs to refresh the permalinks to make the new links work correctly.

Customizing the admin display

The final thing you can do to fully realize your new book custom-post-type is to change its display in the wp-admin panel. You don't need to know the WordPress user who created a given book, but you do want to see the book categories and the thumbnail. Let's go back to functions.php. First, we'll change the columns that are displayed, as shown in the following code:

```
function ahskk_custom_columns($defaults) {
  global $wp_query, $pagenow;
  if ($pagenow == 'edit.php') {
    unset($defaults['author']);
    unset($defaults['categories']);
    unset($defaults['date']);
    $defaults['book_category'] = 'Categories';
    $defaults['thumbnail'] = 'Image';
  }
  return $defaults;
}
add_filter('manage_book_posts_columns', 'ahskk_custom_columns');
function ahskk_show_columns($name) {
  global $post;
  switch ($name) {
    case 'book_category':
      echo get_the_term_list($post->ID, 'book_category', '', ', ', '');
      break;
    case 'thumbnail':
      if (has_post_thumbnail($post->ID))
        echo get_the_post_thumbnail($post->ID, array('40', '40'));
      break;
  }
}
add_action('manage_book_posts_custom_column', 'ahskk_show_columns');
```

The first function says, *don't show author, date, and categories, but do show book categories and thumbnail,* and the second function says, *for the book categories column, print the list of categories, and for the thumbnail column, print the* get_post_thumbnail() *function.*

Revisit the **Books** page in the `wp-admin` panel, and it now looks like the following screenshot:

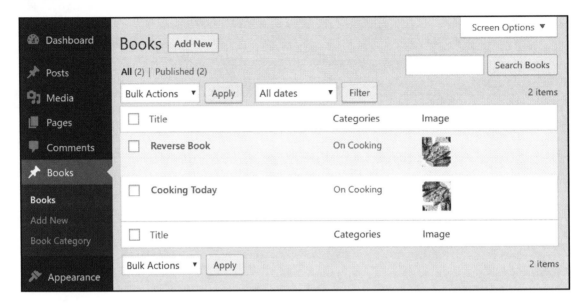

Summary

This chapter was part two of our non-blog website journey with WordPress. I hope you enjoyed the material. We went through the whole process of setting up e-commerce sites, video blogs, photo blogs, and social networks. Along the way, we took a closer look at some interesting plugins and their functionalities, just to make your life easier as a WordPress developer. Finally, we created a custom post type and a corresponding custom taxonomy.

I believe that, at this point, you are well equipped to work with WordPress and use it to build your next great website! WordPress is a top-notch CMS (Content Management System) that has matured tremendously over the years. The WordPress admin panel is designed to be user-friendly and is continuously being improved. The code that underlies WordPress is robust, and is the creation of a large community of dedicated developers. Additionally, the functionality of WordPress can be extended through the use of plugins and themes.

I hope you've enjoyed the information in this book and that you've already started working on your next (or perhaps first) WordPress website. Be sure to stay connected to the WordPress open source community! Thank you for reading; you rock!

Other Books You May Enjoy

If you enjoyed this book, you may be interested in these other books by Packt:

Learn to Create WordPress Themes by Building 5 Projects
Eduonix

ISBN: 9781787286641

- Simple and advanced themes – covers basic syntax and files along with archives and search pages
- Photo Gallery – add simple animation and use the W3.CSS framework to design a photo gallery theme
- Wordstrap – incorporate Twitter Bootstrap into the theme and use the WP_NavWalker Class
- E-commerce Theme – build an e-commerce theme using the Foundation framework

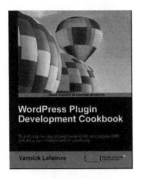

WordPress Plugin Development Cookbook

Yannick Lefebvre

ISBN: 9781849517683

- Prepare an efficient development environment
- Create your first plugins using WordPress action and filter hooksAdd new sections to the administration interface for plugin configuration
- Create new content types using Custom Post Types or Custom Database TablesMake your content dynamic with JavaScript, jQuery, and AJAXAdd new widgets to the WordPress library
- Prepare your plugin to be translated for broad international use
- Get your new creations ready to be shared on the official WordPress site

Leave a review - let other readers know what you think

Please share your thoughts on this book with others by leaving a review on the site that you bought it from. If you purchased the book from Amazon, please leave us an honest review on this book's Amazon page. This is vital so that other potential readers can see and use your unbiased opinion to make purchasing decisions, we can understand what our customers think about our products, and our authors can see your feedback on the title that they have worked with Packt to create. It will only take a few minutes of your time, but is valuable to other potential customers, our authors, and Packt. Thank you!

Index

Made in United States
Orlando, FL
17 January 2024

42591712R00237